Bali

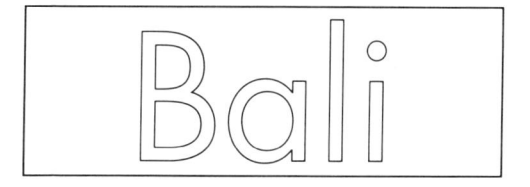

Lynne Maree Smith

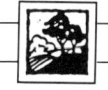

LITTLE HILLS PRESS

© Photographs by the Author and Indonesian Tourist Board.
© Maps, Little Hills Press, 1992, 1997
©This Third edition, May 1997, Revised **December 1997**
Cover by Norman Design
Maps by Angela and Mark Butler, & MAPgraphics
Printed in Singapore

ISBN 1 86315 108 7

Little Hills Press Pty Ltd
37-43 Alexander Street
Crows Nest NSW 2065 Australia
email info@littlehills.com
Home Page: http://www.littlehills.com

All rights reserved. No part of this publication may be reproduced, stored in a retrieval system, or transmitted in any form or by any means electronic, mechanical, photocopying, recording or otherwise, without the prior permission in writing of the publisher.

DISCLAIMER

While all care has been taken by the publisher and author to ensure that the information is accurate and up to date, the publisher does not take responsibility for the information published herein. The recommendations are those of the author and as things get better or worse, places close down and others open, some elements in the book may be inaccurate when you get there. Please write and tell us about it so we can update in subsequent editions.

Little Hills[TM] and are registered trademarks of Little Hills Press Pty Ltd.

ACKNOWLEDGMENTS

Special thanks to Mark Naylor for the surfing section.

Contents

Introduction   7
(Geography, Climate, History)

The People   17
(The Village, Language, Balinese Hinduism, Balinese Calendar, Performing Arts, Art, The Economy, Agriculture)

General Information   41
Entry Regulations, Exit Regulations, Embassies, Immigration, Money, Communications, Miscellaneous)

Travel Information   55
(How To Get There, Tourist Information, Accommodation, Local Transport, Food, Entertainment, Shopping, Recreation)

Badung   77
(Denpasar, Kuta and Legian Resort Area, Bukit Peninsula, Nusa Dua, Benoa, Sanur)

Gianyar   139
(Batubulan, Celuk, Mas, Ubud, Pejeng Region)

Klungkung   171
(Klungkung, Nusa Penida)

Bangli   181
(Bangli Town, Gunung Batur and Lake Batur, Kintamani)

Karangasem 187
(Tenganan, Candi Dasa, the 'Mother Temple')

Buleleng 203
(Singaraja, Lovina Beach, Bali Barat National Park)

Jembrana 214
(Negara, Palasari and Belimbingsari, Gilimanuk)

Tabanan 215
(Tabanan Town, Tanah Lot, Gunung Batukau, Bedugul)

Glossary 220

List of Maps 222

Index 223

Introduction

Bali has been described as the "sanctuary of the gods", the "island of a thousand temples", the "morning of the world" and a tropical paradise. A speck on the world map, it has become the favoured destination for many travellers. An island of contrasts, Bali offers something for everyone: hedonists who desire nothing more than to relax in luxury, sip cocktails and watch the sunset, need look no further; or for the budget traveller, eager to explore the mysteries of an enigmatic island on a shoestring, Bali's the place.

Bali is surrounded by palm-fringed, crystal-clear waters and vibrant coral gardens. Whether white, shimmering sands and pounding surf, or black-crystal beaches and gentle, lapping waves — Bali offers a multitude of water sports. Not far from the coast, hills are meticulously terraced, resembling green stairways to the heavens and majestic volcanoes (the thrones of the gods) loom over the scenery, punctuated by ornate pagodas. The cultivated land, like that created by a landscape gardener, reflects the order and elegance of its people.

Bali's culture is unique and paradoxical. In one sense, the traditional Hindu culture has been preserved intact, despite Western "invasions" and the predominance of Islam in the archipelago. In another sense, the culture is dynamic, and the people, forever curious, welcome new ideas. Bali isn't a fossilised relic, it is alive and well, and for this the gods should be thanked. For essentially, it is the people's pleasure in satisfying the gods that fosters the Hindu culture and adds to the visitor's fascination with the island.

Geography

Nestled in the Indonesian archipelago, Bali belongs to the chain of islands that links South-east Asia with Australia, and divides the Pacific and Indian Oceans. A twinkle among the 13,677 islands in the Republic of Indonesia, Bali remains distinct in its beauty of land and of culture.

For all its fame, the tiny island is a mere 80km (50 miles) from north to south, and 150km (90 miles) at its maximum width, with an area of 5632 sq km (2095 sq miles). Located in the equatorial belt, it is 115 degrees east longitude, 8 degrees south latitude. The north and south are virtually severed by a mountainous ridge of volcanoes, the biggest being the active Gunung Agung (3142m-10,308 ft), "navel of the world" and "throne of the gods".

The Balinese are obsessed with the volcanoes. Although eruptions are devastating to the people and villages, the rich volcanic ashes regenerate the soils, and the volcanic uplands and craters help to retain the constant rain water. The volcanic terrain makes the island ideal for rice growing, and every volcano, lake and spring is revered for its life-giving qualities.

The volcanoes are also the spiritual and directional poles of Bali. *Kaja*, towards Gunung Agung, is the sacred direction, while *kelod* is towards the diabolic sea. *Kangin* faces the rising sun and symbolises rebirth, while *kauh* is toward the setting sun, and is associated with death. Most buildings are constructed according to these poles, and the people even sleep with their heads towards *kaja*.

Bali, in the far east of the chain of mostly volcanic islands that make up Indonesia, is adjacent to the division between Asia and Australasia.

In the 19th century, naturalist Alfred Wallace, a contemporary of Darwin, posited the Wallace Line which separated Asia from Australasia on biological grounds. Bali, the eastern-most island in the chain, exhibited flora and fauna that could be classified as Asian — monkeys and even tigers, roamed in tropical jungles. Lombok, a barren, arid isle, severed from Bali by a deep strait, was home to eucalypti, parrots and marsupials akin to those found in Australia.

Bali is one of 27 provinces that make up the Republic of Indonesia, and the capital is Denpasar, situated in the south in the regency of Badung. The island is divided into eight regencies (*Kabupaten*), each governed by a *Bupati*.

Climate

Placed just below the equator, Bali has a benign tropical climate. There are two seasons, a short, hot, wet season, *musim hujan*; and a longer, cooler, dry season, *musim panas*. The mountains are wet year round, averaging 2,800mm (110 inches) of rain.

The average temperature in Bali is 26C (79F) and the humidity is a relentless 75%. Generally the mountains are about 10C (50F) cooler than the coast, and in the dry season the nights can be chilly. The wet season lasts from November to March, and is the hottest time of the year with temperatures averaging 30-33C (86- 91F) by day, 24-25C (75-77F) by night. April to October is the dry season, when south-easterly winds blow from the Australian interior, easing the temperature by 2-3C (36-37F). Bali often experiences north-east and south-west monsoons, but being close to the equator has no typhoons and cyclones.

It's no secret that the Balinese use the sun as a clock. The island's proximity to the equator guarantees a fairly uniform 12 hours of daylight. The shortest day is in late June, the longest is in late December, and there is only about an hour's difference.

History

Prehistory

While the Balinese trace their origins to the divine, historians view matters differently. The forebears of the Balinese probably migrated to South-east Asia from southern China around 2500 BC. These nomads scattered to various points in the archipelago, mingling with other peoples to become the "Malay" race. Stone Age relics suggest that small bands of hunter-gatherers roamed the island.

By the Bronze Age (300BC), the island was well-populated with small villages that practised farming, and possibly even wet-rice cultivation. The people worshipped various gods who presided over the elements and *cili*, the effigy of the rice goddess Dewi Sri, may have originated from a rice cult at this time. Thrones, sarcophagi and pyramids, all hewn from stone, suggest a sophisticated Megalithic culture had developed. But of all the archaeological finds pertaining to this time, the decorative bronze gong, the "Moon of Pejeng" is the most significant. Enshrined in the *Pura Penataran* in Pejeng, in the regency of Gianyar, the gong is the largest single cast bronze object found in Asia and dates from around 300BC. The motifs that decorate the drum suggest the influences of the Dongson bronze culture of Indo-china.

Towards Hinduism

Indian and Chinese traders had been visiting the archipelago for a thousand years, attracted by spices, sandalwood and gold. So much so, that by the 5th century, Hindu and Buddhist kingdoms were thriving in West Java and Borneo. Bali, having nothing to offer in the way of spices, lacking a suitable harbour, and being almost inaccessible, was probably not on the traders' itinerary. So, historians surmise, the Balinese probably acquired Hindu concepts and artistic motifs from the Javanese, rather than from the Indians themselves.

Most of Bali's history before the advent of stone and copperplate inscriptions, is sheer speculation. The earliest inscriptions date back to the 9th century, and as most are written in Sanskrit (ancient Indian) and Old Javanese (*Kawi*), it is probable that Bali was exposed to Hinduism by this time.

In the 11th century, the relationship between Bali and Java intensified under the Warmadewa Dynasty. The Javanese king, Dharmawangsa, probably arranged for his sister, Princess Mahendradatta, to marry the Balinese prince, Udayana (after whom the university at Denpasar is named). The couple's son, the illustrious Prince Erlangga, ruled a province of eastern Java from 1019 to 1042, while his brother, Anak Wangsa, controlled Bali. From this time all Balinese edicts were written in Old Javanese, and the Hindu epics *Ramayana* and *Mahabharata* were also translated into the language.

Majapahit Empire

During the 13th century, the Hindu Majapahit Empire established a powerful kingdom in Java. In 1343, the Javanese Prime Minister, Gajah Mada, was ordered to subdue the Balinese King Bedulu of Pejeng near Gianyar who refused to recognise Javanese sovereignty. Accompanied by Hindu nobles, Gaja Mada conquered Bedulu, and founded a Javanese court nearby, at Samprangan, near Gianyar. Sri Dalem Kapakisan, a Javanese noble, was later installed as vassal ruler over Bedulu's kingdom.

The introduction of the *Triwangsa* caste system is usually ascribed to this period. The ruling caste, *Satrya*, and priestly caste, *Brahmana*, were Javanese nobles, while the third class, the *Wesya*, were probably land-holding Javanese. The indigenous Balinese were not actually included in the system and were called *Sudra*, or more popularly, *Jaba* (outsiders). The Balinese who refused to participate in the separation of society fled to the mountains, and today they are known as the *Bali Aga* or "original Balinese".

In the late 15th century, as Islamic influences spread through Java, the Hindu Majapahit Empire was threatened with political extinction. Rather than submit to the Islamic Mataram kingdom, the entire Majapahit entourage fled to Bali. The son of the last emperor assembled courtiers, priests, scholars and artists, and crossed the narrow strait separating Java from Bali. Popular opinion suggests that this "exodus" firmly established Hinduism in Bali.

The emperor's son bestowed upon himself the title of Dewa Agung, "Lord of Lords", and in 1515, he established a court at Gelgel near the town of Gianyar. The Dewa Agung unified Bali and the realm was extended as far as Lombok and Sumbawa. And with political prosperity came the "Golden Age". The Majapahit Empire had blossomed culturally in Java, and the renaissance continued in Bali.

Hindu Bali's relationship with Islamic Java waned. While some parts of Western Bali absorbed Islamic influences, the relative isolation, lack of harbours and trade possibilities precluded most of Bali from the "onslaught" of Islam. Today, most Javanese are Muslim, while Bali lives on as a legacy of 15th century Hindu Java.

Over time, the Majapahit nobles increased their power and wealth and as the ruling classes expanded, new realms evolved. By the 18th century there were nine distinct kingdoms: Klungkung, Karangasem, Bangli, Gianyar, Buleleng, Mengwi, Badung, Tabanan and Jembrana. The kingdoms were more or less independent, while acknowledging Klungkung's Dewa Agung as the ultimate ruler.

Dutch Aspirations
In 1602, the Dutch established the Dutch East India Trading Company in western Java. Keen to exploit the spices found in parts of the archipelago, they organised trading posts in Sumatra, Borneo and the Moluccas, and Jakarta was laid to waste and rebuilt as Batavia. Bali had little to offer the Dutch — only impenetrable jungles and perilous reefs.

In the 19th century, Bali entered the limelight. Many trade ships passed by eastern Bali and some foundered on the reefs. This was Balinese territory, and the locals had taken to plundering the wrecks which they regarded as gifts from the gods. As the Dutch controlled the archipelago, and many of the trade ships sailed under their flag, the Dutch felt they had to do something to stop the plundering. In 1846, after another case of looting (to make matters worse, a Dutch ship), the Dutch regent, accompanied by a small garrison, visited Buleleng to negotiate with the Raja. The Dutch were received with hostility, and returning to Java they prepared for an invasion.

Dutch expeditions (1846-1850)
The first Dutch military "expedition" set out to control the regency of Buleleng with 23 warships, mortars, and 3000 men armed with rifles. The Balinese, armed only with spears and *kris* (ceremonial swords), attempted to resist. The palace at Singaraja was razed and 400 Balinese lost their lives. Mads Lange, a Danish trader stationed in Kuta, intervened on behalf of the Balinese and sued for peace. The Balinese rajas signed a treaty of submission, and a Dutch garrison was posted in Buleleng with the main Dutch force leaving the island.

The last Dutch military expedition arrived in Buleleng in 1849 with the largest assembled force ever used in the archipelago: 5000 infantrymen, 3000 mercenaries, and a fleet of 60 ships with 300 sailors. Much to the surprise of the Dutch, the Balinese requested peace negotiations. A treaty was drafted ensuring Dutch control of the realm, and stipulating that the Balinese withdraw to Jagaraga.

The Balinese returned to Jagaraga and promptly mobilised, but the Dutch were more than prepared, and swiftly defeated them. Djilantik and his brothers the Rajas of Buleleng and Karangasem fled to the mountains, and the Dutch returned home, leaving a strong force to control the new territory. Not content with half of Bali, the Dutch returned yet again, landing at Kusamba in the east, with the intention of marching to Karangasem. Djilantik and the Raja of Buleleng, organised a huge force, but this time the Balinese were brutally defeated. The Raja of Karangasem, foreseeing defeat, elected honourable suicide in battle or *puputan*. The Balinese believed that by dying in battle, the soul could reach a state of *nirvana*. And so the court of Karangasem destroyed itself.

By 1882, The Netherlands East-Indies government officially controlled Buleleng in the north, and Jembrana in the west. The south was a different story. The rajas were engaged in power plays, and by the 1880s, Badung and Tabanan had destroyed the regency of Mengwi, splitting the domain between themselves. The rajas, already disgruntled with the Dutch, grew uneasy after an incident in Lombok, where the Dutch intervened in the rajas' control of the Muslim island. The Balinese waited, the Dutch waited ... finally it happened.

Another shipwreck, more looting; this time a Chinese schooner off the coast of Sanur. Via the Dutch, the owner of the craft demanded exorbitant reparations, but the Raja of Badung refused. The Dutch blockaded the coasts of Badung and Tabanan and presented the Raja of Badung with an ultimatum. Once again, the raja refused and the Dutch invaded.

Puputan

It was September 14, 1906. The Dutch met little resistance as they marched to Denpasar. Upon their arrival they were ominously greeted by a seemingly deserted village, except for the solemn beat of drums. The palace gates were flung open and a procession of courtiers, priests, women and children, resplendent in white cremation garments was led by the Raja. Not far from the battalion, the Raja halted the procession, gave a signal, and a priest plunged a dagger into the Raja's breast. Another *puputan*. Everywhere there was death, mayhem, looting and sacking. Puputan Square in Denpasar is a memorial to those who died tragically in the 1906 invasion.

The Dutch advanced to Pemecutan, then to Tabanan. Again and again, the Dutch were met by sacrifice. Finally, in 1908, a battalion was sent to Klungkung, the palace of the Dewa Agung and nominal capital of Bali, demanding that he surrender all power. The palace gates were opened and the Dewa Agung led his sacrificial retinue before the Dutch troops. The last bastion of Balinese royalty died as they had lived, with pomp and ceremony. In less than 16 months the Dutch had annihilated an empire that had flourished for six centuries.

Back in Holland, officials were horrified with reports of the various *puputan*. In the ensuing years, the Dutch instigated a number of "benevolent" reforms. They built schools, roads and clinics, and installed a western-style system of justice. They dusted off historic monuments and generally endeavoured to tidy up. European scholars were invited to study the Balinese culture, and reports of an idyllic island in the tropics attracted many visitors. Tourists were tolerated, but not encouraged, as the Dutch wanted to protect the Balinese from outsiders. But, by the 1930s, influential people like the German painter Walter Spies, the Dutch painter Rudolf Bonnet and the Mexican painter Miguel Covarrubias had made Bali their home. The first tourist joint, the Kuta Beach Hotel, was built by a Californian couple, Robert and Louise Coke, in 1936. They welcomed visitors from America and Europe until the Japanese invaded.

Independence

During the Second World War, the Japanese occupied the island, but intervened little in local politics. After the war, the Dutch were ready to resume control, but the Indonesians had a different idea: independence. On August 17, 1945, Sukarno, the national leader, declared independence. Of course, the Dutch were not about to relinquish the colony and a war of independence, fought mostly in Java, lasted four years. One particular battle fought at Marga, on Bali, saw a modern-day *puputan*, and the leader, Ngurah Rai, a modern-day hero.

On December 29, 1949, The Hague granted independence and Bali became part of The Republic of the United States of Indonesia. Sukarno was president, answerable only to Queen Juliana of The Netherlands, but nevertheless Indonesia was free. The Dutch withdrew in 1956, and in 1963 were ejected from Irian Jaya, thereby losing their last hold on Indonesia.

But independence had its price, and the new republic was fraught with problems. The few schools, roads and hospitals, built by the Dutch were destroyed in the war. The Sukarno administration was awry financially — inflation was 100% and there were whispers of corruption. Martial law was imposed in 1957 following unsuccessful coups, and in 1963, backed by the Nationalist Party, the Communist party (PKI), and the military, Sukarno had a less than successful "confrontation" with Malaya.

Bali was affected by poor economic conditions and the unstable political structure. Land reforms dictated that no one could own more than 7.5 hectares and while many of the Balinese relinquished their land, it was not equitably redistributed. The infrastructure of village life began to crumble, and being remote and Hindu, Bali was neglected by Jakarta.

The Balinese were increasingly discontented. In 1962, a plague of rats devastated crops and the people knew the gods were displeased. In February 1963, the Balinese were preparing themselves for the celebration of *Eka Dasa Rudra*, a ritual of purification held every hundred years at the Mother Temple at Besakih. By March 8, smoke was issuing forth from the volcano — an ominous omen. Some wanted to postpone the ceremony, but Sukarno was expected, as were delegates from overseas. The initial celebrations ensued, Sukarno didn't show, the delegates left, and Gunung Agung blew! Thousands perished, 10,000 were homeless, but news of the disaster was suppressed, and aid was late and erratic.

Bali was suffering physically, Jakarta politically. On September 30, 1965, a small group kidnapped and killed six generals. Some Communist Party (PKI) members seized the radio station in Jakarta, and declared a coup d'état. Seeing an opportunity, the Indonesian army, led by General Suharto, seized control. The coup lasted 24 hours, the bloodshed continued for six months. The PKI was outlawed. A massive purge throughout Indonesia ensued, with Bali in the midst of it. Entire villages were destroyed and Balinese deaths alone were reckoned at 40,000.

In the same year, the Bali Beach Hotel was built in Sanur, funded by reparations from the Japanese following WWII. It marked the beginning of a drive to address Indonesia's national debt problem through tourism -- a strategy that Sukarno had adopted as government policy years before. Ironically though, the hotel was opened at a time when visitors were prevented from entering the country following the coup.

Later in 1968 when General Suharto's party Golkar was officially elected to government with Suharto as president, tourism development was well underway. In the following year, Ngurah Rai International Airport was opened, signalling the advent of mass tourism. The International Monetary Fund and the World Bank urged development through tourism, and in 1972 the Bali Tourist Development Corporation was established. Its first project was the Nusa Dua complex and profits were to be distributed between the corporation, the consortia who built the hotels, and the companies that managed the hotels. While the Corporation was disbanded in 1978, following financial crises, the Nusa Dua complex was ultimately a success and the Corporation's blueprint for tourism development is still used today. But despite all the planning and profits, the direct benefits to Bali were never considered in the equation. Nevertheless, Bali's future seemed brighter and in 1979 at the Besakih complex, a successful *Eka Dasa Rudra* was staged with no ominous rumblings from Agung.

By the mid-1990s President Suharto and his party Golkar had been re-elected five times, with no real challengers. Indonesia's rapid economic growth over the past two decades, coupled with an upsurge in foreign investment, has attracted international interest. And while it seems that Indonesia's policies and actions have been questioned by its neighbours, Bali's political stability is undoubtedly assured, given its place in the tourism spotlight. The social and environmental costs of tourism, and the general prosperity of the Balinese, though, are different matters.

BALI

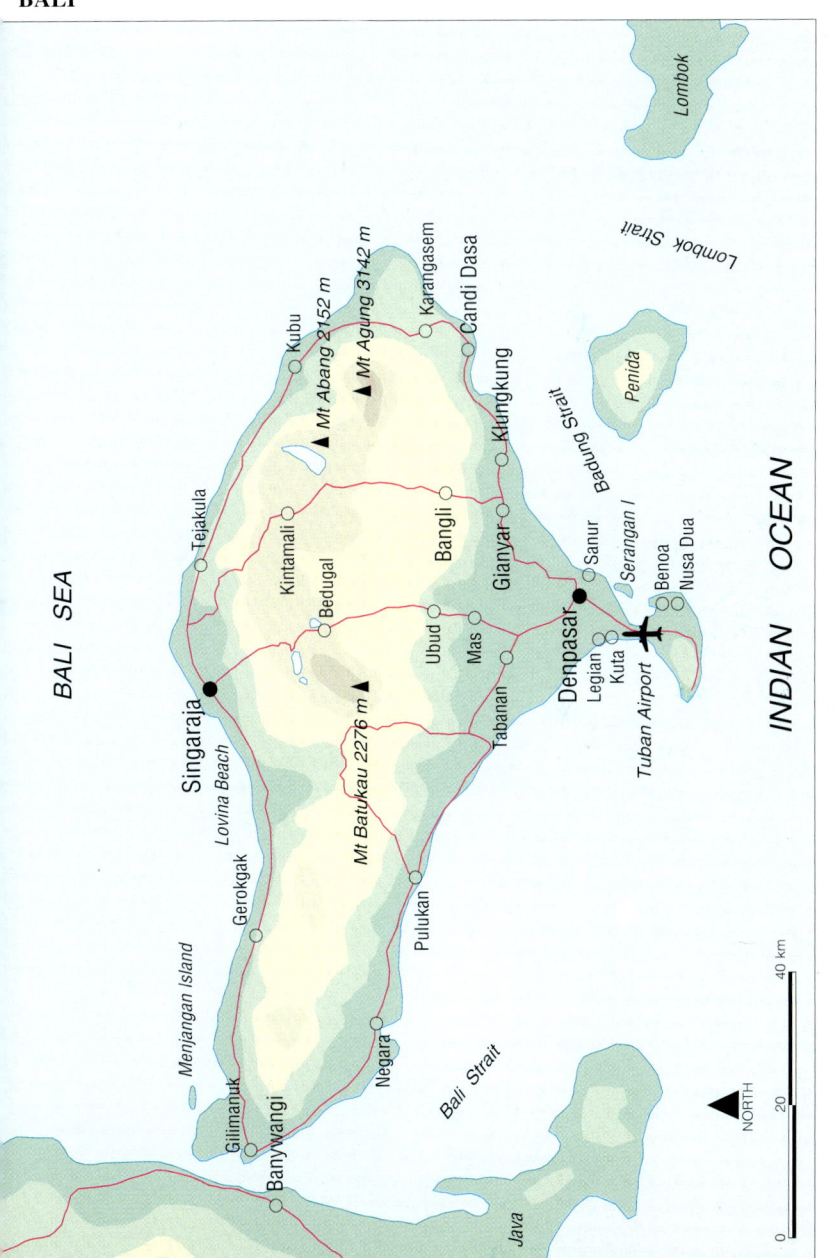

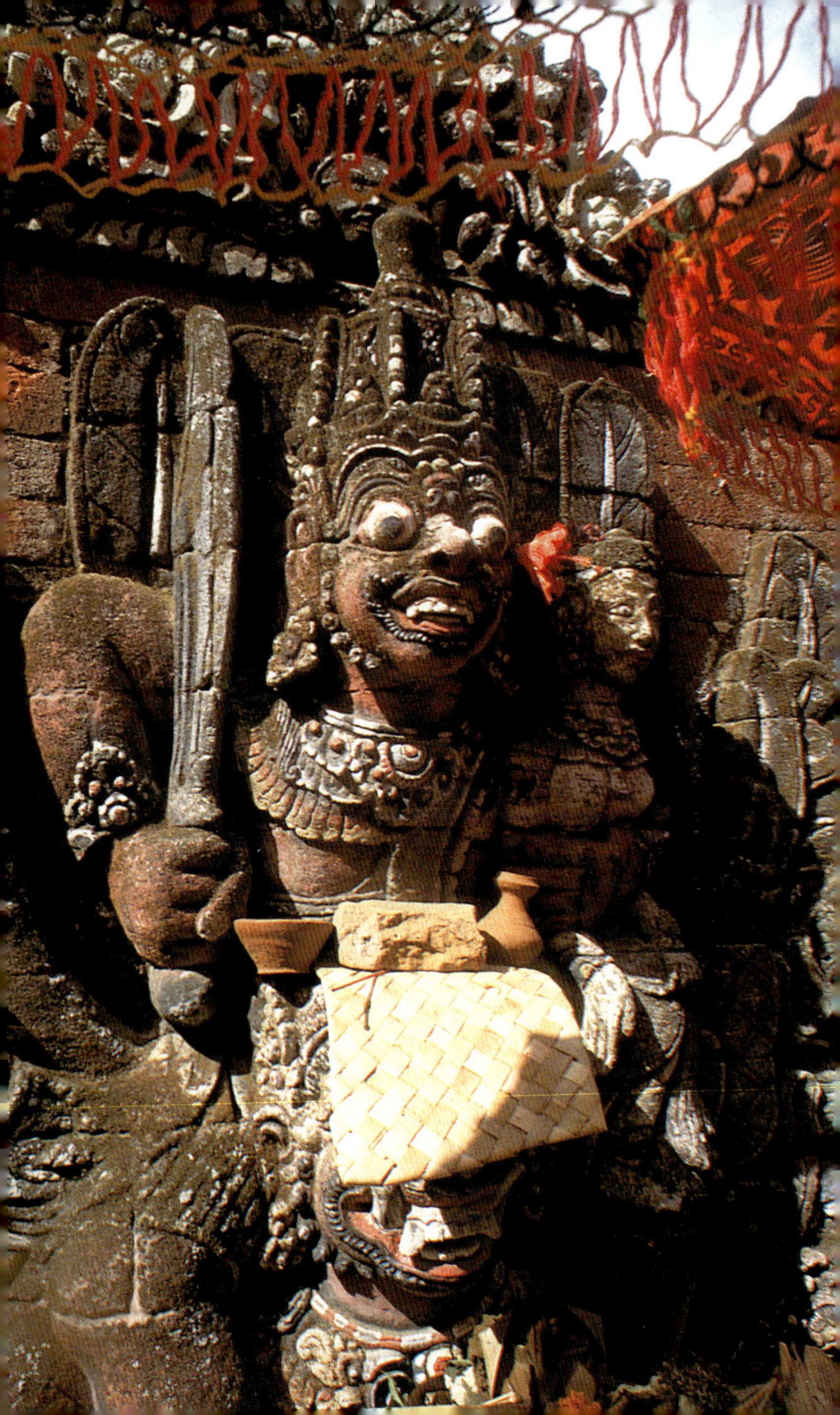

The People

In the 1995 census, Bali was recorded as having a population of 2.9 million. The population is almost entirely Indonesian, 95 per cent of whom are Balinese Hindu. Indonesians are mainly derived from the Malay-type peoples that migrated from southern China to South-east Asia, New Guinea and Australia around 3000BC.

The Caste System

In the 14th century, when Gaja Mada and the Javanese nobles of the Majapahit empire arrived on Bali, they brought with them a Javanese version of the Hindu caste system.

The *Brahmana* were the priestly caste; the *Satrya*, the warrior-kings; and *the Wesya*, the merchants; together they were the *Triwangsa*.

The remaining 90% of the population, the Balinese, were *Sudra*, not recognised as a caste by the ruling classes, and more commonly referred to as *Jaba* or "outsiders". The few Balinese who refused to belong to Hindu society fled inland, and today they are known as the *Bali Aga*, referring to themselves as the *original Balinese*.

The *Sudra* lived a feudal existence, and were dependent on a Hindu overlord who was supposedly endowed with divine rights. The caste system was strictly adhered to, and women were forbidden on pain of death to marry below their caste; men were merely punished.

Today, the Balinese Hindu caste system is not as rigid as its Indian precedent, and social mobility is possible. Although the *Brahmana* women are still forbidden to marry below their caste, inter-caste marriages are increasing in number, and the *Sudra* are able to enter the professional arena.

The caste system is deeply embedded in the Balinese psyche, and while legally, discrimination by caste is forbidden, the system is inextricably bound to the Balinese identity. In fact, in new encounters a name betrays caste.

Naming

Traditionally, there are no family names; rather people's names reflect their caste as well as their order of birth.

The *Brahmana* are called Ida Bagus and Ida Ayu for males and females, respectively; *Satrya* are named Cokorde, Anak Agung, and Prebagus for men; and Anak Agung Isti and Dewa Ayu for women. *Wesya* are named I Gusti and Pregusti for men; and I Gusti Ayu for women. The *Sudra* are simply I for men and Ni for women.

To signify order of birth, *Brahmana* and *Satrya* may be called Putu, Raka, or Kompiang, for the firstborn; Rai for the second; Oka for the third and Alit for the fourth. *Sudra* children are named Wayan, Made, Nyoman and Ketut, repeating the order for the fifth child. Children also have their own special name.

To complicate matters, names may change. When parents have a new child, names may change to reflect the new addition, so that they become "mother of", or "grandfather of".

The Family

Distinction according to sex is more stringent than according to class. In the village limits, women and men have separate tasks. Only men make handicrafts, tend cattle, cook meat and cultivate the fields; whereas women do the housework, look after the pigs and chickens, cook vegetables and rice, and prepare offerings to the gods. The exception being that everyone helps with the harvesting of rice. Nonetheless, women are encouraged to participate in income-earning activities and may dispose of their independent salaries as they desire.

The men are employed to build Balinese-style constructions, but women and girls will be encountered, with huge stone and cement slabs balanced on their heads, walking to Western-style building sites. While women carry their wares on their heads, men carry their loads on poles balanced on their shoulders — maybe that's why the Balinese are so elegantly postured.

Today, women have the same opportunities for education as their male counterparts and are entering the professions. In fact, there's a government department in Denpasar established to lift the status of women. Although women are expected to live with their husband's family, if she should divorce (which is rare) she must leave the children and return to her own family. But during menstruation women are separated from other family members, often sleeping in a different compound. During this time they are forbidden to enter temples — this is because it is sacrilege for blood to be spilt on hallowed ground.

The Village

Traditionally, the social organisation of the island is based on the village (*desa adat*), a complex network of religious, social and economic associations. Within each village are a number of *banjar* or neighbourhoods, and within each *banjar* are family compounds which extend the clan beyond parents and children.

Each member of the family belongs to a number of groups. Before marriage, an individual belongs to either a boys' or girls' club, and has specific duties as a member. Upon marrying, the person then joins the *banjar*, the irrigation association, music clubs and various other groups, and accepts the obligations that accompany membership. In this way, every individual participates fully within the social, religious and economic framework of the village. Indeed, to the Balinese, the group rather than the individual is important. Solitude is not something that the Balinese desire, and those left alone fear visits from mischievous spirits.

Most villages are organised according to spatial orientation, and the most important points of reference are *kaja* (towards Gunung Agung) and *kelod* (seawards). Each village has three temples arranged according to these directions. The *pura desa*, literally the "temple of the village", stands in the centre of the village, while at the northern end of the village is the *pura puseh*, a "temple of origin" dedicated to the spirits of the land. Both of these temples are oriented to *kaja* and the sacred Gunung Agung. On the other hand, the *pura dalem* or "temple of the dead", as well as the village burial ground, face *kelod*.

On a smaller scale, the family compound is also planned in relation to the mountains and sea.

The governing body of each neighbourhood is the *banjar*, a democratic association of married men, who make all the decisions pertaining to the village. The *banjar bale* is the meeting place for the *banjar* as well as all villagers: feasts are prepared, games are held, and dances practised. Sometimes the villagers even sleep there.

Language

The average Balinese who deals with tourists is usually conversant with one of the Balinese dialects as well as the "language of courtesies", Bahasa Indonesia (the official language of Indonesia) and English.

The "language of courtesies" is a complex Balinese language which employs three different levels to indicate the caste or status of the listener: low or *kasar*; middle or *mider*; and high or *alus*. *Kasar*, known as common Balinese, is a Malay-Polynesian dialect. The strange thing is, that when a person of high caste addresses a person of low caste, the high caste will speak in *kasar* and the low caste person will use *alus*.

Although English is widely spoken and most children are taught English at school from the age of 12, Bahasa Indonesia is fast becoming the *lingua franca*.

Bahasa Indonesia

Bahasa Indonesia, which evolved from a Malay dialect spoken in Sumatra, has much in common with other Malay dialects. Since it is a relatively simple and widely-used language, and is not associated with one of the dominant ethnic groups in Indonesia, it has been accepted without serious question. Indeed, it has served as a strong force of national unification. Bahasa Indonesia is taught in most schools, is widely used by the media, and in Bali it is becoming preferable to Balinese.

In 1972, a uniform revised spelling was agreed upon between Indonesia and Malaysia so that communications would improve and literature could be freely exchanged between the nations.

If you're staying on the island, try learning a few words, it's really quite easy. There are basically seven vowel signs each of which has only one pronunciation.
(English has five vowel symbols, but they generate over 20 different sounds.)

a as in cut
e as in set
i as in me
o as in not
u as in you
ai as in bike
au as in now

The consonants are similar to English consonants, but here are a few minor exceptions.
c is "ch" as in chip, but
k is "c" as in car
g as in girl
ng as in ring
h as in help, but with more breath, and it is silent at the end of a word
r is always rolled as "rrr"

The rules for grammar are also quite simple. Sentences are usually ordered: subject, verb, object. There are no articles, like "a" or "the". There are no tenses for verbs (well, none that tourists need learn), as time is indicated by context rather than an inflected form; for instance, words like yesterday (kemarin) and tomorrow (besok) are placed at the beginning of a sentence to indicate time. Questions are usually indicated by question words, but sometimes by raising the pitch of the voice at the end of the sentence. It's also possible to make a question by adding "Kah" to the end of the word which asks the question. Do not try and use this form until you feel comfortable with the language — you can get by without it. Generally, the last syllable of a word is emphasised.

If you want to impress the locals, here are a few words.

Pronouns
I/my - *saya*
you - *kamu*
he/she - *dia*
we - *kami*
they - *mereka*

Titles
Miss - *nona*

Mr - *bapak*
Mrs - *ibu*
Sir - *tuan*
Madam - *nyonya*
child - *anak*

Greetings and Civilities
good morning - *selamat Pagi*
good afternoon (11am-3pm) - *selamat siang*
good afternoon (after 3pm) - *selamat sore*
goodnight - *selamat malam*
sleep well - *selamat tidur*
goodbye (when leaving) - *selamat tinggal*
goodbye (when staying) - *selamat jalan*
please - *silahkan*
thank you - *terima kasih*
you're welcome - *sama sama*
 sorry - *ma'af* ; (and another is)   excuse me - *permisi*

Questions
what - *apa*
who - *siapa*
when - *kapan*
where is - *dimana ada*
where to - *kemana*
from where - *darimana*
how - *bagaimana*
why - *mengapa*
may I - *boleh*
How are you - *Apa kabar?*

Useful Words
well - *baik baik*
good - *bagus*
bad - *jahat*
sick - *sakit*
wrong - *salah*
no - *tidak* (in front of verbs -
but interchangeable with *bukan*)
no - *bukan* (in front of nouns)
not yet - *belum*

walk and street/walking - jalan/jalan jalan
village - *desa*

Useful Phrases
I want it - *saya mau*
I do not want it - *saya tidak mau*
What is your name - *siapa nama*
My name is... - *nama saya...*

Quantity
all - *semua*
some - *lain*
little - *sedikit*
many - *banyak*

Time
today (this day) - *hari ini*
tonight (this night) - *malam ini*
yesterday - *kemarin*
tomorrow - *besok*
week - *minggu*
month - *bulan*
year - *tahun*

Shopping
What's this - *Apa ini*
How much - *berapa*
money - *rupiah*
cheap - *murah*
expensive - *mahal*

Food
food - *makam*
drink - *minum*
chicken - *ayam*
fish - *ikan*
pork - *babi*
fruit - *buah*
rice - *nasi*

Numbers

1 - *satu*
2 - *dua*
3 - *tiga*
4 - *empat*
5 - *lima*
6 - *enam*
7 - *tujuh*
8 - *delapan*
9 - *sembilan*
10 - *supuluh*

Literature

Most literature is derived from Sanskrit which was translated into Old Javanese or *Kawi* around the 10th century. At that time, the Javanese prince, Erlangga (who ruled Bali through his brother), declared that all Balinese edicts should be translated into *Kawi*. Erlangga also oversaw the translations of the two great Hindu epic poems, the *Ramayana* and the *Mahabharata* from Sanskrit. Today only *dalang* (shadow puppeteers), priests and the older Balinese understand *Kawi*, but the language is still celebrated in the puppet shows of the *Wayang Kulit*, in the modern *Ramayana* ballet, *Wayang Wong*, and in excerpts staged in dances and dramas.

The *Ramayana* is an old-fashioned story of the struggle between good and evil. Rama, the hero, embodies virtue and strength, while his antagonist, Rawana, epitomises evil. The *Mahabharata* recalls the exploits and deeds in the battle of the Bharatas (from ancient northern India).

Balinese Hinduism

Signs of Hindu devotion are everywhere. Small gifts of flowers and rice, scrupulously prepared, are laid on the dashboard of a bemo, or on the counter of a boutique. Women and girls, resplendent in *sarong* and *kebaya* place offerings in temples, hotels and crossroads. They stop awhile to pray, or perhaps light incense to attract the attention of the gods. Small clues to the spiritual life of the Balinese.

Most Balinese practise a variation of the Hindu religion called *Agama Hindu Dharma* (the Religion of the Hindu Doctrine) but sometimes known as *Agama Tirta* (the Religion of Holy Water). Balinese Hinduism is a unique mixture of Buddhism and Hinduism, combined with a pinch of animism from centuries past. The basic tenet of Hindu Dharma is that the soul (*atman*) is reincarnated after death. In what form, depends on personal actions or *karma*, and eventually, a soul may achieve unity with the divine (*moksa*).

The Balinese practise their faith with an earthy exuberance, endeavouring to achieve a balance between philosophy, morals and rituals. And balance is everything.

The Balinese are aware of the ever-present forces of good and evil. One cannot exist without the other, and indeed, nothing but a balance between the two will prevent chaos. The people live between the gods and the demons — endeavouring to please one, and appease the other.

Cosmic stability depends on the co-existence of opposites. In the same way, everything is born, dies and is reborn. The soul lives in the heavens or on the earth. Volcanoes erupt and kill, and later the volcanic ash provides fertile loams for cultivation. And those mangy dogs (*cecing*) that howl all night and devour offerings, are merely evil spirits put on earth to balance all things beautiful. The notion of opposites is epitomised in the *kaja-kelod* axis.

Contrary to popular opinion, the educated Hindus subscribe to a monotheistic religion. Ida Sanghyang Widi is the supreme god capable of many manifestations, the most notable being the holy trinity or *trimurti*: Brahma, the creator; Wisnu, the preserver; and Siwa, the destroyer. Belief in one God is the first of the five principles of the Republic of Indonesia, known as the *panca sila*. Even so, the average Balinese, not troubled with resolving a plethora of Hindu gods with the (Islamic) notion of one god, acknowledges a multitude of different deities who watch over the family, village and land.

Temples

Bali has been called the "land of a thousand temples" — what an understatement! Bali might be a small island, but there are many, many more than a thousand temples. Every village has at least three temples, a family compound has one, each rice growing co-operative (*subak*) has a temple, even corporations have them. Some are simple affairs, others are elaborate sprawling complexes of major and minor temples, incorporating pagodas and shrines.

The three important village temples are: the *pura puseh* ("temple of origin"); the *pura desa* ("village temple") in the centre; and the *pura dalem* ("temple of the dead"). The temple of origin is associated with Brahma the creator, and faces Gunung Agung, towards *kaja*, as does the village temple which is associated with Wisnu, the preserver. The temple of the dead is the domain of Siwa, the destroyer, and faces the sea, *kelod*.

Although no two temples are the same, many do share similarities in design. Most temples have three courtyards, each with a split gate entrance, known as a *candi bentar*. The first courtyard is open and spacious with a number of small pavilions (*bale*) where people assemble for prayer and ceremonial preparations. The second courtyard is much the same, while the inner sanctum is the abode of the gods. Leading to the inner courtyard is a set of doors. Open the doors and a wall prevents you from moving forward — you can step either to the left or to the right. The wall is an *aling aling* and it prevents spirits from entering the courtyard, because it's thought that spirits have great problems negotiating corners! Within this courtyard are a number of *meru* shrines which line the northern and eastern walls. The multi-tiered *meru* have odd-numbered roofs, depending on the god to which they are dedicated. Located in the north-east corner is the lotus throne. This is a *padmasana*, the seat of Ida Sanghyang Widi, the supreme god. If there are three thrones, they are dedicated to the supreme god's manifestations as Brahma, Wisnu and Siwa.

Each temple has a *pemangku* who maintains the compound and anyone, regardless of sex or caste, can become one. The high priest, or *pedanda*, presides over ceremonies, and must be of the *brahmana* caste.

Rites of Passage

The Balinese believe that the individual soul is reincarnated several times until it achieves unity with the divine (*moska*). Of course, it takes some individuals a little longer than others to attain *moska* — depending on their deeds or misdeeds (*karma*). When the soul is in the heavens, between incarnations, the gods protect it; but when on earth, its welfare is the business of the Balinese. From birth to death, Bali's Hindus conduct important rites to guide the soul through its various stages.

The rites of passage begin while the child is still in the womb. A pregnant woman is "unclean" (*sebel*) and is not permitted to enter a temple. When the child is delivered, the afterbirth is buried to attract spiritual guides from each of the four cardinal directions to accompany the child throughout its life. There are further rites for the child at 12 days and at 42 days. After 105 days, the child is placed on the ground for the first time and Mother Earth, *Ibu Pertiwi,* is asked to protect it. Before the ceremony the child is not regarded as a human being; the child's soul is more divine than human, as it has just come from the realm of the gods. And at 210 days (one Balinese year) the child is named. One thing you'll never see is a Balinese baby crawling. They are not allowed to crawl, as do animals, so babies are carried everywhere until they can walk.

The passage into puberty is celebrated for both males and females with the tooth-filing ceremony. The ritual must be completed before marriage, and these days it is often incorporated into the marriage ritual. The canine teeth are considered to be animalistic, so they are filed, and this symbolises the levelling of the volatile and beastly aspects of an individual's personality.

Once the daughter has had her teeth filed, her father is no longer obligated to her. However, the father of a son must finance and conduct his son's wedding ceremony, welcoming the bride as his daughter; and the bride must accept her new family and their family gods. A few Balinese marriages are pre-arranged (with the consent of the boy and girl), and fewer still are mixed-caste marriages. The preferred method of entering into wedlock is characteristically Balinese: it is at once dramatic and pragmatic.

Many young men prefer to "kidnap" their brides. The boy "seizes" the girl and after feigned resistance on her part, he carries her off to a pre-arranged retreat. Of course, her family are suitably outraged by the incident, and her father may organise a mock search party to locate her whereabouts - to no avail. The couple make offerings to the gods and consummate the marriage before the offerings wither. Days later, the bride's father will grudgingly relinquish his daughter, but not without payment. The official nuptials, celebrated by the groom's village priest, are merely a formality as the couple have already married in the eyes of the gods.

Cremation

Cremation of the dead is the most important ritual for the Balinese because it liberates the soul from the confines of the body. The body is merely a temporary and unclean vehicle for the soul whose real home is with the gods. The entire ritual is colourful, noisy and exuberant. No expense is spared, and preparations are undertaken with fervour and care. If the cremation is not organised and conducted as the Hindu edicts dictate, the deceased's soul may wander the earth perpetrating mischief, or return to haunt the family who did not undertake the cremation correctly.

Because of the preparation and cost involved, cremation ceremonies are the privilege of a few, and sometimes group rituals are held. In either case the body is interred until the ceremony, or if the ceremony occurs quickly the body is held in the family compound. During this time in limbo, the soul is said to be agitated, eager to resume life with the gods.

The village priest consults the Balinese calender and chooses an auspicious date. The family then constructs a large tower of bamboo and paper, and decorates it according to the caste and wealth of the deceased. Sometimes the body is enshrined in a life-size bull, built of bamboo and plaster.

On the appointed morning, relatives and friends of the deceased visit the family home to pay their respects. At noon, a procession of family and friends, not to mention well-wishers, a *gamelan* orchestra and anybody who cares to join in, leads the tower to the graveyard. Sometimes there are as many as a hundred bearers, bedecked in white ceremonial robes. The family leads the tower bearers with long strips of white fabric. The vital consideration in all this, is that the soul not return home. And with this in mind, the *gamelan* plays thunderously, the people cheer, and the tower is rotated several times — all to confuse the soul and prevent it from escaping before its delivery to the gods.

At the graveyard, the body is placed inside the bull, or sometimes laid on a mound and wrapped in palm leaves. A priest officiates, chanting the last rites, and then the pyre is lit. Afterwards the ashes are collected, and another procession leads to the sea where the remains are thrown to the wind, representing a cleansing of the soul and disposal of the body. The soul sojourns in heaven before returning to earth in a different body. As mentioned, the status of the reborn soul depends on *karma*, or the soul's conduct in the previous life.

A ceremony to end all ceremonies, a cremation is not a time for tears — the soul is freed from the bondage of the material life and draws closer to unity with the divine — it is a time for celebration. The splendour of the ceremony, the colours, music, incense, and fire, all augment the excitement for the passage of the soul from this life to the next.

The Balinese have certainly caught up with technology, though. Some ceremonies use elaborate loud-speaker systems to transmit the rites, and capture the moment on videotape for posterity.

The Balinese Calendar

Keeping an appointment in Bali can be confusing. The Balinese calendar year is arranged according to two parallel systems; the 12 month lunar calendar and the *wuku* or *pawukon* calendar. Festivals are held on auspicious days for both calendars as well as days where the calendars co-incide. Every day is associated with benevolent or malevolent forces, which must be considered before undertaking any activity. To complicate matters, the Gregorian Calendar, which is based on the solar year and is attuned to the changing seasons, is also used.

The lunar calendar is based on the phases of the moon, similar to the system used in India. Each month has 29 or 30 days to adjust to the moon's cycle of 29.5 days; and each month begins the day following the new moon, which means the full moon occurs mid-cycle. Twelve *sasih* months comprise a year. An extra thirteenth month is added every three or four years to compensate for the longer solar year in the Gregorian Calendar.

The *wuku* calendar is originally Balinese, and probably derives from the cultivation period of rice. The year lasts 210 days, and every day has its own god, constellation of the stars, and omen. The *wuku* year is subdivided into shorter cycles that run concurrently. The most important of these are the three, five and seven-day weeks whose conjunctions determine the most holy days.

Festivals and Holy Days

Each temple has an anniversary, and as there are thousands of temples, there is at least one festival every day. The Badung Government Tourist Office in Denpasar publishes a monthly list of imminent temple festivals, available at most tourist centres.

Odalan

This is a temple's anniversary celebration and occurs once each *wuku* year. Preparations for the much-awaited event begin weeks before, and everyone, but everyone, participates. The temple is given a spring-clean and decorated, and large ornate offerings are created. On the first day, the women carry offerings to the temple, resplendent in elegant ceremonial costume, balancing huge baskets of fruit on their heads. In the temple, the priests bless the offerings with holy water, proffering them to the gods and the spirits who devour their essence. Three days later, the pragmatic Balinese are entitled to the leftovers. During the three-day celebrations, the temple compound is enlivened with food stalls, markets, cockfights and music. Toys, balloons and other colourful paraphernalia are not an uncommon sight. At night, dances, shadow-puppet plays and dramas are performed.

Galungan

The most auspicious of events, this 10-day festival celebrates the creation of the world by the supreme God and celebrates the triumph of good over evil. It is a time of feasting, and re-union with one's family. The Galungan festival occurs once every *wuku* year or every 210 days. Should you see *penjor*, bamboo poles decorated with flowers, swaying over roads, you can be sure *Galungan* is near.

Kuningan

This is held ten days after *Galungan* and brings the festival to a close. *Kuningan* honours the souls of favoured ancestors and deities — a kind of "All Souls Day".

If you're in Bali during the Galungan festival you are likely to witness celebrations. However, many banks and office have restricted hours and most are closed on the day of *Kuningan*.

The dates for Galungan and Kuningan are:
1997	February 19;	March 1
	September17;	September 27
1998	April 15;	April 25
	November 11;	November 21
1999	June 9;	June 19
2000	January 5;	January 15

Nyepi

This is the Balinese new year in the lunar calendar. A holy day, it falls on the spring equinox and is observed as a day of silence. On the eve of *Nyepi*, clamorous rites of purification and exorcism frighten the old-year spirits out of their wits. Then, on the day of *Nyepi*, there's silence. No-one ventures outside, no fires can be lit, no work done, and above all no noise. The deathly stillness will convince all the spirits that the island has been deserted and they'll flee. It's expected that some spirits won't be fooled and will return next year. Again, many banks and government offices are closed on *Nyepi*.

The Performing Arts

Some claim that all Balinese are artists — which is probably a slight exaggeration. Nevertheless, the arts are an integral part of Balinese life and are inextricably linked to Hinduism. There are few professionals as most artists perform as an offering to the gods and for the sheer enjoyment. Poems, plays and dances are vehicles for religious and moral instruction, as well as being just plain good fun.

Far from being traditions resurrected for the titillation of tourists, the Balinese continually experiment with different genres, creating new musical and dance forms. Indeed, the Indonesian Academy of Music and Dance, in Denpasar, was established to ensure the continued vitality and creativity of the performing arts.

Dance and Drama

The traditions of Balinese dance and drama are derived from Hindu Java and ultimately, from India. Balinese dancing is a sophisticated and highly stylised form of entertainment. Every movement is symbolic, and is formed in harmony with every other movement, the emphasis being on the eyes, head and arms, rather than the legs. And the entire performance is bereft of emotion. The best performers are those who are inspired by the divine because they will be transported and become their character. Some of the dances involve pure movement, others meld movement with drama, retelling myths and religious stories. Some dances are secular, some sacred.

Wali dances are those performed in the inner sanctum of the temple and are the most revered. The *Rejang, Baris* and *Sanghyang* trance dances are religious, while the *Legong, Kecak* and *Joged* dances are solely for entertainment. There are hundreds of dances in the Balinese repertoire. They range from the classics to the flavour of the month.

The Balinese learn to dance at a very young age, some girls begin at the age of four, and unlike Westerners, they will continue to dance until they can no longer make the moves.

Here's a list of a few of the dances that visitors are likely to see:

Barong (Kris dance)

A morality play recounting the mythical struggle between the witch, Rangda, and the holy Barong. The story is based on the *Calon Arang* myth which tells of the 12th century Javanese king, Erlangga, who conquered his mother, Mahendratta, a bitter woman given to terrorising villages with her black magic. The final scene of the *Barong* dance features the famous *Kris* trance dance, where the Barong's warriors defeat the evil Rangda and prove the goodness of the Barong by committing suicide with their *kris* swords.

Baris

A demanding solo or group warrior dance. A strapping young warrior prepares himself for war, strutting and posturing, while assuming various stylised gestures and expressions. The warrior

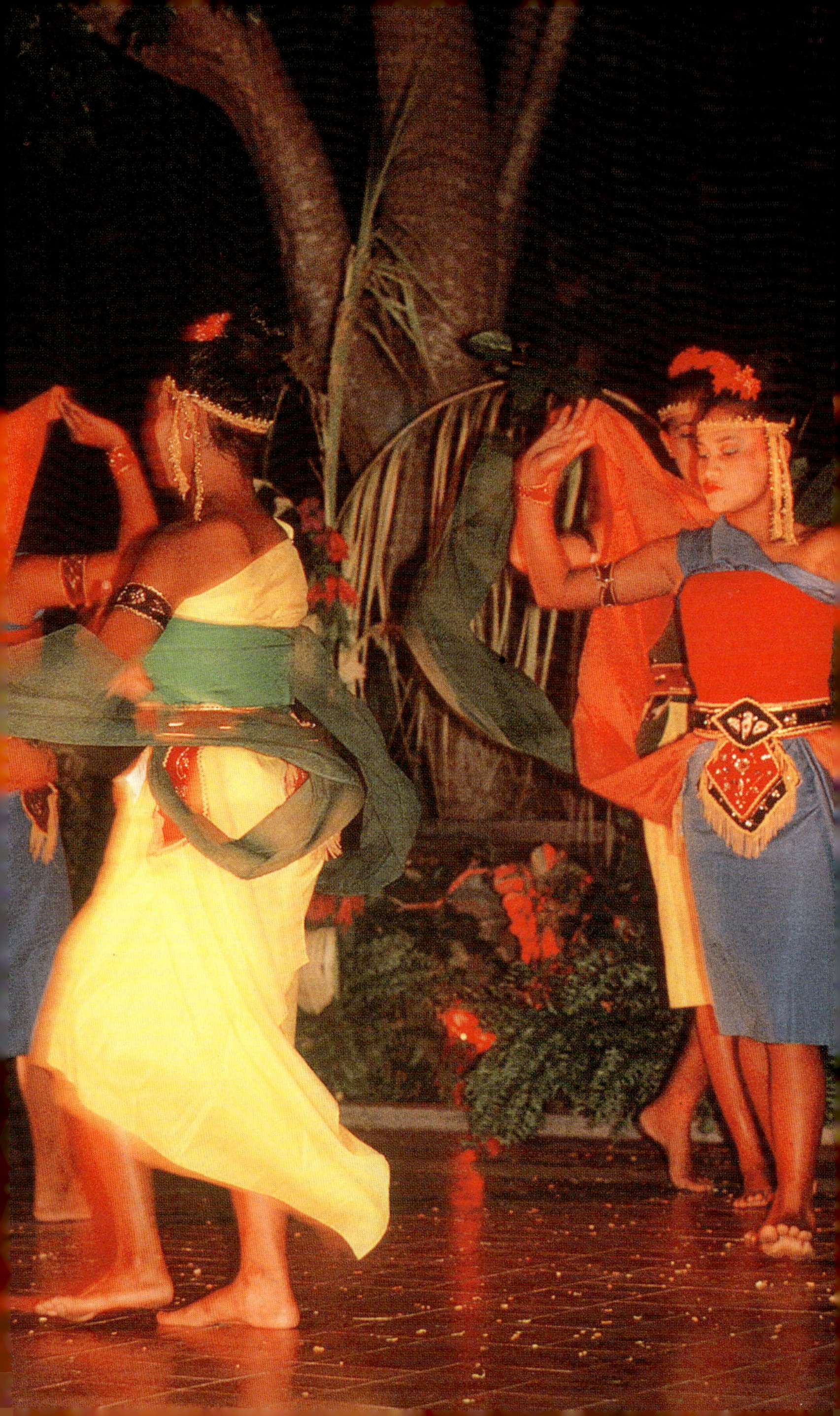

Traditional Baris dance at Nusa Dua

Tirta Empul Spring at Tampaksiring

must exhibit the gamut of emotions equated with a soldier — dignity, ferocity, strength, contempt, and mercy.

Joged Bung Bung

A flirting dance accompanied by a bamboo orchestra. Originally from the regency of Buleleng, the *Joged* features a beautiful young girl who encourages men from the audience to dance with her. Westerners are particular favourites, as even the most lithe and supple of men look unco-ordinated when compared to a Balinese dancer. The audience invariably roars with laughter at the antics of both.

Kebyar Deduk

Kebyar means "lightning" and the dance is one of the most strenuous of all the dance forms. The *kebyar deduk* was created by the Balinese dancer I Ketut Marya, known as Mario, and is performed while in a seated position.

Kecak

The monkey dance. A human orchestra of one-hundred men dressed in chequered sarongs, sway rhythmically, chanting "chucka, chucka, chucka". They provide a musical backdrop to episodes performed from the *Ramayana;* usually the story of the white monkey general, Hanuman, is told, hence the "monkey dance". The dance was created by Walter Spies in the 1930s and was inspired by existing traditions.

Legong

A classical and highly abstract dance performed with exquisite grace by beautiful young girls. There are various stories which accompany the traditional *legong* dances. The dance most often performed recalls the myth of Princess Rangkesari, a beautiful maiden abducted by the king, Lasem. The king attempts to win her favours, but she refuses. When the princess's brother comes to free her, she appeals to Lasem to release her, and warns him of her brother's ferocity. Lasem keeps her captive, and when he ventures out to battle with the brother, he meets a raven, an omen of his impending death. The story finishes unconcluded.

Three girls dance this version, one introduces the story, and the other two, dressed identically, play the parts of the princess and king. The two dancers are tightly wrapped in gold brocade, flattening their bodies — the dance is extremely erotic, but visual sexuality is suppressed.

Elaborate frangipani-laden crowns sit upon their heads and their impassive faces are heavily powdered.

At one moment their movements are perfectly synchronised, the next they separate assuming different roles only to return in perfect accord. The dance is abstract and symbolic, and at times it is difficult to follow the plot.

The *Legong* is probably the most difficult and famous of all the dances. The dance troupe at Peliatan, near Ubud, is said to be the best on the island.

Pendent

Originally a temple procession, danced by male and female *pegmangkus*. The dancers welcomed the gods to the festival, showering shrines with flower petals. These days, the *pendet* is performed by young girls in open dance performances.

Topeng

The name means "mask" and refers to any of the various mask dances. The dancer must convey the character of the mask through gesture and movement. Indeed, the wearer does not assume the character of the mask but is said to be possessed by the mask's spirit. This is why masks are treated with such care.

Music

The Balinese are as musical, as they are dramatic. Music is everywhere — the tones of the gamelan ringing from the local banjar, a boy playing on a *tingklik* (bamboo xylophone), Balinese women singing in the streets or doves "tinkling" overhead as the bells round their necks ring. Sometimes it's difficult to distinguish the noises of nature from those contrived by artists. In fact some historians suggest that music began centuries ago with the chanting and stomping of women harvesting rice.

Most Balinese music derives from the *gamelan*. Few words can describe the frenetic and percussive tones of the *gamelan*. Capable of such soft, haunting music, yet it's usually favoured for its dramatic, fast, thunderous clanging. Some visitors to the island can never appreciate or become attuned to the *gamelan*, mistaking its rippling complexities for a cacophonous din. Many Western musicians are amazed at the complexities of Balinese music, and the likes of Mahler and later, Philip Glass, have been influenced by the *gamelan*.

The term *gamelan* (derived from "*pegamelan*" which means handler), refers to both the orchestra and the instruments. The *gamelan* orchestra is composed primarily of instruments akin to a xylophone, called *gangsa*. The keys are usually bronze placed over bamboo resonators, and beaten with a mallet. The orchestra also has a *riong*, a frame with bronze pots played by four men; a *trompong*, like a *riong* but played solo; a *cengceng*, a frame with cymbals suspended from it; and *kendang*, drums.

The musicians will invariably be male, seated on the ground, and dressed in the uniform of their particular orchestra. The instruments are of invariable pitch, fixed at the time of manufacture. The *gong kebyar* (*kebyar* means "lightning"), is probably the best known of the *gamelan* orchestras. The music is fast, jazzy and syncopated. Kettle drums, pots, gongs, drums and sometimes flutes are paired in rows, and tuned in pairs so that one of the pair is of a slightly higher pitch than the other — achieving a rippling sound.

Puppetry

Wayang Kulit, or shadow play, is the oldest performing art in Indonesia. Inscriptions suggest that it was prevalent by the 9th century, and although the Javanese certainly had puppet shows before this time, the Balinese look upon the *Wayang Kulit* as an indigenous art form.

Probably the all-time favourite Balinese entertainment, the *Wayang Kulit* retells stories from the *Mahabharata* and *Ramayana*. Brightly painted puppets, crafted from cowhide and laced with holes, dance on thin bone handles. Illuminated by lamp, they cast the shadows of gods, clowns and courtiers. Each puppet is instantly recognisable as a character from the story, and each character has a symbolic purpose and stylised movements.

The puppet master or *dalang*, as well as choreographing the performance, narrates, sometimes touching on moral, philosophical, political and social problems. He (sometimes she) is the master, realising all the possible hundreds of characters, subtly combining moral instruction with entertainment. All this and the *dalang* still manages to sit cross-legged manipulating the puppets. And no performance would be complete without the dramatic tones of the *gamelan*.

Art

Painting
Some travellers visit Bali simply to buy paintings. They hop off the plane, catch a taxi to Ubud, acquaint themselves with the going prices, and then begins the buying spree.

Balinese paintings are known for their vibrant colours, iconography, stylised figures and ornate backgrounds, and are almost certainly derived from the *Wayang Kulit* or shadow-puppet theatre. The similarities between the colourful, stylised puppets and the figures depicted in many paintings, illustrate the connection. Of course, the influx of Majapahit Hindus also had an impact on painting styles, not to mention Western artists.

Earliest paintings
The earliest paintings, known as the Kamasan style are traced to the 17th century kingdom of Klungkung, where *Wayang Kulit* figures were incorporated into paintings. Initially, the pictures adorned temples, later becoming decorations for the home. The figures are typically shown frontal, with a three-quarter view of the face rather than a profile as with the puppets. The artists used natural pigments on bark paper, wooden boards, or on woven, unbleached cloth. Themes are mainly derived from the Hindu epics, the *Ramayana* and the *Mahabharata*.

Twentieth Century
In the early 20th century, with no rajas to commission works, many painters laid their brushes to rest. Between the World Wars, a couple of Western artists who'd heard about a haven of artisans, moved to Ubud. The German, Walter Spies, and the Dutch artist, Rudolf Bonnet, established studios in Ubud, encouraging the locals to ignore set formulas, and themselves toying with traditional Balinese methods. The artists used Western-style materials and the themes were often free of

religious symbolism, focusing on daily scenes. Colours were restrained, even monochrome, and the figures comparatively realistic, although light and shade were largely ignored.

A new generation of Balinese painters was born — Made Griya, Gusti Nyoman Lempad and Ida Bagus Anom — all with individual styles. In 1936, Spies, Bonnet and several indigenous painters founded an association called *Pita Maha* devoted to the development of the arts in Ubud, but it disintegrated with the outbreak of the Second World War.

In Batuan, at this time, artists were creating their own styles, some influenced by the Pita Maha. Batuan paintings featured fine lines, painstaking detail filling the entire canvas, and sombre greens and maroons. Themes included fables, legends, the supernatural and later, tourism. I Made Budi, is especially famous for his witty interpretations of tourism, as well as political events.

From the 1950s to the Present

In the 1950s, in Penestanan, a new style emerged influenced by the Dutch painter, Arie Smit, and the Australian Donald Friend. Characterised by strong primary colours and simple, bold lines, the paintings demonstrated a child-like joy of reality. The paintings sometimes referred to as the "naive" or "young artists" style, are extremely popular with tourists, and despite their relatively simple and quick creation, demand the same prices as more complex and technically superior paintings.

There are a few academic painters who have received formal training abroad or at the Indonesian art academies in Yogyakarta and Denpasar. These painters are dedicated to personal styles while still exhibiting Balinese influences.

Carving

The Balinese will carve and sculpt anything: wood, stone, bone, horn, deadwood, even roots. It seems that no stone is left unadorned, no piece of wood bare. From the ornate split gateways of the temples, to the door of your hotel, everything seems to be carved.

Traditionally, stone was carved for temples and buildings. There has always been a demand for stone carvers, because the soft volcanic *paras* used for building, although easy to sculpt, deteriorates quickly. Tourism, however, has altered demand, and many carvers have turned to wood.

Initially, the woodcarvers were *Brahmana*, dedicated to carving for ritual or courtly commissions, and the tradition was passed from father to son. The traditional *Wayang* style was prevalent, depicting religious characters and tales from the *Ramayana* and *Mahabharata* epics.

Under the influence of Walter Spies and the Pita Maha, the style of carving developed to portray realistic, daily scenes. Today, painted carvings made from local soft woods are mass-produced and imitation fruit, garish *garuda* and tacky masks can be bought anywhere. Despite the mindless duplication, there are sculptures carved with genius.

The Art Centre at Denpasar and Ida Bagus Tilems' gallery at Mas, offer rare treasures.

Textiles

Cloth, to the Balinese, is not so much a necessity as a mark of religious and social standing. Even statues and shrines share in the sartorial splendour.

Balinese cloth is amazingly cheap and gorgeous. Buying from the markets is easy, but the best bet is to venture into the weaving factories and cloth shops. And while you're there, have a seamstress transform your purchase into a fine garment.

Batik

Hate to disappoint, but most *batik* sold to tourists is imported from Java. Some factories make hand-figured *batik*, particularly in Gianyar.

Endek

A tie-dyed woven cloth, *endek* is created from the *ikat* method of dyeing. Sections of the fabric are wrapped, and then the cloth is immersed in dye, the wrapped parts remaining undyed. The process can be repeated several times. This creates a muted, wavy pattern.

Kain Prada

These are fine fabrics of woven silk or cotton decorated with gold or silver threads, and are usually made into scarfs.

Geringsing
This is a rare method of weaving, only practised in Tenganan, Karangasem. Both the warp and the weft are dyed in what's called the *double-ikat* method. Colours are made from natural dyes, and are limited to black, red and yellow. One piece of geringsing may take a couple of years to work. Prices are around one million-rupiah range, but the cloth is extremely rare and painstakingly crafted.

Songket
This is the real ceremonial brocade. Gold and silver threads are added on the loom creating a range of patterns from simple lines to intricate lotus flowers and *Wayang Kulit* figures.

Songket is sold in art shops thoughout the island.

Economy

Surprisingly, agriculture accounts for about 40% of Bali's economy, about 10% more than tourism generates. Salt panning, textiles and brickmaking are small industries, and rice, pigs, cattle, coffee, vanilla, cotton and seaweed, are all exported. Despite the fact that Bali is an island, the people have misgivings about the sea and have never been known for their maritime interests. Though, recently, commercial fishing has increased.

Tourism
In 1968, when General Suharto became President of the Republic of Indonesia, the World Bank advised the government to address its national debt problem through tourism—it was good advice. In 1972, the Bali Tourist Development Corporation was formed to create a blueprint for tourism development. The Nusa Dua complex was the first project and profits were to be divided between the Corporation, the consortia who built the complex, and the hotel chains that managed it. Most of the benefits were to be channelled out of Bali, and in fact the direct benefits to Bali were never projected. The Corporation was disbanded in 1978 because of financial difficulties, but the paradigm for development is still used today.

In 1969 when the Ngurah Rai International Airport opened

30,000 visitors landed in Bali. Today about 1.2 million tourists visit Bali annually generating about a third of the economy. Most of the tourism profits however, appear to endup in Jakarta and abroad, rather than with the locals. What's more, the social and environmental costs of tourism to the Balinese, seem to be largely ignored.

Agriculture

It should come as no surprise that rice cultivation dominates the agricultural economy. Rice is usually rotated with other crops, such as peanuts, onions, chilli-peppers and corn.

Rice Cultivation

Rice is not only essential fare but a sacred gift. *Dewi Sri*, the rice goddess, is one of the favoured gods, and worship of this deity predates Balinese Hinduism. Heavy rainfall, natural springs, fertile volcanic loams and constant sunshine make Bali ideal for rice farming. Indeed, such agricultural prosperity has enabled the development of a complex civilisation since early times.

Since the 11th century, all people whose land was fed by the same water channel have belonged to a *subak*, or irrigation co-operative. Distinct from normal village organisations, a *subak* may co-ordinate irrigation of several villages, depending on drainage patterns. The most important duties of the co-operative include the construction of irrigation networks. Developed over the centuries, the irrigation techniques make Balinese rice farming the most sophisticated in Indonesia.

The *subak* also oversees the cultural side of cultivation. All aspects of farming are discussed with recourse to the gods and holy days, and offerings are made to *Dewi Sri* to repel vermin, locusts and evil spirits. When the rice is ready to harvest, the first propitious rice sheaves are used to make a "rice mother" effigy, known as *cili*, later enshrined in the cultivator's household temple to survey and protect the crop. At harvest time, everyone helps, working by day, celebrating by night. *Beras Bali*, the favoured strain of rice, is used primarily for ceremonies, and yields one harvest a year. The introduction of new breeds of rice capable of two or more harvests a year has almost replaced the traditional breed.

General Information

Entry Regulations

Visitors to Bali require a passport which is valid for a minimum of six months upon arrival and a return ticket, and passports should have an empty page to be stamped. Nationals of Australia, Canada, Ireland, New Zealand, Singapore, Thailand, United Kingdom and United States, amongst others, are permitted visa-free entry into Bali. Employment is forbidden on tourist visas or visa-free entry.

Visa-free entry requires that visitors do not exceed a stay of 60 days, and extensions are not permitted.

Health Regulations

Certificates of vaccination are not required unless you have come directly from a country that is infected with Yellow Fever (parts of Africa and South America). In this case you will need to show a certificate of inoculation.

Despite the legal requirements, health authorities advise protection against Typhoid, Malaria, Tetanus, Poliomyelitis and Hepatitis A. See the section on Health below.

Customs Allowance

The following goods may be imported free of customs duty:

50 cigars, 200 cigarettes or 10 grams of tobacco. (Some people do not realise that they can pack quantities of cigarettes bought in their own country prior to travel, the limit pertains only to duty-free purchases.)

All personal effects, 1 litre of alcohol, reasonable amounts of perfume, gifts.

Cameras, video cameras, and a reasonable amount of film, typewriters, binoculars, radios and books are allowed in provided they are taken out at departure.

There is no restriction on the import of foreign currencies in cash or travellers' cheques, but travellers may import no more than Rp50,000 (US$21).

The import of weapons, narcotics, Chinese medicines and literature with Chinese characters, as well as pornographic material, is forbidden. Under the Convention on International Trade in Endangered Species it is illegal to import or export turtle flesh or turtle shell products (including jewellery and ornaments) and ivory.

Exit Regulations

Departure Tax
If leaving Bali by air, the departure tax is Rp25,000 (US$11).
Domestic departure tax varies for different airports and is usually around Rp7000 (US$2.50).
There is no restriction on the export of foreign currencies in cash or traveller's cheques, but the export of Indonesian currency is limited to Rp50,000 (US$21).

Flights should be confirmed three days before departure.

Luggage is charged at an excess over 20kgs. Airline staff will check the weight and any excess is expensive.

Consulates

There are no Foreign Embassies on Bali, and only Australians, Americans and citizens of a few other countries have consular or foreign representatives on the island. If your country is not represented and you lose your passport, you will probably have to travel to Jakarta. Theft or loss of passport must first be reported to the police. Keep a photocopy of your passport and driver's licence for identification at the consulate.

The following foreign representatives and consulates are located in Indonesia:

Australia Jl. Mochammad Yamin 51, Renon, Denpasar,
ph (0361) 235 092
Canada Canadian Embassy, Wisma Metropolitan, Level 5, Jl. Jen Sudirman, Kav 29, Jakarta, ph (021) 510 709
Germany Jl. Pantai Karang 17, Sanur, ph (0361) 288 535

Ireland Irish Consulate, c/- Lane Moving and Storage, Cilandak Commercial Estate, Jl. Cilandak 408, Jakarta Selatan, ph (021) 780 0747
The Netherlands Jl. Imam Bonjol 599, Kuta (0361) 751 517
New Zealand New Zealand Embassy, Jl. Diponegoro 41, Jakarta, ph (021) 330680
Switzerland Jl. Pura Bagus Teruna, Legian, ph (0361) 751 735
United Kingdom British Embassy, Jl. MH Thamrin 75, Jakarta, ph (021) 330 904
United States Jl. Segara Ayu 5, Sanur, ph (0361) 288 478

Immigration

The immigration office (*Kantor Imigrasi*) is at the corner of Jl. Panjaitan and Jl. Raya Puputan, Renon, ph 227 828 (Mon-Thurs 8am-3pm, Fri 8-11am, Sat 8am-2pm).

Money

The unit of currency in Indonesia is the rupiah (Rp), a relatively stable currency tied to the US$. There is no black market for the rupiah. Notes are in denominations of 100, 500, 1000, 5000, 10,000, 20,000 and 50,000; and coins are 5, 10, 25, 50 and 100.

Travellers are advised to take travellers' cheques in the larger denominations as some banks penalise exchange of smaller cheques. Australians travelling only in Bali should feel comfortable with travellers' cheques in Australian dollars. However, many visitors to Bali travel with travellers' cheques in American dollars.

Approximate exchange rates as of April 1997 were:
A$ = Rp1800
U.S.A.$ = Rp2300

Cash and travellers' cheques are very easy to change in the tourist centres and at Bali's Ngurah Rai Airport (if you have arrived without rupiah). You will need your passport as identification to change all travellers' cheques. Banks in your home country will usually be able to organise rupiah in a couple of days, but bear in mind that the importation of rupiah is limited to Rp50,000 (US$21).

Money changers are very competitive in the tourist areas and most travellers find them more convenient than banks. Most of the larger hotels also exchange money, but the rates are usually well below the banks and money changers.

If your hotel has trustworthy facilities for the safe-keeping of your passport and travellers' cheques (most will require two keys to open the safe — yours and the hotel's), it may well be worth the peace of mind to change your money at the hotel rather than carry everything with you.

Major credit cards are accepted by most tops hotels and by a growing number of restaurants and businesses. Many of the banks in Denpasar and the tourist areas will provide cash advances for Visa and Mastercard, but there are no ATMs on Bali as yet.

When dealing with banks, be patient. Always take your passport, and if nothing else, enjoy the air-conditioning.

Banking and Business Hours

Most banks and government departments are open Monday to Thursday, 8am-3pm, and Fri 8am-12pm. Some banks are open on Saturday from 8am-1pm. Most money changers are open from 8am-8pm, and some stay open even later. Retail hours vary considerably, with most shops opening seven days a week from 8am-8pm.

Communications

Telephones

The telecommunications system has vastly improved in the last couple of years. Telkom is slowly modernising the system and its domestic satellite network now reaches all over Indonesia. These days international operators can be connected in a matter of minutes, but demand still tends to exceed supply.

Many phone numbers changed in 1993, increasing most five-digit numbers to six. Should you call an old number a recorded message, in both Indonesian and English, will tell you how to convert the number.

The government-run *Kantor telekomunikasi* has main offices (Kantor Telkom open 24hrs) or branches (Wartel Telkom open 7am - midnight) which offer standardised rates throughout Indonesia, plus a 10% tax. There are also private telephone offices, known simply as *wartel*, offering much higher prices. Local, long-distance and international calls can be made from both Telkom offices and wartel and they also have telegram, telex and fax services.

Telkom Indonesian telephone cards can be purchased with a face value of 60, 100, 140, 280, 400 or 680 units. The standard cost is Rp82.5 per unit (about Rp8250 for a 100 unit card) but some places charge much more than the standard rate. Telephone cards can be purchased from Telkom offices and branches, wartel, postal agents and some money changers.

Telephone books are hard to find, so it's best to use directory assistance for all your enquiries.

Local and Long Distance Calls

A local call is made to any area using the same code. For instance, south Bali (Denpasar, Kuta, Legian, Seminyak, Tuban and Ubud) has an area code 0361, and all calls in this area do not need the prefixed code. All phones permit local calls, whether coin-operated or a card phone. Coin-operated phones usually accept the coins after the person being called has answered.

Long distance calls are made to any area with a different code and can only be made at card phones, Telkom phones or wartel.

International Calls

International Direct Dial (IDD) calls can be made from IDD telephones at Kantor Telkom offices, wartel and through most hotel switchboards. Prices are usually quoted per minute (sometimes for three minutes, and every minute thereafter) but rarely show the 10% tax. Standardised Telkom prices per minute (without the tax) are: Australia Rp 4550; Europe Rp 6180; New Zealand Rp 4550; UK Rp 5200; US Rp 4550.

Public telephones can be used to make international calls billed to your home phone with a telephone credit card purchased in your home country. This is easier said than done, as some people may encounter difficulties connecting to the correct phone number. Home Country Direct (HCD) phones (where you connect with your home country operator so that you can pay with a credit card or reverse the charges) are increasing in number and are available on all IDD telephones or where you see the HCD logo.

Some useful local numbers:
local and long distance operator 100
local and long distance directory assistance 106
overseas operator 101
overseas directory assistance 102
complaints 117
police 110

Post Offices

The Central Post Office is located at Jl. Raya Puputan, Renon, Denpasar, ph 223 565. There are also post offices (Kantor Pos) in Kuta, Jl. Raya Tuban; Sanur, Banjar Taman; Ubud, Banjar Taman; and in Singaraja, Jl. Gajah Mada.

All the Kantor Pos listed above offer post restante services. Mail will be kept for one month. *In theory*, identification is required to collect mail, but just about anyone can search through the mail.

Newspapers and Magazines

Bali Post, a daily Indonesian-language newspaper, focuses on Bali but includes summaries of news from Jakarta and the world. *The Jakarta Post*, Indonesia's major English-language daily, covers Indonesian and international issues (suitably censored, of course), but is difficult to obtain.

The best read for visitors to Bali is *Bali Echo*, a glossy magazine published every two months or so. An informative and well-written magazine, it provides articles on modern cultural issues, interviews with local personalities, as well as reviews on restaurants and hotels. *Bali Echo* can often be found in hotel lobbies and restaurants, or purchased for Rp5000 from most book shops in major tourist areas.

Many international English-language papers are sold by hawkers in the major tourist centres, but there are no fixed prices so they can be very expensive. *The Australian*, *The Age* and *The Sydney Morning Herald* can often be found for Australians wanting news from home, otherwise the *International Herald Tribune*, *USA Today*, *Time* and *Newsweek* are distributed on a relatively regular basis.

Television

The government-run television station, *Televisi Republik*

Indonesia, broadcasts daily from late afternoon to midnight. Indonesian soap operas and entertainment shows are given most air time, but you can catch the evening news in English around 6.30pm. Most hotels have satellite television which receives America's CNN news station as well as *TV Australia.*

Radio

The government-operated radio station, *Radio Republik Indonesia* broadcasts 24 hours a day, and features news programs, chat shows and sporadic English news bulletins. *Hot FM* (93.5Mhz) is a commercial Indonesian pop music station, while *Top FM* (89.7Mhz) is the Kuta-based pop and easy-listening music station featuring the American Top 40 on Sunday afternoons. *Bali FM* (100.9Mhz), broadcast from Denpasar, is an English-language radio station, while *Radio Plus FM* (106.5Mhz) prides itself on quality cultural and news programs.

Health

Inoculations

Inoculations are not required by law for entry into Bali, except if you have come directly from parts of South America or Africa. In this case you will require a valid certificate of vaccination against Yellow Fever. Despite the legal requirements, health authorities recommend vaccination against Typhoid, Tetanus, Poliomyelitis and Hepatitis A, as well as protection against Malaria. Authorities recommend that you consult your doctor about 6 weeks before departure.

Typhoid can be fatal and is contracted through contaminated food, water or milk. Vaccination is advisable, particularly if you intend to venture beyond the tourist centres. The symptoms of Typhoid are a very high fever, abdominal pains, headaches, diarrhoea and red spots.

Hepatitis A and B have similar symptoms — yellowing of the skin and eyes, exhaustion, fever and diarrhoea, persisting for months. Treatment involves rest and total abstinence from alcohol. Medical authorities recommend inoculation against Hepatitis A which is spread through contaminated food or water. Hepatitis B is a much more serious virus spread by sexual contact or contaminated blood, and the need for vaccination depends on lifestyle.

Cholera is prevalent in parts of Asia, but there is no effective vaccination available. Spread via contaminated food and water, symptoms include watery diarrhoea, vomiting, cramps and weakness. While there is no vaccination available against Malaria, anti-malarial tablets are recommended, especially if you intend to visit the mountains. A course of tablets is recommended throughout your visit and following, depending on the treatment. Malaria is spread by infected mosquitoes, so protection against mosquito bites is as important as the tablets. The common symptoms are flu-like: recurring headache, fever and shivering. Malaria can be fatal and can appear within 12 months after a bite.

Poliomyelitis, while not common in the Western world, still lurks in Asia. Most Westerners will have had the vaccine at some time in their lives, but should check with their doctor to ensure they are protected.

While most of the dogs on Bali aren't the kind one would pat, it is important to avoid them and other domestic animals. Likewise for monkeys. If bitten or scratched by an animal, it is possible to contract rabies. The wound should be cleaned thoroughly, an antiseptic applied, and medical treatment sought. Authorities recommend vaccination *after* a bite.

Water

The water is not safe for Westerners. Bottled water is recommended for drinking, and is widely available. It's also advisable to use bottled water when cleaning your teeth.

Hotels will often supply a carafe of purified water daily in each room and this should be safe to drink. Despite suggestions to the contrary, ice is safe for Westerners.

In the past few years the Indonesian Government has vigorously enforced the use of purified water for ice in hotels and restaurants catering to tourists.

Bali-belly

Many travellers complain about Bali-belly. Do not drink the water. Don't even think of brushing your teeth in it or putting your toothbrush under the tap. Avoid seafood in isolated places, raw salads and vegetables washed in tap water, and food left out in the sun. While drinking tap water is a major contributor to

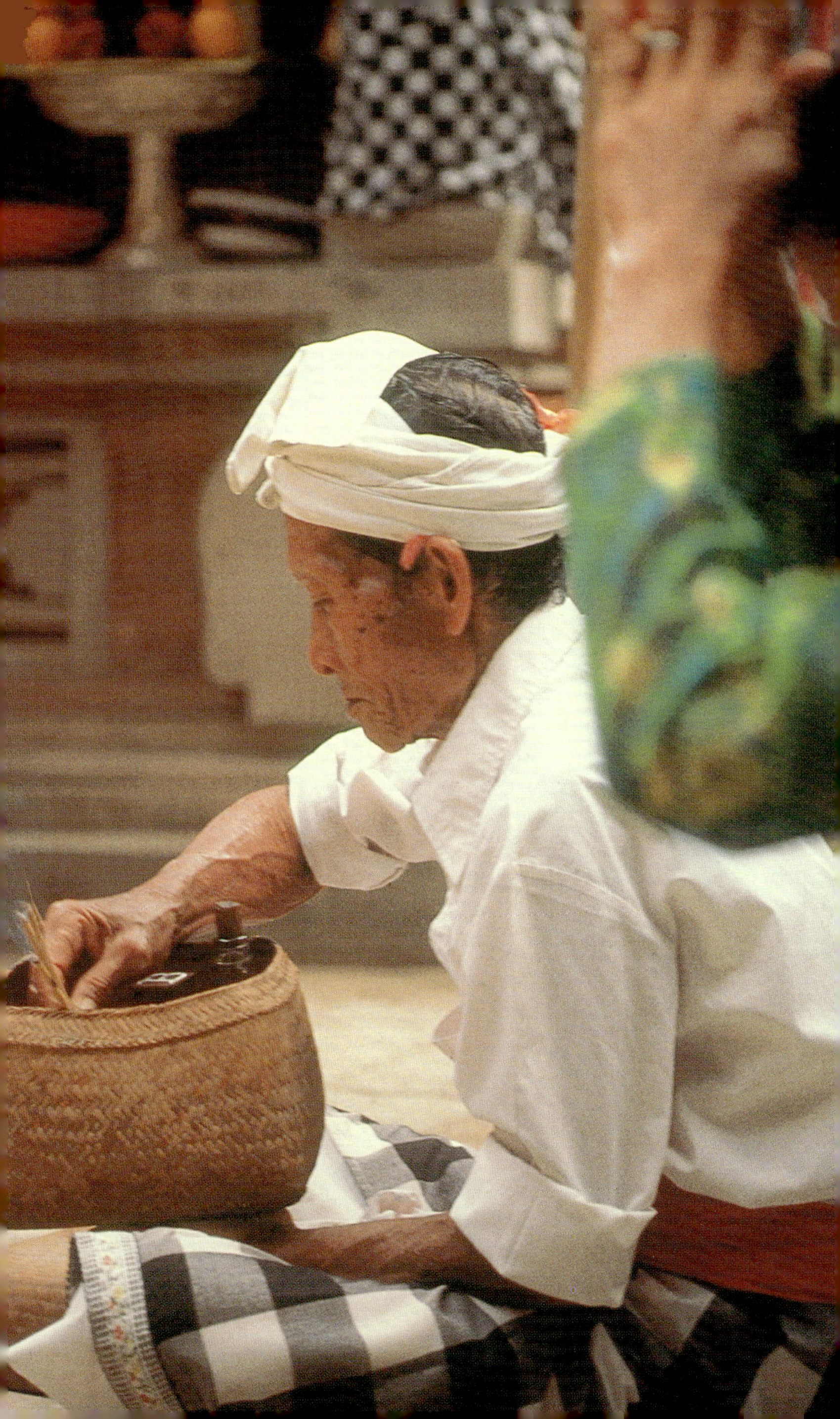

On Kuta Beach

Bali-belly, many travellers fall victim despite scrupulously watching their water intake. The heat, humidity, spicy foods, fruit juices and increased alcohol intake can all contribute to diarrhoea. If you have tummy problems, avoid juice and spicy foods and reduce your food intake. Most importantly, ensure that you do not dehydrate. Anti-diarrhoea treatments can be effective, but if you don't change your diet, the symptoms will persist. Seek medical advice if the attack is particularly severe, lasts more than a couple of days, or is accompanied by a fever.

Precautions

Chemists (apotik) can be found all over Bali, but it's often best to pack a small first-aid kit to take with you.

An antiseptic is a must as cuts and scratches are susceptible to infection in the tropical climate. Wash the wound carefully, apply an antiseptic and keep the area dry until it has healed. Pack Lomotil or the like to stem diarrhoea and rehydration salts to keep hydrated. Heat rashes and fungal infections are common occurrences in hot, wet climates, so it's handy to pack an anti-fungal powder.

And don't forget a hat and sunscreen!

Medical Care

Medical assistance is obtainable at any time and most doctors speak English. *Sanglah Public Hospital*, Jl. Kesehatan Selatan 1, Sanglah Denpasar, ph (0361) 227 911-5. *Wangaya Public Hospital*, Jl. Kartini, Denpasar, ph (0361) 222 141. *Rumah Sakit Umum* (Public Hospital) Jl. Ngurah Rai, Singaraja, ph 22046, 41 046.

If you simply need to see a doctor, the clinics at Kuta, Nusa Dua and Ubud are open 24 hours: Kuta, Jl. Raya Kuta 10X, ph 753 268; Nusa Dua, Jl. Pratama 81A-B, ph 771 324; Ubud, Darma Usadha, Jl. Abangan Tjampuhan, ph 975 235.

For *emergency dental treatment* see Dr Indra Guizot, Jl. Patimura 19, Denpasar ph (0361) 222 445, 226 834.

For minor gum or mouth infections, it's worth trying a little teatree oil (antiseptic) or clove oil (for its numbing qualities), which are widely available throughout Bali.

Miscellaneous

Shipping
Items under 10kg can be sent through the post office and can be registered and insured. Customs have to inspect so only wrap after inspection. Customs closes at 1pm so arrive early. Air cargo is charged by the kg. Bali Delta Express, Jl. Kartini 58, Denpasar, ph 223 340; Bali International Cargo, Jl. Raya Sanur 2, Denpasar, ph 288 563; and Alpha Sigma, Jl. Raya Imam Bonjol 98, Denpasar, ph 227 768 are all reputable and efficient.

Measurements
Metric measurements are used for all weights and measures.

Time
GMT + 8 hours, AEST - 2 hours. As Bali is close to the equator, daylight hours vary only slightly, generally 5am to 5pm.

Electricity
The current is 220 volts 50 cycles AC and uses a two-pronged plug. Many hotels hire adapters or these can be purchased from most duty-free stores.

Dress Requirements
Entrance to a temple requires a sarong and sash, though long pants and sash suffice. Sarongs and sashes are always available at the temples. Nude bathing is not tolerated and is in fact illegal. Dress sensibly when dealing with banks, consulates, etc. Pack a hat and sunscreen.

Conduct
The carefree attitude of the Balinese belies a strict code of conduct and morals. *Some tips:* Always *remove your shoes* when entering a private residence. The *left hand* is associated with toilet activities so give and receive with the right hand. It is *rude to point* and never, *never pat anyone on the head*. The head is considered to be the seat of the soul. I've also been told it is *rude to blow your nose* in public.

Tipping

While not customary, tipping is gaining favour and if someone has provided a service it's appreciated. However, many hotels and restaurants add a 10% service charge, so there's no need to tip. Porterage at the airport is usually about Rp1000 per bag (and you thought they were just being helpful!).

Mandi and Toilets

In recent years, toilets and bathrooms throughout the south of Bali have been modernised to accommodate Western habits. Sooner or later, however, you may encounter Indonesian-style bathrooms. The tub filled with water is not a bath. You stand next to the tub and pour water over yourself with the pot. As for the toilets, there are still the floor-level, starting-block variety to be found in more remote parts. In these areas the locals are less inclined to use toilet paper and the toilets are easily blocked. Use the pot to wash down the waste for the starting-block variety.

Police

For all police emergencies call 110 or contact your hotel.
Denpasar. Jl. Gunung Sanggiang, ph 110.
Kuta. Jl. Raya Kuta, ph 751 598.

Drugs

Once upon a time Bali was a haven for mind-altering substances. Not so now. The drug penalties are extremely harsh and Indonesian gaols are said to be hell! There is no distinction between small and large quantities, and importation and possession are treated the same. In fact, it is an offence not to inform the authorities of offenders.

Photography

Generally, it is advisable to purchase film duty-free before arriving on the island. Slide and print film is easily purchased in the major centres, but check that the film has not been sitting in the sun. Camera batteries in Bali are suspect, so take spares.

In Denpasar, Sanur, Kuta, Ubud and Singaraja there are one-hour developers, and the going rate is around Rp16,000 to develop 36 prints. Given that the standard of developing has greatly improved and that film does not endure well in the humidity, it is worth having films developed on the island. If you do not have a filter avoid taking photos between about 10am and 2pm as the sun is overhead and photos will look dull and washed out.

Theft
In the last couple of years, the number of thefts on Bali has increased. Always be aware of your passport and travellers' cheques and keep them close to the body, preferably inside clothes. Bum bags and the like only advertise that you're carrying these goods.

Pickpocketing often occurs in crowded places and the locals, even though embarrassed by the incident, will not tell tourists their wallet is being lifted. The most prevalent type of theft is usually by deceit. Guys, but sometimes girls, will devise an elaborate story about a poor family member, etc, which usually results in the victim handling over large wads of money. Beware of rush tactics (many tourists are duped by the sense of urgency) and never ever accept an invitation to see someone's village. Offers of assistance, be it for a car, camera, etc, will usually be very costly.

Also be wary of monkeys, especially at Ulu Watu and in the Monkey Forest at Ubud. These rascals are particularly adept at steeling sunglasses or anything shiny, and often use the element of surprise. I have seen hapless victims smacked on the head, their sunglasses stolen in seconds. Usually there is a Balinese guide nearby, and for a few thousand rupiah the items will be returned. The trouble is the monkeys tend to scratch the glass.

Travel Insurance
A must. But read the fine print. The medical facilities for emergencies are restricted so make sure your policy has provisions for your safe and swift removal from the island.

In the case of theft, most insurance policies will require a police report, so contact police on the island as soon as possible.

Churches
There are many church services held on Bali and often the larger hotels can help with locations and times. Churches belonging to Christian denominations are present on the island. **Roman Catholic:** *St Francis Xavier*, Tuban, Kuta. Jl. Kepurdung,

Denpasar. Mass - Sunday 8am; Grand Bali Beach Hotel, Sanur, Legong Room, Saturday 5pm; Bali Hyatt Hotel, Sanur, Hibiscus Room, Saturday 6pm; Bali Sol Hotel, Nusa Dua Conference Hall, Sunday 5pm; Nusa Dua Beach Hotel, Garuda Room, Sunday 6pm. **Pentecostal:** Jl. Karna, Denpasar. *Protestant Church:* Hotel Bali Beach, Garuda Room, Sunday 6.30pm. *Evangelical Church:* Jl. Melati, Denpasar.

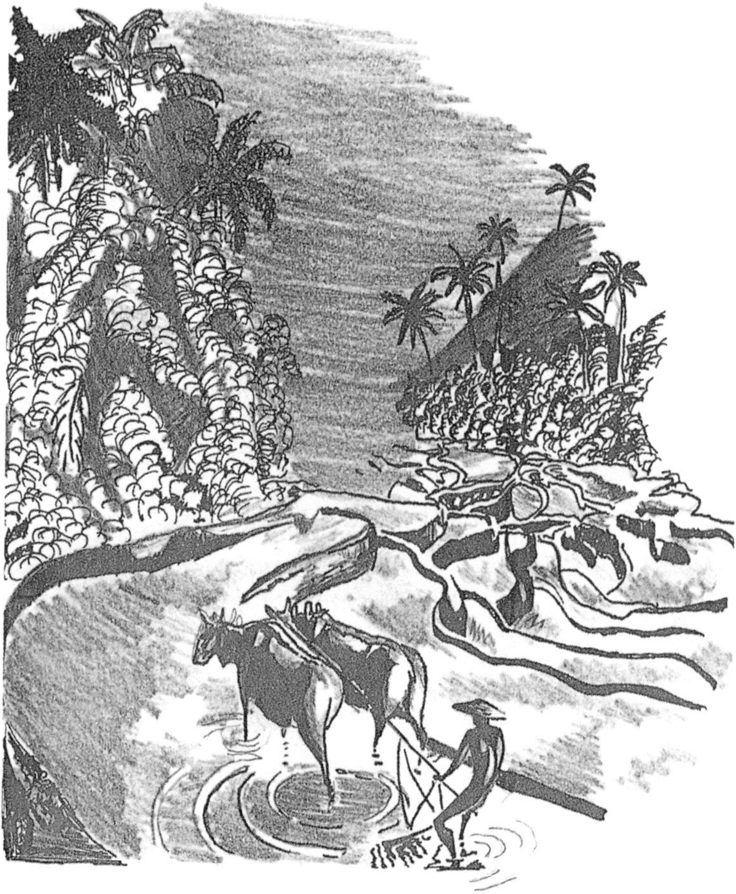

Travel Information

How to Get There

By Air
Cathay Pacific flies direct to Denpasar Mon, Wed, Thur, Sat from Hong Kong.

Continental has flights to Denpasar from:
Los Angeles, San Francisco via Honolulu and Guam (the hub) Tues, Wed, Fri, Sat.

Ansett has flights to Denpasar from:
Sydney -	Wed and Sat
Melbourne -	Wed and Sat
Perth -	Sat and Sun
Darwin -	Wed and Sat
Adelaide -	Sat
Brisbane -	Sat

Qantas has flights to Denpasar from:
Sydney -	Sat and Sun direct
Melbourne -	Mon, Thurs and Sun
Perth -	Tues, Sat and Sun direct
San Francisco -	Mon, Fri, Sat via Sydney
Los Angeles -	Mon, Tues, Sat via Sydney
Los Angeles -	Mon, Thurs, Sun direct
Singapore -	Sat, Sun via Sydney and Mon, Thurs, Sun via Melb
London via Perth -	Thurs, Sat

Singapore Airlines flies to Denpasar daily from Singapore and from London via Singapore.

Garuda Indonesia (national carrier), has flights to Denpasar from:

Sydney -	daily
Melbourne -	daily except Thursday
Perth -	daily
Adelaide -	Mon and Fri
Brisbane -	Mon, Wed, Fri, Sat
Darwin -	Wed, Sun
Auckland -	Tues and Sat
London -	Mon, Wed and Sat
Singapore -	daily
Hong Kong -	daily
Honolulu -	Mon, Tues, Thur, Sat, Sun via Biak
Los Angeles -	Mon, Wed, Fri, Sat, Sun, via Honolulu and Biak.

From Java

There are several options for those wishing to travel overland from Java to Bali. Java is served by a dense network of bus routes and rail services. The two-month Indonesian tourist visa allows considerable time to island hop, as long as entry is via an official immigration gateway. Many tickets sold through local agents on Java offer passage from Jakarta, Yogyakarta or Surabaya straight through to Denpasar or even Kuta or Ubud, and include the half-hour ferry jaunt. Travelling the opposite way is just as easy to organise through local agents.

By Air

Garuda and the domestic airlines such as Merpati and Sempati have flights between Denpasar and major provincial capitals, and prices tend to be very competitive. A one-way fare from Jakarta to Denpasar costs around Rp300,000. Garuda also offers a *Visit Indonesia Pass* for US$300 for three one-way flights (with various possible extensions) but you must fly into and out of Indonesia with Garuda. You cannot be an Indonesian resident.

By Train

It is possible to begin the trip to Bali by train from Jakarta through Yogyakarta to Surabaya or along the north of Java from Semarang to Surabaya. There are first-class and economy class seats, but given the length of the journeys, first-class with its air-conditioned carriages, comfortable seats and complimentary meals would seem to be the ticket.

For instance, the 16-hour trip from Jakarta to Surabaya on the first-class air-conditioned *Mutiara Utara* night express train costs about US$33 one-way. From Gubeng Station in Surabaya, take the *Mutiara Timur* train, which departs at 11am and 9.30pm for Banyuwangi on the eastern tip of Java. This 8-hour trip costs about US$4. Then you transfer to a bus which takes the ferry across to Bali and continues on to Denpasar, all for US$1.

By Bus

There are regular bus services from Jakarta, Yogyakarta or Surabaya, including the ferry crossing, to Denpasar's Ubung bus and bemo terminal. The 26-hour trip from Jakarta to Denpasar costs about Rp23,000 economy, or from Yogyakarta, the 16-hour trip costs about Rp17,000 economy. Then from Surabaya to Denpasar costs about Rp12,000 and takes 10-12 hours. Some buses will travel on to Kuta and Sanur, if yours doesn't, it is very easy to catch a taxi or charter a bemo.

There are many local operators both in Bali and Java organising shuttles across the islands and prices vary with levels of comfort.

By Ferry

Any form of transport from Java to Bali has, of course, to link up with the ferry. The journey across the Bali Strait from Ketapang in East Java to Gilimanuk takes about 30 minutes and private and government ferries ply the route, leaving at 15 to 20-minute intervals. But if it's vacation time, waiting to board can take hours. From Bali you can trip across to the island of Lombok from Padangbai on the east coast. The ferry trip takes about 4 hours or so and departs every 2 hours (tickets range from Rp4700-Rp8750). The Mabua Express catamaran departs from Benoa Harbour twice daily to Lembar on Lombok. Tickets for the 2-hour journey range from US$18-US$25.

Tourist Information

There is a tourist information centre at the airport, or visit the Bali Government Tourism Office in Denpasar at Jl. S. Parman, Niti Mandala, Renon, Denpasar, ph 222 387 or in Kuta at Jl.

Bakung Sari, Kuta, ph 251 419. While not really helpful with specific information, the offices will provide you with a map and a calendar of events. There are also branch offices on the island and information on these is included in the relevant sections.

Accommodation

Bali offers a wide range of accommodation from opulent 5 star hotels to spartan *losmen*. Visitors can choose to stay in the confines of a resort offering around-the-clock services or opt for medium-priced accommodation close to the action. Likewise, there is no shortage of options for the shoe-string traveller.

In the past few years some stunning properties in the mid-price range have found a home on Bali. For instance, *The Serai* in Candi Dasa, on the east coast, is a luxury, modern resort with rooms for around US$130 In Ubud, *The Chedi*, perched above the Ayung River, provides perfect isolation and its restaurant is lauded well beyond Bali. *The Waka di Ume*, the house in the rice fields, in Ubud, offers tranquillity amongst the rice fields and Balinese-style new-age hospitality.

Prices vary according to location, amenities, availability of air-conditioning and hot water, as well as the season (book early during December to February). They are usually quoted in US$ and do not include the 10-15% service charge nor the 10% government tax.

I have listed a range of hotels in the sections on the various towns, but please remember that the prices quoted should be used as a guide only. Rates can change quickly, although you can probably be sure they won't be reduced.

Another thing. Many hotels call themselves "cottages" and "bungalows", when in reality they are two-storey cement blocks. If booking your accommodation through your travel agent, it's wise to ask what your accommodation entails and just what amenities are included.

The most economical and expedient way to book your accommodation is through your travel agent at home. Many tour agencies offer flight and hotel packages at reduced rates, including hotel and airport transfers, making your holiday relaxed and carefree.

Local Transport

Taxis

The number of metered taxis has increased markedly in the past few years, especially in the southern tourist centres. Thank the Gods! They're a vast improvement on the bemo touts. Not only can they be hired for trips to restaurants and the like, but they're generally willing to go to all sorts of tourist destinations like Tanah Lot and Ulu Watu. Oftentimes, it's cheaper to hire a taxi for two people than it is to travel on a "guided tour".

Having said that, many are loath to turn on the meter, pulling tactics such as covering the meter with a cloth or pretending the meter is broken. Insist on using the meter before jumping in, or hail another.

Although booking a taxi through your hotel may cost you an extra Rp1000, the taxi will be in a much better condition and for really long journeys an air-conditioned taxi is a must!

Metered taxis charge Rp1500 flagfall and about Rp500 per kilometre.

Public Bemo

The most convenient and cheapest form of transport is the public bemo. Not to be confused with bemo available for charter, the public bemo ply the routes between Denpasar and just about every major provincial town on the island.

Public bemo operate from dawn to dusk, and although they don't operate to a timetable they are frequent. The fares are fixed, but unfortunately tourist prices are gaining favour, and vary for different bemo. You can often ask the going rate but sometimes the locals clam-up and you may have to bargain with the fare collector. For public bemo terminals, see the entries in the sections on the various towns, as well as the section on Denpasar for the central bemo terminal.

Private Bemo

The all-pervading "transport" touts are as pestilent as the watch hawkers that line the streets of Kuta. Forever soliciting, they seem to have little success. Although they bargain, they demand exorbitant prices and unless you're desperate for a ride, an encounter with these people is simply an exercise in exasperation. If you're travelling in a group a shared fare may be cheap, but I'd sooner take a taxi.

Dokar
Dokar are pony-driven carts, and during Dutch colonisation were the most luxurious means of transportation. Although superseded by machines they are still to be found in poorer places and, of course, for the pleasure of travellers.

Do-it-yourself
Driving around Bali might be the best way to see the island, but it's not the safest. It's not so much that the Balinese drive fast — in fact they travel on average at about 40kph. They're not really impatient, rude or tense. They're *gila* (crazy)!

Perhaps it's the overcrowding. The roads are often narrow and pot-holed, and a lot of bicycles and motorbikes use them. In fact, trying to pass motorbikes five-abreast, with families perched precariously and women side-saddle, can be a little disconcerting, if not terrifying. Not to mention contending with the stray dogs, cats and chickens that feel compelled to amble across the road with little fear of their impending peril.

There are a few rules: drive on the left-hand side, overtake on the right, always honk before overtaking (most motorbikes don't have mirrors) and the bigger the vehicle, the more right of way. Good luck!

Before you hire a car, you'd be advised to acquire a good map. Many of the roads in Denpasar and around Kuta are one-way, and you may have to circumnavigate the area several times before finding an inroad. Of course, there are maps and there are maps. Periplus Maps are highly recommended for their accuracy and detailed legends. (You'll need a good map to find the nearest petrol station.)

You'll also need an international driver's licence. The Traffic Police Department (Polisi Lalu Lintas, Jl. Seruni, Denpasar, ph 227 711) issues temporary driving permits, but it is probably easier to procure an international driver's licence in your home country (rather than suffer the vagaries of the Balinese bureaucracy). You must carry a permit and the vehicle's registration papers at all times, as this infringement carries a fine, and the police pull drivers over regularly.

Petrol (*bensin*) costs around Rp700 a litre and there are few petrol stations so keep an eye on the fuel gauge. The station on Jl. Puputan in Denpasar is open 24 hours.

Car rentals

If you do decide to drive, the Suzuki Jimny, which fits up to four people and costs around US$45 a day, is popular. Prices are fixed, but bargaining is permissible for longer periods. Insurance is often not included in the price, and while it may cover the vehicle if it is a write-off it may not cover minor damage. Be warned. It's the minor damage that'll cause you a major headache in the long run. With this in mind, scrutinise the vehicle, and agree on the defects with the owner before hiring the car. And get them in writing. If you wish to travel beyond Bali, check with the rental agent first. Many agents do not permit their cars to leave the island.

Oh, and another thing, rental agencies will often want your passport as security. Some will accept a large deposit, but whatever the outcome, you'll probably have little bargaining power when you return the vehicle.

Then when you're through the hiring process, check your map and get yourself to the nearest petrol station — there'll be just enough petrol to get you there.

The following rental agents are reputable:
Avis Rent-A-Car, Jl. Veteran 5, Denpasar, ph 224 233; Jl. Raya Kuta, Kuta ph 751 474; Jl. Danau Tamblingan, Sanur, ph 289 138.
Bali Car Rental, Jl. By-pass Ngurah Rai, Sanur, ph 288 539.
Toyota Rent a Car, Jl. Raya By-Pass Nusa Dua, Jimbaran, ph 701 747; Ngurah-Rai Airport, International Arrival Halls, ph 753 744.

Motorbike rentals

Motorbike casualties, particularly tourist casualties, occur with monotonous regularity. Only the most experienced riders should entertain ideas of riding on Bali. There are numerous agents offering a wide selection of bikes, and rental starts from about Rp10,000 a day (less if you rent for long periods).

*Shop around for the best deal, remembering that safety is of the utmost importance — consider the state of the motorbike.

*Always carry the registration papers and your licence with you.

*If you intend to travel by motorbike take your own helmet because the plastic affairs that accompany the bike are inadequate. Besides, riding without a helmet is illegal.

*Don't leave your passport with the rental agent.

*You should possess an international motorbike licence, if not, you can spend hours at the police station in Denpasar going through the rigmarole of being tested. Licences are not difficult to procure, but be patient and dress respectably.

Bicycles
Cycling is yet another form of transport on this wonderful island. There are plenty of bikes to hire at very reasonable prices (Rp2000 per day), but make sure that the bike is roadworthy.

> **For serious bikers: don't ride at night or the middle of the day; take plenty of water; and wear a hat.**

The following table gives some idea of the distances involved in touring Bali.

Distances from Denpasar to:

Amlapura -	78km (48 miles)
Bangli -	40km (25 miles)
Batubulan -	8km (5 miles)
Bedugul -	46km (29 miles)
Besakih -	61km (38 miles)
Celuk -	11km (7 miles)
Gelgel -	43km (27 miles)
Gianyar -	27km (17 miles)
Gilimanuk -	128km (80 miles)
Kintamani -	68km (42 miles)
Klungkung -	40km (25 miles)
Kuta -	9km (6 miles)
Mas -	22km (14 miles)
Negara -	95km (59 miles)
Nusa dua -	23km (14 miles)
Sanur -	7km (4 miles)

Singaraja - 78km (48 miles)
Tampaksiring - 37km (23 miles)
Tanah Lot - 31km (19 miles)
Ubud - 25km (16 miles)
Ulu Watu - 30km (19 miles)

Day Tours

Most hotels offer day tours, as do the numerous tour agents. The island is so small that it's possible to travel from say, Kuta in the south, to Singaraja on the north coast, in about three hours. So even if you plant yourself in one place it is still possible to cover all of Bali.

Most tour agencies as well as hotels offer similar trips around Bali. The following tours can be taken from just about anywhere on the island and prices will depend on your agent, the comfort level of the transport, where the tour departs from and the number of people on the tour. It is also possible to choose your own destinations, but check out the prices of standard tours before putting together your own combinations.

You may soon notice that most English-speaking Balinese are also amateur tour directors. Depending on the individual, sometimes you'll get a better tour from the guy that tends the bar in your hotel, than from a licensed agent. The Balinese are enamoured of their island and generally have a good understanding of the history and culture. However, there are two qualifications to the above. The Javanese, while just as enthusiastic about the tourist dollar, do not match the Balinese's enthusiasm for the island. Secondly, there are many attractions on Bali that forbid non-licensed agents to accompany Westerners, and this is well-policed at the Besakih complex, for instance. Make sure you get what you're paying for!

Furthermore, any purchases you make along the way will earn a commission for your "agent", so shopping in the villages is not necessarily cheaper than shopping in the tourist centres.

Kintamani Volcano Tour

If taken from the south, the tour to Kintamani is usually 8 hours long, stopping along what has become known as the "handicraft highway" to Ubud, then onto Kintamani to view Gunung Batur, an active volcano, and the third highest mountain on Bali. The stops usually include Batubulan (a centre for stone carving), Celuk (known for silver and gold works), Mas (a village of wood carvers), Ubud (famed for its paintings), Goa Gajah (the Elephant Cave and 11th century monastery), Gunung Kawi (the Royal Tombs) and Tampaksiring (the holy spring of Tirta Empul). The tour's "highlight" is the buffet lunch (Rp15,000) in the huge cement viewing gallery in the village of Kintamani. Apart from the packs of hawkers that greet all tourists to Kintamani and the awful buffet food, Kintamani does not afford the best view of Gunung Batur. The view is good, but Penelokan and the villages in the crater beside the lake provide better vantage points to view the volcano.

Besakih or Mother Temple

The Besakih Complex or Mother Temple is the temple for all of Bali. Rather than one temple, it is a multitude of temples sprawling down the side of Gunung Agung, the sacred mother mountain and "navel of the world". The highest mountain on Bali, Agung is an active volcano which last erupted in 1963, days before the 100-year Eka Dasa Rudra purification ceremony, killing thousands of Balinese.

When departing from the south, the tour follows one of either two routes. The first route is via Batubulan to Tampaksiring taking in the same villages as the Kintamani tour, while the second travels south-east via Klungkung. Klungkung was once the seat of royalty for the regency of Klungkung, and the site of a magnificent palace and court. All that remains of the palace's former glory is the Kerta Gosa or Court of Justice with its ceiling friezes depicting the machinations of the court and the service of justice. The tour invariably stops at Bukit Jambul to sample the buffet lunch while taking in the panorama of rice terraces. This tour also stops at the fishing village of Kusamba and Goa Lawah the very smelly bat cave.

Tanah Lot

This is usually an afternoon tour concluding with a sunset view of Tanah Lot, a temple perched on an outcrop of rocks on the south-west coast. Depending on the weather, the view can be spectacular or very disappointing. Stops along the way include Alas Kedaton (the holy forest of monkeys), and the temple of Taman Ayun at the former royal centre of Mengwi.

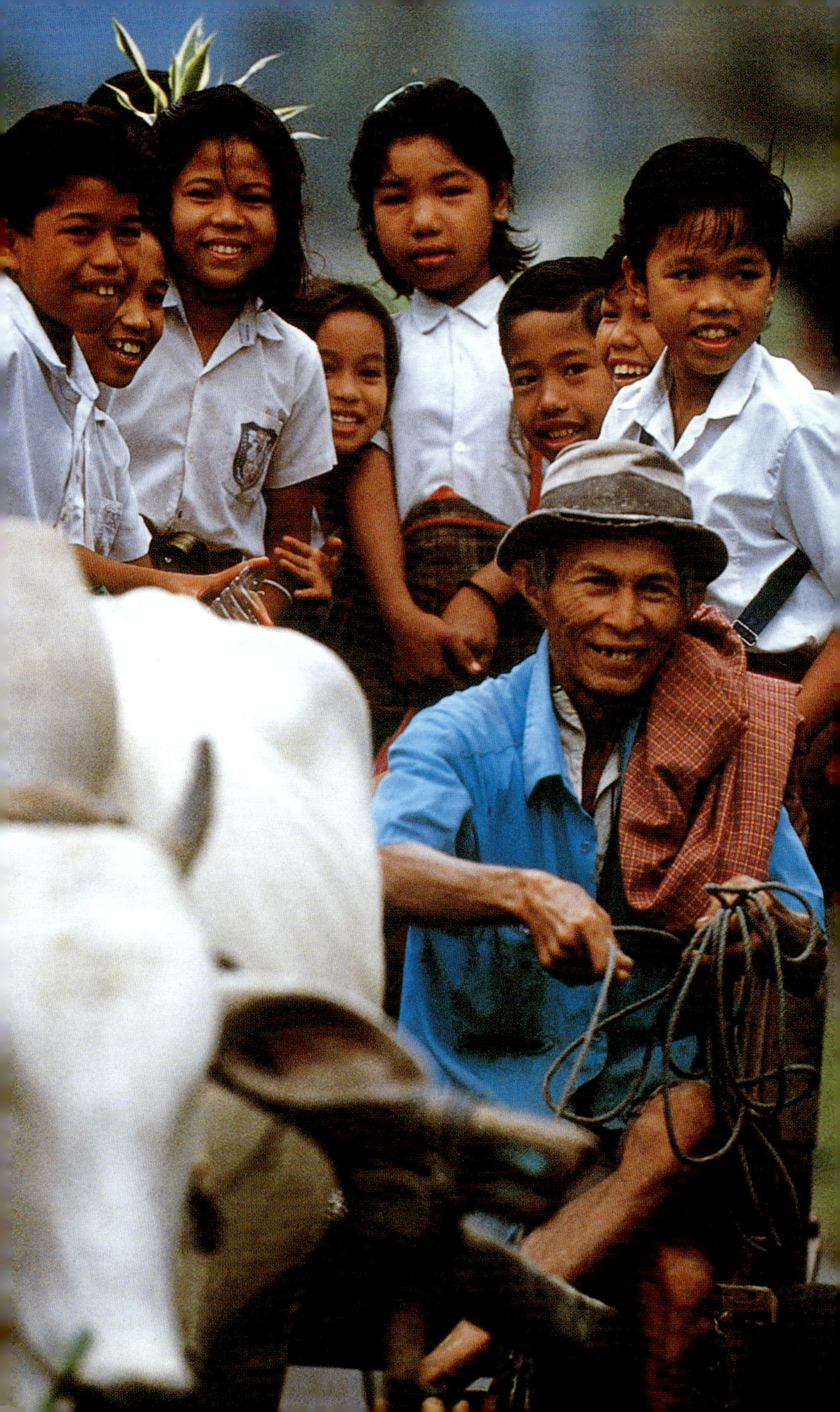

A typical street stall in Legian

Visitors at the Royal Tombs of Gunung Kawi

Cruises

Various companies offer cruises around the island. Book a day trip, or groups can charter a yacht for extended trips to other islands in the archipelago. *Trade Wind Yacht Charter* (PT *Tourdevco)* is highly recommended, and can be located at Bali Benoa Port, ph 231 591. Bali Hai Cruises, Benoa Harbour, ph 720 331 and Wakalouka Cruises, Benoa Harbour, ph 723 629 both sail to Lembongan Island on modern catamarans.

Sights, attractions and suggested tours are listed in the relevant sections. The tours listed above are merely a selection of the kinds of tours available and are by no means exhaustive.

Food and Drink

Balinese daily fare is simple. Most meals are created around white rice or *nasi*, and there is little variation. Brightly coloured rice cakes *(jaja)* are the usual Balinese breakfast, and other meals involve rice mixed with vegetables, peanuts and sometimes meat (beef being the exception). Spices, especially chilli, are sprinkled with gay abandon.

There are no real meal times. Women prepare and cook the food in the morning, leaving it in pots covered with palm leaves, for leisurely consumption throughout the day. It seems that eating is one of the few activities the Balinese choose to do alone.

Festive Foods

Feasts for the gods are a different matter. Ceremonial food is a community effort focused in the kitchen of the temple. The men usually slaughter the animals in the early hours of the morning, and then cook the meat in the temple, and the women tend to the rice and vegetable dishes. When the preparation is complete, the food is divided and some laid on banana-leaf squares as offerings to the gods, the leftovers are for the cooks.

A feast might entail *babi guling* (roasted suckling pig), *betutu bebek* (duckling roasted in banana leaf), *nasi goreng* (fried rice mixed with meat and vegetables), perhaps *mei goreng* (fried noodles) and definitely *lawar* (a salad of finely shredded meats, coconut, papaya and spices). Of course, no banquet would be complete without a sate, usually chicken (*ayam*), pork (*babi*), goat or turtle meat, which are skewered and smothered in a peanut sauce. *Rijstaffel*, the much-lauded Dutch "rice table" creation, is a variety of side dishes served with steamed rice.

Popular dishes of the archipelago include *soto ayam* (chicken broth), *ikan* (fish) cooked in various spices and sauces, *nasi padang* a very spicy but cold Sumatran dish, and *gado-gado* (rice salad with peanut sauce).

Meals are accompanied by *sambal* sauce, a concoction of shallots, turmeric, ginger, garlic, cardamom seeds and red peppers. It's hot!

Restaurants

In the tourist triangle, there is a multitude of restaurants specialising in a multitude of cuisine. As in any country, a busy restaurant usually means that the food is good and the produce fresh. Indonesian food is common, but real Balinese food is rare, and both are modified for Western taste buds. If you really want to sample genuine Balinese food, go no further than the various night markets (*pasar malam*). Watch that the meat is not left for the delight of insects, and that any food washed in water is thoroughly cooked. The treats offered by the itinerant cooks with carts are generally not recommended and you'll see few Westerners availing themselves of these goods. I think the same applies as to the night markets. The food is authentic, but look to the preparation.

Drinks

In the tropics, cold drinks take on a whole new meaning. Every restaurant, *warung* and bar serves iced juice: any fruit you'd care to mention is blended with ice, and sometimes coconut milk. The addition of avocado makes this already luscious drink, nectar for the gods.

If you venture into the warung and markets you'll probably encounter *es campur*. Made from any number of fruit bases, it's a lumpy and brightly coloured concoction, adored for its sweetness. The main ingredients are shaved ice and palm sugar syrup, combined with tapioca, coconut, agar-agar (gelatin) and other floaters, to taste.

Water, tea and coffee (Bali Coffee is packaged for the tourist market) are all consumed in copious amounts on a daily basis, but the Balinese have also created some wicked brews.

The distinctive Balinese drink, *brem* (not unlike sweet sherry) is a sweet wine distilled from red or white rice. Yeast is added to cooked rice which is wrapped in palm leaves, and after a week, wine can be squeezed from the rice.

Tuak is a mild wine made from the frothy juice of palm flowers, and takes about a day to ferment. Tuak varies in strength and sweetness from early collection (about 1% alcohol) to that left until evening or even the next day (5% alcohol).

Bali's own moonshine, the colourless *arak*, is distilled from rice wine and has an obnoxious smell. An acquired taste (although it may take only one or two drinks to acquire), it is often consumed straight or with soft drink. Actually, *brem* mixed with *arak* isn't a bad drop.

Beer drinkers will feel at home in Bali. There are a number of local brews that are inexpensive, or imported Australian and European beers are available throughout the island. As for wine, most of the larger hotels and restaurants sell imported wines but the Indonesian tax on wine is very high, making wine prohibitive. In fact, most imported wines have at least a 600% mark-up on their home country's retail price! A couple of companies, foremost Hatten wines, are experimenting with local grapes grown in Singaraja, and are producing reasonably priced wines. The taste test? I'll let you be the judge.

Fruit

Balinese fruit is a real treat. Pineapples, papaya, coconuts, bananas, mangoes and avocados are plentiful and cheap. There are some taste sensations that you may not have encountered.

Rambutan - tastes like a cross between a lychee and a grape, and has an unmistakably hairy, red skin. This is definitely my favourite.
Mangosteen - white, segmented flesh, with a purple, black or brown skin. Tastes exquisitely sweet.
Salak - has a hard almost spiky skin with the flesh also hard, and tastes slightly bitter.
Blimbing - has green or yellow skin and its cross-section is star-shaped.
Durian - do not let the odious smell of this fruit deter you. It

tastes wonderful.
Nangka - jackfruit.
And of course there's always fresh, icy cold fruit juice.

Coconut Palms

The coconut is revered by the Balinese, probably because every inch of the plant can be used for something. The coconut palm provides: oil for cooking and lamps; sweet water for drinking; the flesh makes milk for cooking; the wood is used for building and furniture; the leaves wrap offerings for the gods; the "palm cabbage" and flesh of the coconut are edible; and the gum from the flower buds is used for palm beer. Copra, the dried flesh from the nut, is exported.

Entertainment

There is no shortage of entertainment on Bali. Local dance, puppet and theatre performances provide amusement for those who desire cultural titillation, while at the other end of the spectrum, pubs, bars and discos cater to those who seek less cerebral pleasures.

See the **Entertainment** section for each village for listings.

Shopping

Bargaining

If you've come to shop, you've come to the right place. In Bali, the simple "tagged-item-hand-your-money-over" syndrome, is only half the story. There are other approaches you may not have encountered.

There's the highly animated and sometimes anxiety-provoking form of shopping, called bargaining. This is the traditional means of purchasing items and it's expected. There are two ways to approach bargaining. Ask the price and then make a counter offer that's about 30% of the original price. The vendor's next price will probably be 5% less than their original price, then it's up to you to make a counter offer higher than your original 30% offer. The final price is usually about 60% of the vendor's original offer. Once you have agreed on a price you cannot renege.

Alternatively, if you've been shopping around, make the first offer, with your final price in mind.

Prices will vary according to the season, the seller's profit margin for the day, and her or his estimation of the buyer. And the theory is, the more you buy at the one shop, the better the bargains should be. The much-touted morning prices are usually cheaper. As the Balinese are superstitious, they believe that their first sale will bear on the day's business, and are often happy for a good to be sold cheaper than usual just to clinch the first sale.

The secret to bargaining is to maintain your humour. It's the spirit of the transaction that counts. The Balinese will feign offence and disgust at your first offer, and you are welcome to do the same. Do not take it personally. Be as animated and as excitable as the vendor. If the sale is made, those sighs and looks of incredulity will turn to smiles.

It's simple in theory. If it's any consolation, everyone feels cheated at least once — put it down to experience. The most important fact is that you bought something you wanted.

Just when you think you've adapted to bargaining, they spring fixed prices on you. There are places where bargaining is inappropriate, for instance, most hotels, shopping centres, supermarkets and restaurants have fixed prices. But when it comes to *losmen*-style accommodation bargaining can be appropriate if you want to stay for a week or if it's the off-peak season (April to October). In the south, many boutiques and jewellery shops have fixed prices but are very competitive.

And then there's the hawkers. On the beach, walking down the street, sometimes even in the hotel grounds, are pedlars importuning you to buy, buy, buy. Whether it's perfume, watches or jewellery — the stuff isn't worth buying. Worse than the rubbish they're soliciting, is the fact that they seem to be having a negative effect on tourism. Many travellers cite hawkers as the reason they hated Kuta and Legian. Whatever ploy you use to discourage them, be it ignoring them, being courteous, or telling them where to go, they persist. They're damnable and if the authorities cared about the future of the south, they would outlaw them. They're a blight on the island.

Likewise with the amateur masseurs. They'll give you a good rubdown on the beach (Rp6,000 for an hour) but if you want the real thing many hotels have professional masseurs whose rates start from Rp25,000.

Batik and Other Fabrics

Surprisingly, the majority of *batik* is machine-made and imported from Java. Nonetheless, exquisite hand-made *batik* can be found in the village of Gianyar. Traditional Balinese hand-woven fabrics are probably the best buys, and can be purchased in shops in Gianyar and Singaraja.

In Singaraja (on Jl. Veteran in between the library and tourist information service) is Puri Agung Sinar Nadi where women weave silken fabrics on the premises.

In Tenganan (about a kilometre out of Candi Dasa proper), women still practise the art of double *ikat*, which involves tie-dyeing both the weft and warp threads before weaving. Known as *geringsing*. The cloth is quite expensive and elegant.

Leather Goods

Kuta is the best place to buy leather. The shops are very competitive and the goods are more fashionable than in the other tourist centres. In most places the price is negotiable, but fixed-prices are gaining popularity. Like any other purchase, shop around and assess the market.

Leather jackets are made to order, but it's advisable to ascertain your correct measurements from a jacket that fits, before you leave home. For instance, arm length, shoulder width, wrist, shoulder to waist, and waist measurements are good figures to take with you. Some people have walked out of leather shops less than impressed with their purchases.

Paintings

Ubud is the place to buy paintings.

Visit the **Neka Gallery** and the **Puri Lukisan Museum,** both in Ubud, to familiarise yourself with the different styles. You'll find the staff at both places very helpful, and they will divulge information on different styles, quality and prices. The nearby villages of Pengosekan and Peliatan have communities of artists famed for their distinctive styles. Batuan (on the road to Ubud or Gianyar) is well-known for black and white ink paintings and the sombre, dark Batuan style of painting.

Silver

Kuta and Legian are recommended for silver purchases. Celuk is often said to be the best place for silver, and while you can see silversmiths working, the prices are much higher than in the south and the designs tend to be the old-fashioned filigree. Beratan, a village on the outskirts of Singaraja, is also known for the "dynamic Buleleng" style of silver. Again, the silver there tends to be the old-fashioned ornate style.

Unfortunately, silver tarnishes in high humidity, especially on perspiring skin, so it's an idea not to wear purchases until you return home. Also, don't clean the silver in the various dips available, because it removes the protective oxidised coating, making it tarnish permanently.

Woodcarving

Mas is probably the best place to window shop, but the best place to buy woodcarvings is Batuan. Prices differ as to the intricacy of the carving and quality of the wood. There are many types of wood, from the indigenous "white" jackwood and mottled coconut, to the imported teak and ebony. But be careful, your beautiful ebony statue might just be painted jackwood.

Recreation

Bungy Jumping

Take a leap of faith on Bali! *The Bali Bungy Co* has a 45-metre (150 ft) tower certified to international standards. One jump costs US$49 but they sometimes offer two for the price of one. They will also organise free transportation within the Kuta, Sanur and Nusa Dua areas. Bali Bungy Co, Jl. Pura Puseh, Legion Kelod, Kuta, ph 752 658.

Golf

The *Grand Bali Beach Hotel* in Sanur, ph 288 271, has a nine-hole course, but the course at the *Bali Golf and Country Club* in Nusa Dua, ph 771 791 is recommended. Featuring a championship-standard, 18-hole, par 72-course, its fairways are excellent for all levels of experience. The course was designed by Robin Nelson and Rodney Wright, and it hosted the Alfred

Dunhill Masters Tournament in 1994. Both courses have equipment for hire.

Better still, the *Bali Handara Kosaido Country Club,* ph 288 944, in the regency of Tabanan, is said to be one of the best courses in Asia and one of the most beautiful in the world. A championship golf course, it was built in an extinct volcano and is surrounded by lush gardens. The fast par-72 course was designed by Australian Peter Thompson and is spread over 100 hectares. Because the course is somewhat out of the way, it's often empty. But Bedugul and its environs are gorgeous and well worth the visit. It's also much cooler in the mountains and a walk around the golf course can be very enjoyable. The Country Club has fine accommodation and rents out all golfing gear.

Diving and Snorkelling

Bali's underwater world is stunning. Surrounded by coral reefs, the island has warm, clear waters perfect for snorkelling and diving. Whether you're experienced, a novice, or simply want to sit in a glass-bottomed boat, the sights are not to be missed.

The areas of Nusa Dua, Sanur, Menjangan Island, Lembongan and Nusa Penida are frequently visited by divers. Tulamben, on the east coast in the regency of Karangasem, is the site of a shallow wreck of a WWII US cargo ship and now home to colourful corals and tropical fish. Scuba and snorkelling gear can be hired on the beach.

Most hotels in Nusa Dua and around Tanjung Benoa offer diving expeditions, but *Bali Marine Sports Dive Centre,* Jl. By-pass Ngurah Rai, Sanur, ph 289 308 has PADI qualified instructors for first-timers and is highly recommended, as is *Wisata Tirtha Alpha,* Jl. Pratama Tanjung Benoa, Nusa Dua, ph 272 116.

Water Sports

Tours for parasailing, jet-skiing, windsurfing or water-skiing are all available throughout the south. If you want to have a go at any or all of the above, head to Sanur. Both the Grand Bali Beach Hotel and the Bali Hyatt Hotel have offices on the beach where you can rent equipment.

Most hotels in Nusa Dua offer equipment for water sports but you'll find equipment hire much cheaper further along the beach at Tanjung Benoa.

Surfing

by Mark Naylor

Bali really is a surfer's dream come true. Mainly because it's cheap, accessible, tropical, has perfect coral reefs and beach breaks, and has consistent large and powerful swells coinciding with favourable trade winds.

Bali's most consistent surf (and its driest months) coincides with the Southern Hemisphere's winter months, June to August. By the same token, Bali receives good waves almost all year round.

Bali has two main surf seasons:

1. By far the surfers' most popular is the dry season, from late March through to September or October.

This is dictated by wind direction and the fact that large swells are generated in the southern Indian Ocean by severe storms at this time of the year. For surfers of a lesser standard Kuta Beach, Legian Beach, Canggu and many lesser-known spots are recommended.

A word of warning: these beaches still receive large swells and can be very dangerous.

2. From October to late February is Bali's wet season and there is a change of wind direction.

This means the trade winds favour the Sanur side of the island. Swells during these months can be large, and sometimes wild and out of control, being generated by cyclones off the north-west coast of Australia.

Although it may be the wet, humid, and sometimes unbearable time of the year, it can pay dividends as far as being less crowded and it is possible to surf the lesser-known reef breaks (of which there are many).

Other Islands

Nusa Lembongan is the closest island to Bali being only a few hours' boat ride.

A great escape to some great waves. Some high quality reef breaks include "shipwreck" and "lacerations".

These are the two most popular breaks, and both can be terrifyingly shallow, and crowded, due to lack of easily accessible breaks. There are a few secret spots on the island reached by a short boat ride.

Kuta is the place to hang out for surfers. There you'll find numerous surf shops, as well as *Tubes* on Poppies Lane 2, a surfers bar, with free tide charts and plenty of other surfers to compare notes with. Mambo, Hot Buttered, Hot Tuna and various other surf outlets are represented. *Lili's Surf Shop*, Jl. Legian in Kuta, is owned by Gede Narmada, one of Bali's best surfers.

Boards can be hired in Kuta, but if you want to bring along your own gear most airlines won't permit a board if luggage is more than 20 kgs. Check with your airline first.

Water Skiing
Lake Bratan, in Bedugul, has become the water skiing capital of Bali. Boats, skis and ramps are available from the Bedugul Hotel in the arcade on the shores of the lake.

Whitewater Rafting
Several companies offer whitewater rafting on the Ayung River which flows through Gianyar. *Sobek* in Sanur, ph 287 059 organises all kinds of different tours and their guides are highly experienced. *Ayung River Rafting*, another reputable company can be contacted in Ubud on 261 367 or in Denpasar on 238 759.

Water Parks
Waterbom Park, Jl. Kartika Plaza, Tuban. With numerous water slides, swimming pools, water games and picnic areas (not to mention a bar and restaurant for weary parents), this park has

enough activities to keep most families occupied for a day. Certified lifeguards are scattered throughout the park for kids' safety. Open 9am-6pm daily.

Wildlife Parks

Bali Barat National Park. Most of Bali's mountainous west is designated as Bali Barat National Park (Taman Nasional Bali Barat). Covering an area of 760-square kilometres of woodlands, rain forests, swamps and coastal plains, it is home to a diverse range of animals and 160 bird species. Visitors entering the park must be accompanied by a guide and possess a permit, and are not allowed in 90% of the park. Guides and permits can be arranged at the National Park Headquarters in Cekik at the crossroads, 3 kilometres south of Gilimanuk.

For more information see Bali Barat National Park in the chapter on Buleleng.

Taman Burung Bali Bird Park, Batubulan, Jl. Serma Cok Ngurah Gambir, Singapadu, Gianyar, ph 299 352 (30 minutes from Kuta). Set in 2 hectares of tropical gardens, the park boasts over 1000 birds with 150 exotic species and a large collection of birds of paradise. The park also has a small rain forest with walk-in aviary and a number of Komodo dragons. Open from 9am-6pm daily and there is a restaurant in the grounds.

Indonesia Jaya Reptile & Crocodile Park, Banjar Binong, Desa Werdi Bhuwana, Mengwi, ph 243 686. This park has over 500 crocodiles, as well as the famed Komodo dragons, and features snake shows. Open from 9am-6pm daily.

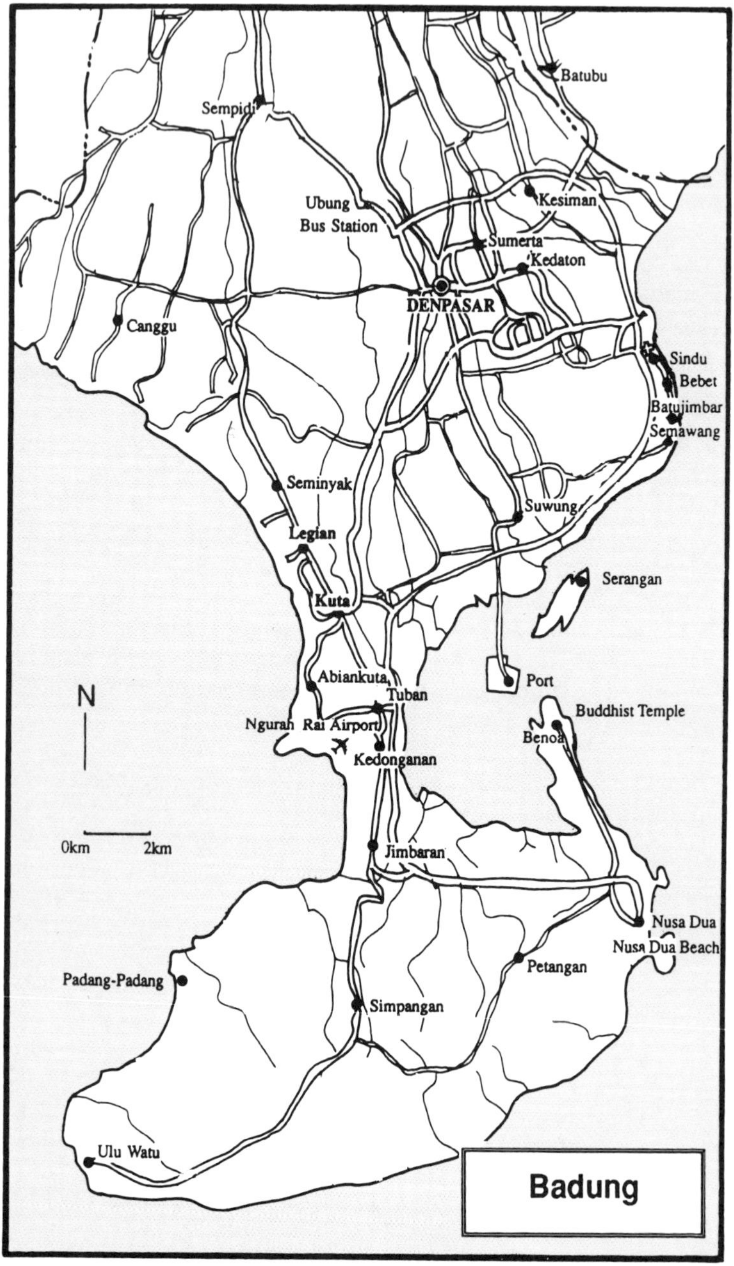
Batubu
Sempidi
Ubung
Bus Station
Kesiman
Sumerta
Kedaton
DENPASAR
Canggu
Sindu
Bebet
Batujimbar
Semawang
Seminyak
Suwung
Legian
Serangan
Kuta
Port
Abiankuta
Tuban
Buddhist Temple
Ngurah Rai Airport
Benoa
Kedonganan
N
0km
2km
Jimbaran
Nusa Dua
Nusa Dua Beach
Petangan
Padang-Padang
Simpangan
Ulu Watu
Badung

Badung

The regency of Badung is the most populated area in Bali, and encompasses the capital city, Denpasar, and the tourist areas of Kuta, Legian, Sanur and Nusa Dua. A narrow strip of land, Badung extends north to the slopes of Gunung Batur and south to the tip of the Bukit Peninsula.

Badung is blessed with fine rivers and fertile volcanic soils which the Balinese have dauntlessly nurtured to yield their crops. But far from being simply an agrarian land, Badung is also favoured with clean beaches, wild surf and stunning postcard-like sunsets.

By sea, it is the most accessible area in the south, and since the 1920s, when Mads Lang established his post at Kuta, Badung has steadily been influenced by Java and the West. But it wasn't until the international airport was built at Tuban in 1969, that the regency really expanded. Since then, the government has seen that tourism remains centred in Badung, so that the south has experienced whirlwind changes ahead of the rest of the island.

History

Badung has had a rather short, but nevertheless illustrious, history. The earliest known example of writing was discovered at Belanjong, near Sanur, suggesting that Hinduism had reached the area by 914AD. But Badung was not recognised as a powerful political force until the 18th century.

By 1891, the Pemecutan family, Badung's ruling clan, had extended its territories to include most of Mengwi its neighbouring regency. Meanwhile, the Dutch had conquered the north and the west by the mid 19th century, and were waiting for an opportunity to take the south. Following the Pemecutan expansion, the Dutch only needed to defeat one royal family.

The Balinese had taken to plundering trade ships that

foundered on the surrounding reefs, and the Dutch used this as a pretext to intervene. In 1906, the Dutch landed at Sanur and marched to Badung (present-day Denpasar) where they were met by the Raja of Pemecutan and thousands of resolute Balinese adorned in cremation attire. Rather than surrender, the Balinese chose ritual suicide or *puputan*. While it wasn't the first *puputan* in Bali, nor the last, it marked the demise of Balinese sovereignty in south Bali. The Dutch, however, never really managed to take control of the southern part of the island. Following independence in 1945, Badung became the focus of Balinese political and social energies.

Denpasar

In 1958, Denpasar emerged phoenix-like as the capital of Bali. While Den*pasar* means "next to the market", it seems that the market has encroached on the village, and that the two are one. But it's a burgeoning market at that, where old is pitted against new. Western-style concrete buildings dwarf classical Balinese architecture. Satellite disks dot the skyline. Bemo, motorbikes and carts vie for space on narrow streets originally built for horse-driven dokar. Dust, smoke and fumes, not to mention the cacophony of horns, brakes and people, blend to create a vexing atmosphere. Denpasar is the antithesis of most people's expectations of Bali.

Look at it this way. The Balinese seek to achieve a balance between opposites, and anything less than a balance means chaos, and possibly destruction. If Bali is as paradisiacal as many people claim, something had to be diametrically opposed. And Denpasar, with its limited charms, is it.

With a population of 400,000, Denpasar, market-cum-city, is one of the richest places in Indonesia. Many say that it's a small-scale replica of Jakarta, and that the youth of the city look to the Indonesian capital for inspiration. The national language, Bahasa Indonesia, is spoken almost to the exclusion of Balinese dialects, and the educated Hindus preach of one supreme God, reconciling their beliefs with the creeds of a united Indonesia (*panca sila*).

The new suburbs of Renon and Niti Mandala in the city's

south-east are home to various government departments including the Governor's Office, Immigration Office and the Japanese and Australian Consulates. Their wide, grand, landscaped streets are another indication of the concentration of wealth in Denpasar.

> ## Getting Your Bearings
> The main street, *Gaja Mada*, runs from east to west, and is lined with shops, restaurants and small businesses. *Jalan Veteran*, the other main street, intersects with *Gaja Mada* at the statute of Batara Guru (the Lord Teacher). The field across from the statute is Puputan Square where the last Raja of Badung led his court to ritual suicide.

Some Words of Advice
Denpasar is not a place for tourists to stay. Spend the day looking around, but a day in Denpasar can be enough for a lifetime. If Kuta and Legian are noisy, dusty and overcrowded, double that and you've got Denpasar.

How to Get There

By Public Bemo
From Ngurah Rai Airport, the dark blue bemo depart from the main road, outside of the airport compound, and arrive at Denpasar's Tegal bemo station.

These bemo only operate during daylight hours and cost about Rp800. The trip takes about 40 minutes.

In Kuta, dark blue bemo leave from the famed Bemo Corner frequently and arrive at Tegal station. The fare is Rp2000.

By Hiring a Bemo
From the airport, bemo can be chartered for around Rp10,000. It's always advisable to complete negotiations before boarding the vehicle. Bemo are no longer permitted to park in the airport car park, so they ply the road in front of the compound. I'd recommend taking a taxi.

By Taxi
From the airport, a ticket can be purchased at the taxi stand outside customs for a fixed-fare to Denpasar (Rp9000 for the 25-minute journey). Better still, blue and yellow metered taxis can be hired outside the compound and generally cost about half the fare of fixed-price taxis. Flagfall is Rp1500 and about Rp500 per kilometre.

By Car
Denpasar is 9km (6 miles) from Kuta and the drive takes about half an hour. See the **Travel Information** chapter for distances.

Tourist Information
The tourist office that serves the regency of Badung is on Jl. Surapati 7, Denpasar, ph 223 602, opposite Puputan Square. It's open Monday to Thursday from 8am to 1pm, and on Friday and Saturday from 8am to 11am.

The office provides a map and information on monthly activities and festivals.

Accommodation
There is no shortage of accommodation in Denpasar, especially losmen, but only the Indonesians or business people stay here for the night.

Prices are in US$ for one night's accommodation and should be used as a guide only. **The telephone code is 0361**.

Natour Bali Hotel, Jl. Veteran 3, ph 225 681. Just north of Puputan Square, this hotel is charming but the rooms are very plain. Oh! and the reception, swimming pool and restaurant are inconveniently located across the road. Room $60-$90.

Hotel Denpasar, Jl. Diponegoro 103, ph 226 363. Recently rebuilt, the Hotel Denpasar is about as good as it gets in Denpasar. Room from $90.

Pemecutan Palace, Jl. Thamrin 2, ph 223 491. Small, sparse rooms looking out to the royal reception pavilion. Room $35.

Tohpati Bali Hotel, Jl. By-pass Ngurah Rai 15, ph 235 408. Suite $176.

Adi Yasa, Jl. Nakula 23, ph 222 679. Pleasant and well-kept, this

losmen is a favourite with backpackers. Room Rp8000-Rp12,000.
Bali International Youth Hostel, Jl. Mertesari 19, Banjar Suwung Kangin, Sidakarya, ph 263 912. Located in the southern suburbs, it has a pool and rooms sleeping 2 or 4 people. Also provides free transportation to and from the airport.

Local Transport

Negotiating Denpasar on foot is probably the easiest way to see the place, then you don't have to worry about traffic jams, parking, or the one-way streets.

By Public Bemo

The bemo transport system can be frustrating and to make matters worse, it doesn't adequately cover all the major roads in Denpasar. There are no official transport maps, and sometimes it's difficult to locate pick-up points. Worse still, bemo services between terminals often take circuitous routes because of the various one-way streets, and return journeys may take a different route for the same reason.

There are some clues to the various city routes, though. Each bemo is colour-coded and has its major stops on the side or back of the vehicle. Wave to signal the driver and be sure to state your precise destination. Foreigners are charged a standard fare of Rp500 to any destination in Denpasar.

The major services between Denpasar's main terminals are Ubung (grey-blue) to Batubulan; Kereneng to Batubulan; and Tegal (yellow but sometimes blue-green) to Ubung, then south-east to Kereneng and back to Tegal.

Kereneng-Sanur bemo are dark green and take the most direct route to Sanur. Tegal-Sanur bemo are dark blue and terminate at the Sanur roundabout.

As Denpasar is "bemo central", it's the best place to find public transport to just about anywhere on the island.

The four main terminals are:
Tegal station on Jl. Imam Bonjol is south of the city on the road to Kuta and provides services to the south of Bali including all other terminals in Denpasar:

Airport	Rp800
Kuta	Rp800
Legian	Rp800

Sanur	Rp800
Nusa Dua	Rp1200

Ubung terminal runs city services to Tegal, Batubulan and Kereneng and provides services to the north:

Kediri	Rp1500 (change for Tanah Lot)
Mengwi	Rp1700
Negara	Rp2100
Gilimanuk	Rp4500 (for services to Java)
Bedugul	Rp3000
Singaraja	Rp3300 (change for Lovina)

Kereneng terminal on Jl. Kemoning (off Jl. Hayam Wuruk), to the east, is mainly for services in Denpasar, but also has a direct bemo service to Sanur (Rp500).

Batubulan terminal has city services to Ubung, Kereneng and Tegal terminals and runs services for eastern and central Bali:

Ubud	Rp1000
Gianyar	Rp1000
Tampaksiring	Rp1800
Klungkung	Rp1200
Bangli	Rp1200
Padangbai	Rp2500
Candi Dasa	Rp3200
Amlapura	Rp3000
Kintamani	Rp3500

Suci terminal, near the corner of Jl. Hasanudin and Jl. Diponegoro, has services to Suwung for Serangan Island.

Eating Out

Denpasar has the widest selection of authentic Chinese and Indonesian restaurants on the island — probably because they don't have to cater to the insignificant tourist market.

Probably for the same reason, many restaurants stop taking orders after 8.30pm.

Restaurants

Akasaka, Jl. Teuku Umar, ph 238 551. A reasonably priced and extensive Japanese menu, this restaurant is also a karaoke club and discotheque.

Atoom Baru, Jl. Gaja Mada 106, ph 222 733. Busy Chinese

restaurant catering for large groups. Lots of good soups and some seafood.

Hong Kong, Jl. Gaja Mada 99, ph 234 845. This up-market Chinese restaurant is air-conditioned(!) and offers a huge selection of reasonably-priced meals, including a few Western dishes.

Kak Man, Jl. Teuka Umar. Specialises in traditional Balinese food, and for this reason alone should not be overlooked. It's also very reasonably priced.

Puri Agung, Natour Bali Hotel, Jl. Veteran, ph 225 681. Specialises in Dutch East Indies-style food and they make a great *rijstaffel* (a Dutch hotch-potch of Indonesian foods) for Rp10,500.

Restaurant Betty, Jl. Sumatra 56. This Indonesian-style warung has a vast menu, is cheap and the food's good.

Rumah Makan Padang, Jl. Diponegoro. This is one of the better Sumatran restaurants. Specialising in Padang food which is very spicy but served cold, you can choose from the display and the waiter will gladly explain the contents.

Night Markets

The night markets or *pasar malam* are invariably cheap and good, and as the Indonesians and Balinese frequent the markets you can be assured of sumptuous delights.

Kerengeng, just off Jl. Hayam Wuruk next to the bemo station of the same name, opens around 5pm and has over 50 stalls serving Indonesian and Balinese food. Trestle tables and chairs are set up throughout the market. And it's open until dawn!

The New Dewata Ayu Pasaraya (NDA) Food Station, top floor, NDA Department Store, corner of Jl. Teuku Umar and Jl. Sudirman. This is the largest night market and has a wondrous array of stalls specialising in various regional and international cuisines. You pay at the counter and the food is brought to your table. Closes at 9pm.

Nightlife

Denpasar is bereft of pubs, bars and night clubs, apart from the *Akasaka Karaoke Club,* Jl. Teuku Umar, ph 238 551, so those looking for the action head to Kuta or Sanur.

There's a couple of cinemas, for instance the *Wisata 21* on Jl. Thamrin, ph 423 023, has five screens. Most films are shown with the Indonesian subtitles and the original soundtrack is retained. See the *Bali Post* for programs.

Entertainment

Sadly, most of the dance performances in Denpasar are mediocre. STSI (the College of Indonesian Arts, see below) is recommended, but Ubud really is the place to be captivated by some of the best dancers on the island.

Kecak dance is performed nightly (6.30-7.30pm) at the Werdhi Budaya Cultural Centre, Jl. Nusa Indah in the open-air amphitheatre. *Barong Leak* is performed daily 9.30-10.30am in the same theatre.

The College of Indonesian Arts (STSI), Jl. Nusa Inda (near the arts centre). Anytime during the morning you can watch student dancers and musicians practising in both the traditional and modern art forms.

Shopping

As mentioned, "pasar" means market and Denpasar's full of them. The Kumbasari Market, Jl. Gajah Mada, on the east bank of the Badung river (in the middle of the city) is a huge concrete building crammed with three floors of vendors: fruit and vegetables on the ground floor, household goods on the second, and clothes on the third.

Antiques

You'll really have to scrutinise the merchandise or you may have purchased a genuine fake.

The Arts of Asia Gallery. Tucked behind a shopping centre (Jl. Thamrin 27, Block C5), is one of the best-known antique shops in Bali, and the proprietor, Verra Darwiko, is very knowledgeable.

Books

Corsica Books, Jl. Sumatra. This bookshop has a good selection of books on Bali.

Coffee

Not surprisingly, Bali produces some fine coffees. Toko *Bhineka Jaya*, Jl. Gaja Mada 80, ph 222 053, has a wondrous array of coffees to satisfy the most discerning of coffee connoisseurs.

Electronics

Few people realise that electronic goods in Denpasar are quite cheap and there are many shops from which to choose:

Denpasar Electronic, Jl. Veteran 25, ph 227 479.
Palapa Agung Electronic, Jl. Sumatra 8, ph 225 721.
Surya, Jl. Gaja Mada 128, ph 222 254.
Toyobo Electronic, Jl. Diponegoro, ph 222 613.

Gold

Despite the claims of the jewellers from Celuk, Denpasar is the best place to buy gold, and there are quite a few gold shops to visit. Just take a stroll down Jl. Sulawesi and Jl. Hasanuddin. Very yellow in colour, most of the gold is 22kt and is sold by weight. **The prices are often comparable with those in Singapore and Hong Kong.**

Textiles

Denpasar has many fabric shops, particularly along Jl. Sulawesi, or you can venture into the *Kumbasari Market* (third floor).
Dua Lima and *Toko Murah*, both on Jl. Sulawesi, are reputable fabric shops.
Pertenuan AAA on Jl. Veteran (near the Bali Hotel) is one of the larger weaving factories in Bali, and sells the renowned *endek*.

Sightseeing

The striking thing about Denpasar is the old juxtaposed with the new. Change in Bali has accelerated since the 1970s, much of it unfolding in Denpasar, but this market-cum-city still holds many reminders of its former history.

Puputan Square

Puputan Square is considered to be the geographic heart of Denpasar and is named in honour of the 1906 event. The statue in the corner is a monument to the heroic men, women and children who sacrificed their lives rather than succumb to the invasion of the Dutch militia.

Puputan Square is a good starting point from which to explore the metropolis.

Museum Bali

On the eastern side of Puputan Square is the Museum Bali. Erected in 1932 by the Dutch, and with the subsequent assistance of Walter Spies, it attempts to present a historical account of Balinese culture within an architectural framework.

Housed in Tabanan, Karangasem and Buleleng styles of architecture, the museum illustrates the two types of construction in Bali: temples and palaces. The split gate, outer and inner courtyards, and *kulkul* drum typify the temple; while the thatched roofs, ornate windows and verandahs characterise the palace.

The main two-storey building, located at the back of the entrance courtyard, houses traditional artefacts from Bali's prehistory, including a massive stone sarcophagus. There are also two black and white photographs documenting the 1906 puputan at Badung.

The first pavilion was designed in the Singaraja style of architecture and contains textiles including *endek* (ikat), *geringsing* (double ikat) and silk songket. The second pavilion, built in the style of an 18th century Karangasem palace, houses religious and ceremonial artefacts. The third pavilion is reminiscent of Tabanan palaces and displays the masks, costumes and puppets associated with music and dance.

The museum's contents are a little disappointing, as some items are poorly labelled and rather haphazardly arranged. Nonetheless, the museum is worth visiting for the examples of architecture, and it does give the visitor an idea of the history and culture of the island.

The museum is open: Tuesday to Thursday 7.30am-1.30pm. Friday 7.30am-11.30am. Saturday to Sunday 8am - 12pm. Closed Monday. Admission Rp200.

Pura Jagatnatha

Next to the museum is the relatively new state temple, Pura Jagatnatha. A "world" temple, it's dedicated to Sanghyang Widi, the supreme God. The idea of one supreme god marks a shift from a polytheistic to a monotheistic philosophy for Bali's intellectual Hindus. The intellectuals have their eyes cast towards Jakarta, so it's said, and reconcile their Hindu beliefs with those of a predominantly Muslim Indonesia. Hence, all gods are manifestations of the Supreme God.

Surrounded by high walls with several entrances, the temple is one of the busiest in Bali. Unfortunately, it is closed to the public except for festivals, and even then, locals seem reluctant to welcome foreigners. A strict dress code is enforced, so don't expect to go in without a sarong and sash, and shoulders should be covered. Opposite Pura Jagatnatha is the new military headquarters. You'll probably see some of the militia wandering around town.

Pura Moaspahit

In the city proper, one of Denpasar's oldest temples is the Pura Moaspahit on Jl. Sutomo, just north of Pasar Badung. Although a significant building, it's often by-passed by travellers. The temple is a relic of the Majapahit empire and, it's believed, parts of the building were brought over from Java in the 14th century during the Majapahit exodus to Bali. The plain, red brick facade, you might notice, is atypically Balinese. However, much of what you'll see today is purely reconstructed as most of the temple was destroyed in the earthquake of 1917.

The Pura is guarded by two massive statues: Batara Bayu, the god of wind; and Garuda, messenger of the gods. On the facade are the gods Yama and Indra.

Puri Pemecutan

Just near the central bus station on the corner of Jl. Thamrin and Jl. Hasanudin stands Puri Pemecutan. Once the site of the royal palace for the Pemecutan Empire, it was rebuilt in 1907 as a hotel, after the original palace was destroyed in the 1906 *puputan*. The design emulates the palaces of the former Badung kingdom, and the palace houses *lontar* manuscripts of traditional literature as well as a fine collection of paintings. Alas, it is yet another attraction often missed by travellers.

Catuh Mukha Statue

The four-sighted statue (it stares in four directions) at Denpasar's main intersection (corner of Jl. Gaja Mada and Jl. Veteran), represents the god Bhatara Guru (Siwa). Built in 1972, it was a somewhat belated erection to commemorate the *puputan* of 1906.

Werdhi Budaya Cultural Centre
Located in the complex on Jl. Nusa Indah, the centre was built in 1973, and the permanent exhibition, although poor in comparison to the Museum Neka in Ubud, is worth seeing. Designed by Bali's most beloved architect, Ida Bagus Tugur, the Centre attempts to display the cultural and artistic aspects of Bali neglected by the Bali Museum. Again, many of the exhibits and works are poorly labelled, but for Rp3000 or thereabouts, an enthusiastic lover of art will show you around.

STSI (Academy of Dance)
The Sekolah Tinggi Seni Indonesia, formerly ASTI, is the Academy of Dance, located in the grounds of the Cultural Centre on Jl. Nusa Indah. A tertiary-level institution, it offers courses from undergraduate to masters level.

Visitors are welcome to observe dance and musical rehearsals at their leisure, or attend the regular dance and dramatic performances on the open-air stage. But the best time to visit is around June-July during the four-week Bali Arts Festival, as there is a comprehensive program of gamelan and dance performances, as well as art and craft exhibitions.

Kesiman
Take a drive through the old village of Kesiman and observe some fine examples of Badung architecture. The temple, Pura Kesiman, has a fine split gate in the old-Badung style, as opposed to the new Gianyar-style, reinforced concrete. The old palace, Puri Kesiman, is now a private residence and it's worth taking a peek.

The Kuta and Legian Resort Area

Kuta, so it's said, was a sleepy fishing village, and a hideaway for criminals, reprobates and exiles. While cynics might say that little has changed, Kuta does have some endearing qualities. It has fine restaurants, great surf, and postcard-like sunsets. It's a shopper's paradise, a drinker's fantasy, and a claustrophobe's nightmare. Dogs howl in competition with the local *gamelan* orchestra, and crowing roosters remind ragers it's time for bed.

Short sun-filled days melt into hot nights of oblivion. Kuta's not for everyone, but it sure does attract the crowds.

Kuta's history is less than illustrious. In the 14th century, it was the port for the Majapahit Empire, and in the 18th century became a slave port for the exchange of the indigenous peoples between the Balinese and Javanese rajas. But by the 19th century, thanks to the Danish trader Mads Lange, Kuta had developed into a thriving village. Lange built a strong trade empire centred in Kuta and managed to ingratiate himself with the Raja of Badung, as well as the Dewa Agung. Later he became an agent for the Dutch government and was pivotal in the negotiations between the Balinese rajas and the Dutch in the tumultuous 1846-1850 period. From this time, Kuta was a port of call for ships to resupply and repair.

In 1936, the Californians, Robert and Louise Koke, came to Bali and were captivated by its beauty. They built the Kuta Beach Hotel, the first tourist joint, and until the Japanese invasion of 1942, welcomed guests from America and Europe. But it wasn't until the 1960s that tourists began to take stopovers in Bali, and Kuta beach was *the* place to stay. Long-haired hippies, enamoured of the place, found families willing to let rooms and *losmen* were born.

Opportunists, aware of the value of a dollar, established restaurants and shops, and Kuta grew into a spirited, even crazy village. Ever since, tourists have sought the sultry sunsets, sand, surf, shopping and sex, and Kuta has become one of the most prosperous villages on the island.

In the early 1970s, Legian was still a separate village, a place of respite for those indifferent to Kuta's offerings. Now the two villages are virtually one, incorporating Seminyak to the north, and Tuban to the south. The Kuta-Legian resort area is self-contained, and there is no need to venture beyond its limits — but, there is much, much more to Bali.

Swimmers Beware!

The goddess of the sea is said to claim a victim each year, but most tourists explain deaths by drowning due to the sometimes perilous undertow and strong currents. The stretch of beach between Kuta to the south and Legian to the north is staffed by livesafers and it's advisable to swim between the flags.

90 Bali

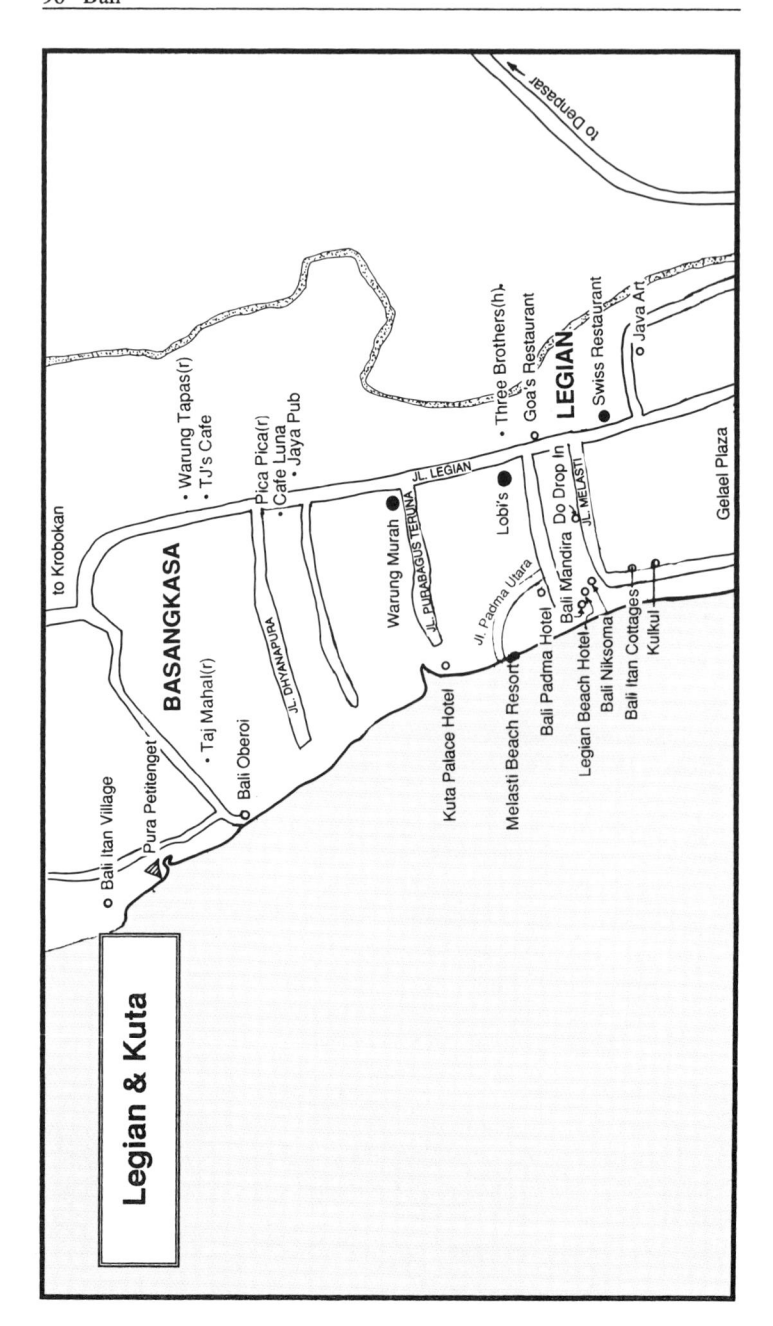

Badung 91

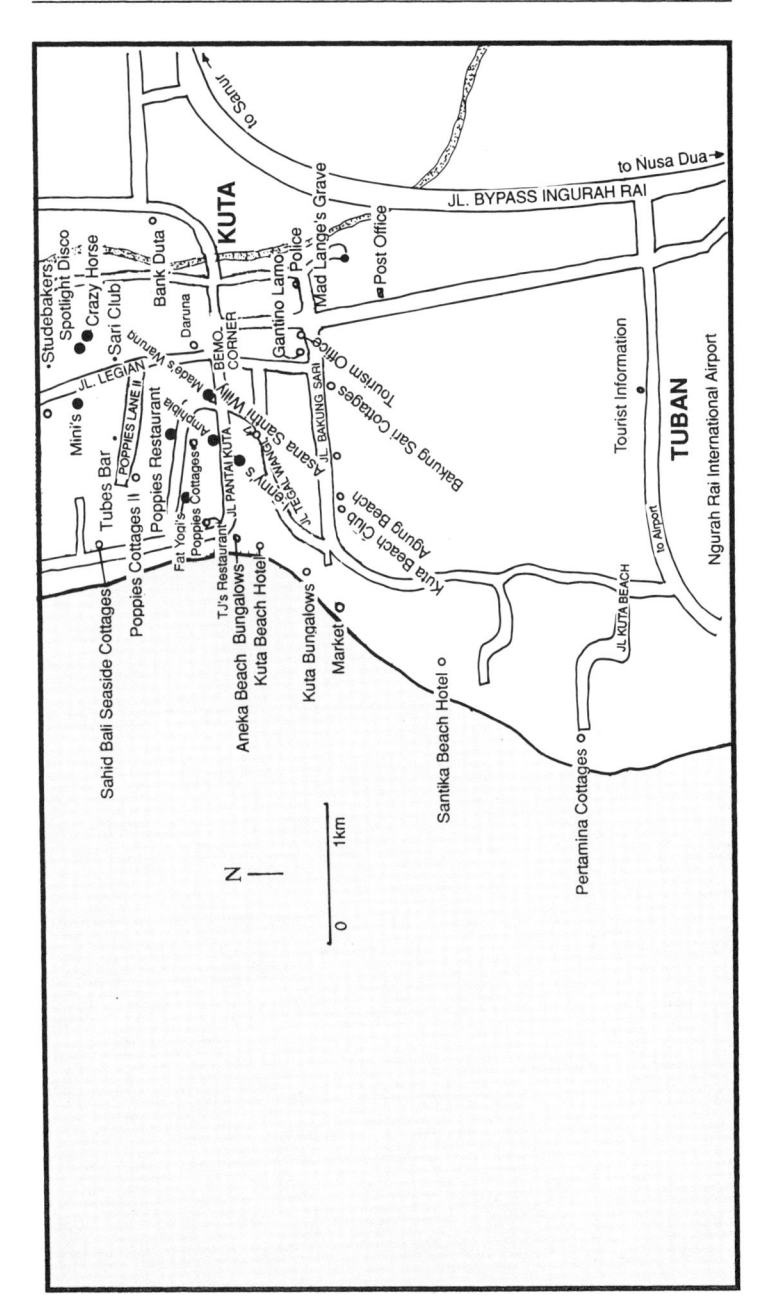

Getting your Bearings

Kuta proper stretches north from the *Patra Jasa Beach Resort* (formerly *Pertamina Cottages)* to Jl. Melasti, while Legian is the area north of Jl. Melasti to Jl. Double Six.

Seminyak stretches from Jl. Double Six (north of Legian) to *The Oberoi*, and is fast becoming the place to stay. The restaurants, hotels and shops are mostly trendy, and the bars and clubs attract a fashionable crowd. Yet it's quieter and less frantic than Legian or Kuta, and there are less hawkers (thank the gods!).

Tuban properly denotes the airport area, south of Kuta, up to the *Patra Jasa Beach Resort*.

The main drag, Jl. Legian, runs parallel with the coast, starting south in Kuta at Bemo Corner,and running north through Legian to Seminyak. The Kuta-Legian-Seminyak resort is largely contained between the coast and Jl. Legian.

How to Get There

Most travel agents organise transfers from the airport with accommodation. But those without prior reservations will have no problem finding transport.

By Public Bemo

From the airport, provided you're not over-burdened with luggage and it's still daylight, take a public bemo from Jl. Airport Ngurah Rai, just outside of the gates (Rp500). These dark blue bemo travel via Kuta's Bemo Corner as far as Jl. Melasti, then to Denpasar's Tegal terminal via Jl. Legian. However, they skip most of north Legian, Seminyak and Tuban to the south. If you need to get to these areas I suggest hiring a metered taxi.

By Hiring a Bemo

Probably not the nicest introduction to Bali are the mobs of bemo drivers that beseech tourists to hire their vehicle. The fare is negotiable and you should consider the price of a taxi when bargaining. Clearly state the hotel where you want to be dropped or you could end up at the tout's friend's hotel. Unlicensed bemo are not permitted into the airport compound, but this does not prevent these persistent people from annoying tourists. Take a taxi.

By Taxi
The easiest and most expensive form of transport from the airport is by fixed-fare taxis. Simply purchase a ticket from the taxi desk in the arrival section of the airport. The fare to south Kuta (as far as Poppies Lane 1) is Rp6500, Rp8500 to Legian (Jl. Double Six) and Rp12,000 to Seminyak.

There are also yellow and blue metered taxis outside the airport compound and they can be hired for around half the price of the fixed-fare taxis: flagfall is Rp1500 then about Rp500 per kilometre.

Tourist Information
Badung Tourist Office, Jl. Bakung Sari, ph 751 419 (Mon-Sat 7am-5pm). The staff are very helpful, particularly with bemo routes, festivals and worthwhile tourist attractions.
Bali Travel Service, Jl Benesari (near the corner of Jl. Legian), Kuta, ph 753 540 (daily from 9am-8pm). The staff are extremely helpful and can arrange travel throughout Indonesia. The office also stores luggage and is a postal agent. In the same complex, the *Bali Tourist Office* will provide a map and list of events for the month, but that's about all.

Information on entertainment can be found in the local free tourist newspapers, the fortnightly *Bali News* and the monthly *Bali Tourist Guide* which are distributed through tourist information centres and some hotels.

The glossy *Bali Echo* provides a wealth of information on restaurants and entertainment, as well as articles on culture and the arts, and can be found in book shops and hotels.

Accommodation
Accommodation in the Kuta and Legian resort area ranges from 5 star hotels to very cheap losmen. While it's good to be close to the action, Kuta can be very noisy and the larger hotels can be very crowded. Many new hotels have been built in Seminyak (north of Legian) and Tuban (south of Kuta), and most provide shuttle services into Kuta and Legian. So it's possible to be near

the shops, night life and restaurants, but enjoy quieter environs. Around December and July it is imperative that rooms are booked in advance.

Prices for one night's accommodation are in US$, do not include a 10-15% service charge nor the 10% government tax, and should be used as a guide only.

The telephone code for all of south Bali is 0361.

Seminyak

The accommodation in Seminyak tends to be either luxury five-star or standard accommodation, with little in between.

5 star Hotels

All the luxury hotels have full amenities and offer various restaurants, pools, sporting facilities and 24 hour room service, as well as shuttle services into Kuta and Legian.

Bali Imperial, Jl. Dhyana Pura, ph 730 730. Spread over four and a half hectares, the Bali Imperial has rooms with either ocean or garden views. Tennis courts, swimming pools, sauna, indoor jacuzzi, spa, massage rooms and library are some of the facilities guests can enjoy, as well as various restaurants and bars. Rooms from $130.

The Legian, Jl. Kayu Ayu, Petitenget, ph 286 543. Recently opened, The Legian is the latest offering from the operators of *The Chedi*, in Ubud, and The Serai, in Candi Dasa. Located on the beach, and far away from the throng, these towers of elegant suites have five-star amenities. Rooms from $240.

The Oberoi, Jl. Kayu Ayu, Petitenget, ph 751 061. 75 rooms. *The Oberoi* is very grand but discreet. Coral rock bungalows are scattered throughout landscaped gardens and have their own private courtyards. Facilities include restaurants, bars, tennis court, swimming pools, water sports, bank, shops, beauty salon and outdoor theatre. And, of course, the hotel has its own secluded beach. Some villas include a private swimming pool. Rooms from $230; villas from $400.

Villa Rumah Manis, Jl. Legian, ph 730 606. Formerly the Bounty Riverview, it's near a river rather than the beach. Built in the traditional Balinese village style, this hotel is perfect for small groups. Each bungalow is a spacious two-storey villa with private garden, plunge pool and alfresco dining area. Villas can accommodate up to five guests. Rooms from $90.

3 star Hotels
All the 3 star hotels have a restaurant, bar and pool, but are usually a short walk to the beach.

Bali Sani Suites, Jl. Petitenget, ph 754 050-4. Each room features a garden or ocean view from a private terrace or balcony. The hotel has its own shopping arcade and beauty salon, as well as restaurant and pool. Rooms from $95.

Hotel Intan Bali (formerly Intan Bali Village), Jl. Pura Peti Tenget, ph 752 191. Comfortable rooms with terrace or balcony. This beachfront hotel has its own shopping arcade and various restaurants including a 24-hour cafe and night club. This hotel is about five kilometres from Legian but has a shuttle to Legian for all guests. Rooms from $70.

2 star Hotels
Most of the 2 star hotels have a swimming pool and restaurant but are a short walk to the beach.

Bali Holiday Resort, Jl. Dhyana Pura, ph 753 547. Set in landscaped gardens, this hotel is well-catered to families and each room has a private balcony. Rooms from $60.

Tjendana Paradise, Jl. Dhyana Pura, ph 753 373. This large hotel offers spacious rooms with private balcony or terrace, and even has its own disco. Rooms from $50.

Kuta and Legian

5 star Hotels
Bali Padma, Jl. Padma 1, Legian, ph 752 111. This is a value for money hotel boasting 2 tennis courts, 2 squash courts, fitness centre, five restaurants, and the crowd-pleasing O'Barrel Pub. With 400 rooms, The Padma is very big and can be very crowded especially in the peak season — ideal if you want to meet lots of people, but a little stifling if you're looking for a romantic getaway. All rooms have full amenities and 24-hour room service. Rooms from $120.

3 star Hotels
These hotels usually offer very good facilities but without

sporting attractions. Most rooms have air-conditioning, hot water, a telephone, a television and include breakfast. Rates for one night's accommodation are in US$ and do not include the tax and service charges.

Bali Mandira Cottages, Jl. Padma, Legian, ph 751 381. Located on the beach, this hotel has tennis and squash courts and welcomes families. Room from $80.

Hotel Intan Legian, Jl. Melasti 1, Legian, 751 770. Formerly the *Bali Intan Cottages*, this hotel is a short walk to the beach and has two swimming pools, tennis courts, fitness centre, two restaurants, four bars and offers motel-style rooms as well as bungalows. Ideal for the 18-35s. Rooms from $65.

Hotel Jayakarta, Jl. Pura Bagus Teruna, Legian, ph 751 433. Formerly the Kuta Palace Hotel, the Jayakarta is on the beachfront and has a tennis court and fitness centre. A shuttle service operates daily for guests. Room $75.

Melasti Beach Resort, Jl. Padma Utara, Legian Beach, ph 755 971. Right on the beach, with only 50 rooms, the Melasti is a quiet hotel with large comfortable rooms. Huge pool, and tennis and squash courts available.

Natour Kuta Beach Hotel, Jl. Pantai Kuta 1, ph 751 361. One of Kuta's original hotels, it's located on the beachfront and was recently renovated and expanded. Boasts all mod cons and services such as beauty parlour, florist, chemist, business facilities and travel agent. Rooms from $60.

Legian Beach Hotel, Jl. Melasti, Kuta, ph 751 711. Located on the beach, the Legian Beach Hotel has a games room, tennis courts, squash court, fitness centre and swimming pool and spa. Rooms from $70.

Ocean Blue Club Kuta, Gang Benasari. This hotel caters for the 18-35s and does not permit children. It even has its own night club — the Wet'n'Wild. A great place to meet other party-minded travellers. Room from $60.

Poppies Cottages, Poppies Gang 1 and Old Poppies, Poppies 2, Kuta, ph 751 059. A short walk to the beach and close to the action, both of these properties have traditional Balinese-style cottages. Self-catering facilities available. Exceptional for the price, but best to book. Room from $60.

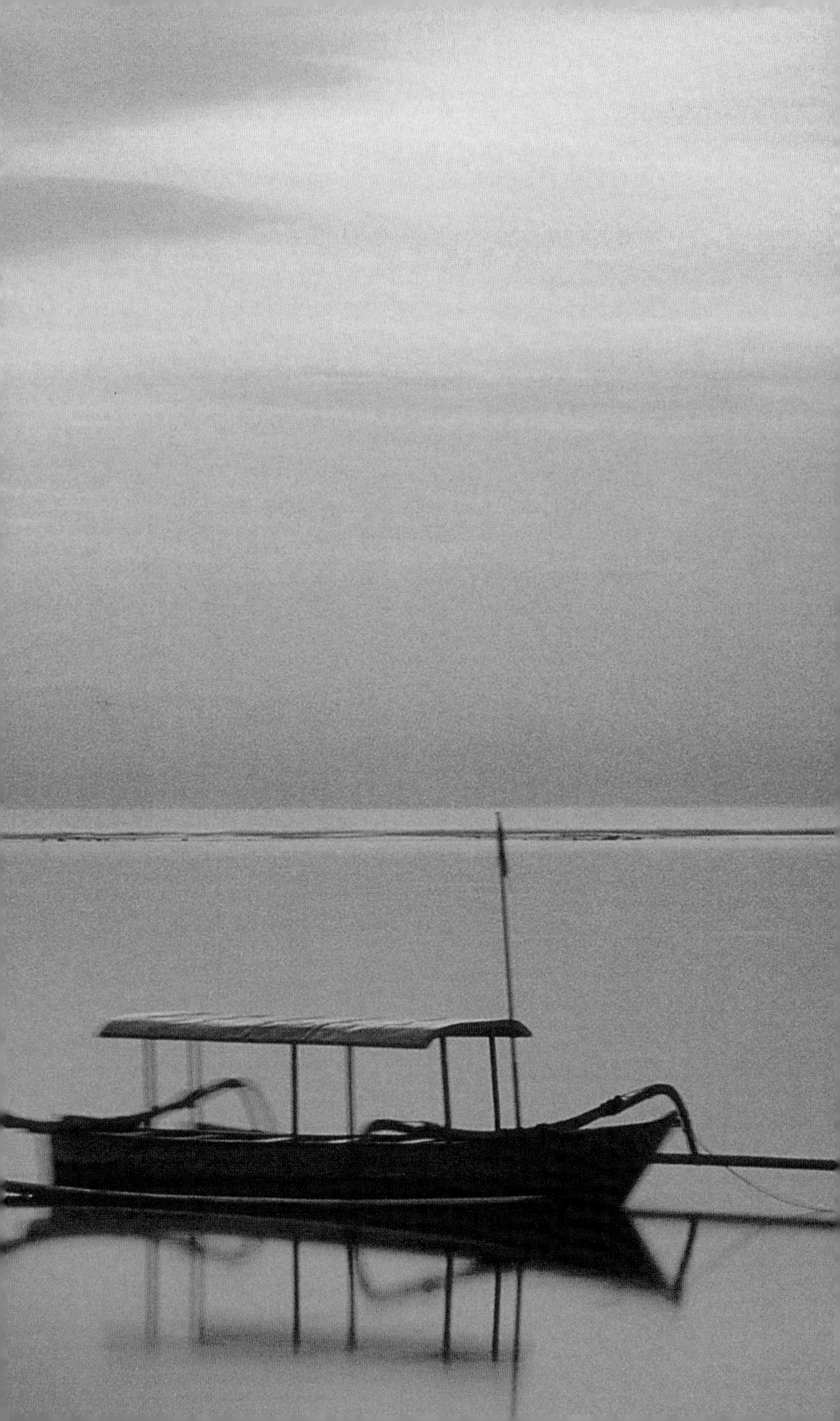

Boardriders making their way to the point at Nusa Dua

2 star Hotels
These hotels usually have a restaurant and swimming pool, offer rooms with air-conditioning and hot water, and sometimes breakfast is included.

Aneka Beach Bungalows, Jl. Pantai Kuta, ph 752 892. Across the road from the beach, suited to families. Room from $40.

Bounty Hotel, Jl. Legian, Kuta, ph 753 030. Minutes from the beach and shops, this hotel is for 18-35s and has a 24-hour pool bar overflowing with Aussie drinkers. Room from $50.

Kuta Beach Club, Jl. Bakung Sari, Kuta, ph 751 261. A ten-minute walk to the beach, value-for-money accommodation. Room $40.

Ramayana Seaside Cottages, Jl. Bakung Sari, Kuta, ph 751 865. A few minutes from Kuta beach, this hotel is ideal for young singles who want to be close to the action. Room $50.

1 star Hotels
These hotels usually offer adequate facilities for the budget-conscious traveller. Rooms may or may not have air-conditioning and hot water — check first. Rates include the tax and service charges.

Agung Beach Bungalows, Jl. Bakung Sari, Kuta, ph 751 263. Close to the beach, rooms comfortable. Room $30.

Bakungsari Cottages, Jl. Bakung Sari, Kuta, ph 751 868. Has restaurant and swimming pool, and although near the action is surprisingly quiet. Room $25.

Garden View Cottages, Jl. Padma Utara 4, Legian, ph 751 559. In a quiet back lane a few minutes' walk from the beach, the cottages are clustered in fours, so they're less crowded. Room $40.

Kuta Bungalows, Jl. Legian Kelod (Gang Benesari), Kuta. A walk from the beach, with restaurant and swimming pool. Room $28.

Kuta Village Inn, Jl. Bakung Sari, Kuta, ph 753 051. Rooms are small and basic, but good value. Has swimming pool and restaurant. Room $28.

Budget Accommodation
There's an abundance of *losmen* in Kuta and Legian with rooms for as little as US$5 a night. Prices are often negotiable, depending on the duration of stay. Location is of the utmost importance — Kuta can be very noisy — as is cleanliness. **The best idea is to shop around.**

Tuban

Staying in a hotel in Tuban can be an attractive idea as you'll be close to the action, but far enough away to enjoy a little peace and quiet. Also, the larger hotels are usually built on bigger grounds and so don't seem so crowded. Around December and July it is imperative that rooms are booked in advance. Prices for one night's accommodation are in US$, and should be used as a guide only. The telephone code is 0361.

5 star Hotels
All hotels have various restaurants and bars, swimming pool, and sports facilities, as well as 24 hour room service.
Kartika Plaza Beach Hotel, Jl. Kartika Plaza, Tuban, ph 751 067-9. On the quiet southern end of Kuta beach, the Kartika Plaza is built on 12 hectares of landscaped gardens. The three-storey hotel boasts tennis courts, squash courts, a fitness centre, mini-golf and children's playground, as well as various swimming pools and restaurants and bars. Room from $120.

4 star Hotels
All hotels have a restaurant and bar, swimming pool, and rooms have hot water, air-conditioning and 24-hour room service.

Bali Dynasty Resort, Jl. Kartika Plaza, Tuban, ph 752 403. A short walk to Kuta, the Bali Dynasty is located in lush gardens and is a quiet but grand hotel. The hotel has a "disco" and families are well catered for. Room from $105.
Patra Jasa Beach Resort, Jl. Tuban Beach, Tuban, ph 751 161. Formerly *Pertamina Cottages*, this was originally an executive haven. At the southernmost point of Tuban surrounded by tropical landscaped gardens, the Patra Jasa has a secluded beach protected by a coral reef, and spacious Western-style rooms with old-world charm. The hotel has full amenities including tennis courts, fitness centre, a swimming pool with a slide, and a children's club. Room from $130.

3 star Hotels
All hotels have a restaurant and bar, swimming pool, and rooms have hot water, air-conditioning and 24 hour room service.

Prices are in US$ and do not include the government tax and service charges.

Bali Rani, Jl. Kartika, Tuban, ph 751 369. Five minutes walk to the beach and recently refurbished, this hotel is ideal for families. Room from $65.

Rama Baruna (formerly Rama Beach Cottages), Jl. Wana Segara, Tuban. This beachfront hotel is value for money and has swimming pools, tennis courts and children's playground. Either standard motel rooms or cottage rooms. Room from $65.

Risata Bali Resort, Jl. Wana Segara, ph 753 340. A short walk to the beach, this hotel has a 24 hour restaurant, swimming pool and fitness centre. Comfortable standard rooms. Room from $55.

Santika Beach Hotel, Jl. Kartika, Tuban, ph 751 267. This beachfront hotel is value for money and caters well for the family. Has swimming pools, tennis courts and children's playground. Room from $70.

2 star Hotels

Most hotels have air-conditioning and basic facilities but ask about the hot water. These hotels are often much better value than the same range in Kuta—and they're quieter! Prices in US$.

Bakung's Beach Cottages, Jl. Kartika Plaza, Tuban. Close to the beach, the hotel is value for money and is a comfortable walking distance to Kuta. While called "cottages", the hotel is motel-style. Room from $25.

Local Transport

Really, the best way to get around Kuta and Legian is to walk — how else could you manage to stop at all those shops!? But you may need transport to some of the outlying attractions.

By Public Bemo

Kuta's transport hub is **Bemo Corner**, on the crossroads of Jl. Pantai Kuta and Jl. Legian. Dark blue bemo originating from Denpasar make a round trip through Kuta from Bemo Corner as far as Jl. Padma and back to Bemo Corner. They'll stop anywhere along the route to pick up and fares within the Kuta area are about Rp300. This service runs during daylight hours at roughly ten-minute intervals. See **Local Transport** in the **Denpasar** section.

To travel to any major villages from Kuta, first go to Denpasar.

To Denpasar, public bemo pick-up at Bemo Corner and unload at the main market or Tegal terminal (see **Local Transport** entry in the **Denpasar** section).

To Sanur, catch a bemo to Tegal terminal in Denpasar, then change at Kereneng terminal for Sanur. There are no services running directly between Sanur and Kuta and Legian.

To Ubud, first go to Tegal, then change at Batubulan for Ubud.

By Hiring a Bemo

Along Jl. Legian are a species of predatory bemo drivers that incite momentary mirth, followed by frustration. The prices are negotiable, but shop around and ask other travellers. Travelling from the south of Kuta to Seminyak should cost around Rp5000 during the day and up to Rp8000 at night, perhaps more after midnight. Negotiate the fare before you board the vehicle. (I'd sooner take a taxi!)

By Taxi

In recent years, blue and yellow metered taxis have increased in number, and are highly recommended for those without a car. Not only will they ply the village routes but they can also be hired to travel to isolated destinations like Ulu Watu (and they can be much cheaper than hiring a bemo). They can be hailed in the street or will pick-up at hotels. If booked through your hotel they'll probably cost Rp1000 more, but you can bet you'll get a better standard of vehicle. Also, some drivers like to pretend their meter doesn't work or cover it with a cloth, and would rather bargain for the fare. Just be firm and insist on using the meter — they usually relent.

Taxis cost Rp1500 for flagfall and about Rp500 per kilometre.

By Car

The best way to see Bali is to hire a car. Unfortunately, navigating the one-way streets in Kuta can be nightmarish (not to mention slow) and finding a park, miraculous. The closest petrol station is on Jl. Kuta Raya.

For more information on driving around Bali and car rental agencies see the **"Local Transport"** entry in the **"Travel Information"** section.

Eating Out

Kuta has a multitude of eateries from the plushest restaurants to inexpensive warung. Many nationalities are represented so that you can choose to dine in restaurants offering cuisine from Indonesia, Italy, Mexico, Spain, China, Germany, Japan, Sumatra ... the list goes on.

There are some excellent restaurants that are included in the sections on Seminyak and Tuban, but they require a taxi ride from Kuta. For instance, *La Lucciola* on Kaya Aya Beach north of Seminyak offers modern Italian in a grand al fresco setting (dinner reservations essential).

But then, perhaps you'd prefer a burger. You won't have to venture too far to find cappuccinos, jaffles, sandwiches, chocolate cake, milk shakes, burgers, steak, baked dinners, vegemite, KFC, McDonald's, ice cream parlours — Kuta and Legian have them all.

Seminyak

Seminyak has some great restaurants and cafes, and new places are opening all the time.

Asian

Goa 2001, Jl. Raya Seminyak (across the road from Ryoshi), ph 730 592. Large bale-style restaurant and bar offering Thai, Indian and Balinese food and a sushi bar. The restaurant is often very busy and noisy, and there's usually a DJ playing retro hits. Moderately priced.

Indian

Taj Mahal, Jl. Kayu Aya, ph 730 525. Large and busy Indian restaurant with its own tandoor. The food is good and reasonably priced.

International

TJ's Cafe, Jl. Raya Seminyak, ph 730 576. Open-air dining with special Mediterranean, New Orleans and South American buffet nights. Also offers BBQ specials for Sunday lunch.

Italian

Cafe Luna, Jl. Raya Seminyak (across from Goa 2001). Very trendy cafe specialising in pizzas, pasta and salads. New Age decor and music create a mellow atmosphere. Open nights only.

La Lucciola, Oberoi Road, Kaya Aya Beach, ph 261 047. Set in a grand pavilion on the beach, the view pans out to palm trees, sand, and surf. The menu is modern Italian at its best, and the service smart. Open breakfast, lunch and dinner, although it's wise to book for dinner. Good wine list and wines available by the glass. Expensive but well worth it. La Lucciola is not really in Seminyak, but is much further north on Kaya Aya Beach. Nevertheless, most taxis will know where to go and there are always plenty of bemo outside for the return journey.

Japanese
Ryoshi, Jl. Raya Seminyak 71. Simple and modern Japanese restaurant for those desperately seeking sushi, tempura, robata and soba. Moderately priced, especially for Japanese.

Spanish
Pica Pica Tapas Bar, Jl. Dhyana Pura 7, ph 730 485. Modern Spanish restaurant specialising in bite-size tapas and steaming paellas, as well as steaks and seafood. Buzzing atmosphere and great service. Moderate to expensive.

Kuta and Legian

Bakery
Za's, Jl. Legian Kelod. One of Legian's oldest cafes, it's renown for its breakfast menu but also serves pastas, curries, etc for lunch and dinner. Inexpensive.

Chinese
Viva's, Jl. Legian. Basic warung-style eatery with large menu specialising in Chinese food, as well as excellent seafood. Inexpensive to moderately priced.
Golden Palace, Jl. Raya Kuta, ph 752 304. Traditional Chinese food and dim sum, and excellent seafood dishes. Moderately priced.

German
Mama's German Restaurant, Jl. Legian 99 and 354, ph 757 209. Surprisingly authentic food with sausages, pork knuckle and steaks a highlight, not to mention the cakes and desserts. Mama's always seems to be busy verging on a beer-hall atmosphere. Some German beers available. Moderately priced.

Indian
Griya Delta, behind Panin Bank, just off Jl. Legian. One of the few Indian restaurants on the island boasting its own tandoor, it serves the gamut of curries. Moderately priced.

Warung Kopi, 427 Jl. Legian, ph 753 602. The menu is mostly Indian but with some Arabic and Mediterranean thrown in. Very popular and inexpensive tourist joint.

Indonesian

Gantino Lamo, Jl. Bakung Sari. Basic warung serving a wondrous assortment of Padang dishes. Inexpensive.

Sama-Sama, Jl. Padma Utara, Legian, ph 757 191. Basic warung-style eatery serving excellent and inexpensive Indonesian meals and some Western dishes. It is highly recommended.

International

Fat Yogi's, Poppie's Lane 1, ph 751 665. Cafe-style eatery offering wood-fired pizzas, breads fresh from the oven, and Western snacks. Good atmosphere and inexpensive.

Kopi Pot, Jl. Legian, Kuta, ph 752 614. Owned by the Poppie's group, this warung-style cafe serves Indonesian and Western meals. The Indonesian meals are particularly good and the satays and nasi goreng highly recommended. Inexpensive.

Made's Warung, Jl. Pantai Kuta (just past Bemo Corner). The menu is extensive from Padang to cappuccino, and a lot in between, but it's all average. One of Kuta's oldest warung, many people visit Made's just for people watching. Moderately priced.

Poppie's, Poppie's Lane 1, 751 059. One of Kuta's oldest restaurants, it's reputation extends far beyond the island. Ten years ago it was *the* place to eat, but today it just seems dated. The food is good ranging from seafood to Indonesian and Western. Amidst waterfalls and pools, the setting is pretty but the restaurant is crowded. It still draws the crowds so it's best to book a day in advance. Wine available. Moderate to expensive.

Yanie's, Jl. Tunjung Mekar, Legian, ph 751 292. Menu ranges from BBQ steaks, grills and hamburgers to curries. Basic, inexpensive tourist fare.

Japanese

Kurumaya, Padma Hotel, Jl. Padma 1, Legian, ph 752 111. Excellent teppanyaki with sizzling showmanship. Expensive.

Ryoshi, Jl. Legian (past Poppies Lane 1), ph 755 026. Good sushi, tempura, robata and soba served in simple Japanese setting. Moderately priced.

Mexican

Poco Loco's, Jl. Padma Utara, Legian, ph 756 079. Modern Santa Fe-style restaurant, offers all the Mexican favourites with a few

Indonesian-style specials thrown in. The service is friendly and atmosphere up-beat. It really has a great buzz which is why it's always busy. If you don't book you may be forced to sip Margaritas at the bar while you wait. Has wine by the glass or carafes of sangria.

TJ's, Poppies Lane 1. Well-run Mexican and Californian-style restaurant set around a water garden. Enchiladas, tacos, tostadas — all taste sensations! Up-market and popular, it's prices are Moderate to expensive. Small wine list.

Seafood

Mini Seafood, Jl. Legian 36, Kuta, ph 751 651. Open market-style setting, Mini offers a wide range of seafood cooked to your specifications. It's all very fresh and reasonably priced. Wine available.

Swiss

Swiss Restaurant, Jl. Pura Bagus Taruna, Legian, on the right just before Jl. Melasti (near the Swiss Consulate). Bratwurst, fondue and many other Swiss favourites. Has live music or dance performance nightly. Busy and bubbling atmosphere, with the host often taking time out to entertain his guests.

Tuban

Chinese

Mandarin, Jl. Kartika Plaza, 751 369. Good selection of Cantonese and Szechuan meals and fresh seafood including wonderful chilli crab. Live music nightly. Moderately priced.

Golden Lotus, Bali Dynasty Hotel, Jl. Kartika Plaza. Specialises in Szechuan and Cantonese cuisine. Moderate to expensive.

Indonesian

Kaisar, Jl. Kartika Plaza. Balinese and Indonesian specialties. Moderately priced.

Melati, Kartika Plaza Beach Hotel, Jl. Kartika Plaza. Excellent Indonesian and Asian dishes avoiding the stock of tourist favourites. Reasonably priced.

Ratna Satay Terrace, Holiday Inn Balihai. Roof-top restaurant with spectacular views will satisfy satay-lovers and those hankering for spicy food. Expensive.

Italian

Palm Cove, Jl. Kartika Plaza. Great gourmet pizzas with a

Balinese touch and standard Italian fare. Moderately priced.
Segara, Kartika Plaza Beach Hotel, Jl. Kartika Plaza. Pool-side restaurant with usual selection of Italian favourites and some more modern Italian specials. Expensive.

Seafood
Bali Seafood Market & Restaurant, Jl. Kartika Plaza, ph 753 902. Huge market-like restaurant with a menu to match. You can get just about any seafood you desire, cooked the way you like it. Good for groups. Moderately priced. The restaurant will arrange free transport.
Kuta Seafood Theatre & Restaurant, Jl. Kartika Plaza 92, ph 755 807. Another market-like seafood restaurant offering a huge range of seafood cooked to your requirements, but with 90-minute show featuring a dance trip through Indonesia (from 7pm).

Fast Food
Pizza Hut and KFC can be found on Jl. Raya Kuta. There is also a KFC and Swensen's Ice Cream Parlour in the Gelael Plaza, Jl. Legian 10, and Burger King is just opposite. McDonald's and another KFC, can be found further along Jl. Legian.

Where the Action is...

If Kuta and Legian are busy by day, they're just warming up. Once sated on the culinary delights it's off to the bars for light refreshments and respite, before assaulting the night clubs.

Many of the pubs, bars and night clubs stay open until at least 1am, some much later. Despite what many think, Kuta and Legian are quite safe. The streets are well-lit and quite busy well into the morning hours. Muggings have been reported, though, so I wouldn't recommend walking unaccompanied. There's enough activity in Kuta and Legian to confine your night activities to the area. However, two good night spots, *Gado-Gado* and *Double Six*, are further north in Seminyak and are too far to walk. Either call a taxi or bargain with the bemo boys.

Seminyak

Some of the best night spots on Bali are to be found in Seminyak. Party-goers will like the old favourites, *Double Six* and *Gado-Gado*, while those desperate for a rave should head to *Warisan* on Friday nights. Many restaurants clear out their tables after 11pm ready for a party and venues change all the time, so check around for notices. *Cafe Luna* and *Goa 2001* have DJs and are usually buzzing by 11pm. Or if you want live music head to Jaya Pub or Warung Tapas.

Bars and Pubs
Goa 2001, Jl. Raya Seminyak. This barn-like restaurant-cum-bar is very popular, especially after 11pm. Sometimes charged, sometimes mellow, the DJs invariably know how to work the crowd. Open until 2am.
Jaya Pub, Jl. Seminyak (not far from *Goa 2001*), ph 752 973. This small bar has live music nightly. It attracts a more sophisticated crowd.
Warung Tapas, Jl. Seminyak. Open-style Spanish bar and restaurant has live music several nights a week and visiting musicians are often invited to jam. Friday night parties are often huge with people spilling onto the street.

Nights Clubs
Double Six, Jl. Double Six, ph 753 366. This up-market club has a sizeable dance floor and two bars attracting Bali's chic locals and expatriates. European DJs spin current club hits from around the world. Open Monday, Thursday and Saturday nights until 6am with a cover charge of Rp15,000-20,000.
Gado-Gado, Jl. Dhyana Pura, ph 752 255. Almost a sister to *Double Six*, *Gado-Gado* is open alternate nights, attracts a similar crowd and plays similar music, but the dance floor is bigger. Both clubs arrange transport from the Bounty Hotel in Kuta. Depends what you like!
Taj Mahal, Jl. Kayu Aya, ph 730 525. This cavernous restaurant is gaining notoriety for its parties. After 11pm the tables are cleared to make way for the dance floor and DJs play club hits. The nights may change so it is worth it to call for more information.
Warisan, in the Italian restaurant north of *The Oberoi*, ph 754 710. Set in a rice field, Warisan hosts Friday night techno dance parties to satisfy ravers. Rumoured to be moving to Saturday nights, so call first to check dates.

Kuta and Legian
Bars and Pubs
For those into *pub crawls*, you've come to the right place. Peanuts Pub Crawl (ph 751 920) has become a local ritual for tourists, starting at Casablanca at 6.30pm, and finishing at Peanuts 1 & 2.

Bagus Pub, Poppies 2, Kuta. Huge tourist restaurant and bar very popular with young tourists and surfers.

The Bounty, Jl. Legian, Kuta. Usually overflowing with loud and drunken revellers.

Casablanca, Jl. Buni Sari (south of Bemo Corner), Kuta. Busy pub, and live music featured twice weekly when the Peanuts Pub Crawl stumbles in.

Hard Rock Cafe, Jl. Raya Legian 204, Kuta, ph 755 661. Regular live bands, some playing original music, draw a big crowd, but the drinks are expensive. Bands nightly except Monday and open until 2am.

Lips, Jl. Legian, Kuta. Dingy and small country and Western pub with occasional live bands, but mostly taped music.

O'Barrel, Bali Padma Hotel, Jl. Padma 1, Legian, ph 752 111. Up-market pub with live music (usually covers), always busy.

Rum Jungle Road, Pura Bagus Teruna, Legian, ph 752 111. Behind the restaurant, the second bar has pool tables and guest guitarist.

Tubes, Poppies 2, Kuta. Kuta's surf bar is fully furnished with surfing notice boards, paraphernalia and pool tables. Open and spacious, it is inviting to surfers and non-surfers alike.

Discos and Night Clubs
There are plenty of night clubs in Kuta and Legian, but also see the venues listed in Seminyak, north of Legian, and Tuban, south of Kuta.

Bali Rock Cafe, Jl. Melasti, Legian. Restaurant and bar with small dance floor plays rock'n'roll hits from the 50s, 60s and 70s. Open until 1am.

Bruna Reggae Bar, Kuta Beach Road, Kuta. Popular with the surf crowd, this bar has a reggae band playing nightly from 11pm, then a DJ spins reggae hits. Small dance floor. Admission Rp8000 minimum.

Peanuts 2, Jl. Legian, Kuta (north of Peanuts 1). Huge cavernous night club with large dance floor and mirror ball attracts young tourists and locals with dance hits. Three bars, one street-side generally with mediocre band thrashing rock'n'roll covers and another with pool tables. Usually overflowing when visited by the Peanuts Pub Crawl. Reasonably priced drinks.

Sari Club, Jl. Legian, Kuta. Very popular bar and night club drawing a young and trendy crowd. DJs spin current dance hits (though no techno) for nightly parties. The drinks are reasonably priced, there's no cover charge and closes at 3am.

Studebakers, Jl. Legian 81, Kuta (near Hard Rock Cafe). One of a chain, this night club has lots of promotions and competitions to woo party-goers. The open-air venue is spacious and popular, and hosts parties nightly. Admission charged. Also open for breakfast, lunch and dinner.

Tuban

BB's Discotheque, Bintang Bali Hotel, Jl. Kartika Plaza, Tuban, ph 753 292. Very popular with the locals, hosts party nights with DJs. Check the Alun Alun Lounge in the Bintang Bali for live jazz. Open 7pm-2am.

The Fun Pub, Dynasty Hotel, Jl. Kartika Plaza, Tuban, ph 752 403. Laid back venue with pool tables, and live band requesting karaoke victims.

Zero Six, Jl. Wana Segara, Tuban, ph 753 196. Open-air venue on the beach features a large dance floor and hosts DJ techno dance parties as well as live bands. Usually only crowded for events. Check posters.

Entertainment

Kuta has never had a reputation for its cultural attractions, but many tour agencies will organise trips to performances held out of the area. Prices can be as high as Rp20,000-Rp40,000 for a ticket when admission is only about Rp6000, so sometimes it's cheaper to find your own transport. In Denpasar at the Werdhi

Budaya Cultural Centre, Jl. Nusa Indah, the Kecak is performed (6.30-7.30pm) nightly in the amphitheatre. Many of the larger hotels host cultural dinner shows but they tend to be expensive. The *Legong* is performed at Hotel Melasti, Jl. Padma Utara, Legian, ph 755971 on Friday nights (US$10) at 7.30pm; and at the Natour Kuta Beach, Jl. Pantai Kuta, ph 751 361, on Monday nights at 8pm (US$12). The Natour Kuta Beach also hosts the Ramayana Ballet on Friday nights (US$12).

Many bars and pubs around Poppies 2 have large video screens blaring out the latest action thriller, and some hotels have video screens as well. Look for notices on lamp posts for details. There's a cinema in the same complex as McDonald's on Jl. Legian in Kuta. *Legian 21* (ph 752 222 ext 4000; program information call 423 023) has three air-conditioned cinemas showing current mainstream films at 6pm, 8.45pm and 10.45pm.

A performance you may hear without even leaving your hotel is the tones of the local *gamelan* orchestra practising in the banjar. Another free but not so welcome act is that of howling dogs or *cecing* — those despicable pariahs that are the antithesis of everything Balinese.

Shopping

Kuta and Legian are a bargain-shopper's paradise: from small boutiques selling "designer" goods, adjacent to dusty little shops displaying dusty little items, to pedlars offering beachwear.

Further north in Seminyak along Jl. Raya Basangkasa a number of boutiques have sprouted specialising in ladies fashion, menswear, curios and homeware. For instance, Rags, Kaya Gaya and The Range have displayed their designer fashions on the catwalks. Warisan (of the restaurant fame), Ibid and Transit Gallery, to name are few, design original homeware. Window shopping is possible because few pedlars bother annoying tourists.

For paintings and carvings, go to Ubud and Batuan.

Books

Bookshop, corner of Jl. Benesari and Jl. Legian, Kuta. Has a huge selection of books in English ranging from novels to non-fiction on Bali and Indonesia. Also stocks newspapers and maps.

Cassette Tapes

There are copious cassette shops throughout Kuta and Legian. The quality has improved and most shops have quite good selections. Since Indonesia signed a copyright agreement, cassettes shops are supposedly 100% legal. Cassettes sell for around Rp12,000 and CDs are more expensive at around Rp26,000.

Mahogany, Jl. Legian, Seminyak (down from *Cafe Luna*). Large selection of tapes (from Rp10,000) and CDs (from Rp30,000) and the staff are very helpful.

Clothes

In the last couple of years Kuta has developed a reputation for its rag trade. Many young designers from all around the world have come to Bali to establish their own businesses. Years ago, cheap mass-produced beachwear was ubiquitous. Now, there's still plenty of cheap clothing, but there are also some very chic boutiques with designer fashions. Most of the boutiques have fixed prices and by Kuta standards they're expensive, but by international prices they're a bargain. Most take credit cards, although the vendor will charge about 6% which is the rate the banks charge. For those into surfwear, Hot Buttered, Hot Tuna and Mambo, to name a few, have stores throughout Legian and Kuta. The clothes are cheaper than in Australia, but they are made in Indonesia.

Baik Baik. A young Balinese designer with a flare for the dramatic, works with traditional and modern fabrics styles.

Biasa, Jl. Raya Seminyak. Balinese designer fashions for women.

Galang Dua Koleski, Jl Pantai Kuta (not far from Bemo Corner). Has a treasury of fine antique-style clothes, with lots of lace and intricate embroidery.

Indigo, Jl. Legian. A chain store specialising in batik shirts for men and women, as well as casual wear. The styles are definitely more "up-market" than those sold in the markets.

Kuta Kidz, Bemo Corner. Illustrates the Balinese philosophy of dressing children in miniature adult fashions.

Mr Bali, Jl. Legian. One of the original menswear shops and now, one of a chain.

Rags, Jl. Basangkasa 28A, Kuta. Jeans, shirts and shoes for men with some imported European fashions as well.

Wild Woman, Jl. Legian 66, Kuta. Lots of lace and embroidered evening wear.

Curios
Borneo Art Shop, Jl. Legian, Kuta.
Kaliuda Art Shop, Jl. Legian, Kuta.
Kuta Art Market, Jl Bakung Sari, near the beach.

Jewellery
The filigree silver for which Bali is so famous is mostly made in Celuk. Go there to see the silversmiths at work, but buy in Kuta, the prices are much cheaper. Kuta also has the best range of fashion and costume-style jewellery, and although the prices are fixed they are still competitive. To ensure the jewellery is sterling silver, look for the .925 stamp.

A word of advice. If you buy jewellery with stones inlaid, don't wash them in soap, the glue deteriorates and the stones usually fall out.

Suarti, Jl. Legian 404 and Jl Bakung Sari. Chain of designer jewellery stores known for their huge range of modern designs. All silver is sterling .925.

Leather Goods
Kuta is the best place to purchase leather goods. If you want clothing, most shops will make the garments to measure. Buying off the rack, though, is recommended, then you'll know exactly what you're getting.

Photography
If you have any camera problems go to Prima Photo on Jl. Thamrin in Denpasar. But if you simply want to develop your film, there are a number of one-hour processors along Jl. Legian.

Sightseeing
Tour companies, as well as hotels, offer a variety of tours around the island. Prices differ as to sights, number of people travelling, and the state of the transport. The guides usually speak fluent English and are so enamoured of their island it can be contagious. (See **Day Tours** in the **Travel Information** chapter for more information.)

Besakih

This tour takes about eight hours and visits Batubulan, Celuk (famed for its silver), Mas (woodcarving), Gianyar, Klungkung, Kerta Gosa, Goa Lawah (Bat Cave) and Bali's state place of worship, the "mother temple", Pura Besakih. The temple is actually a huge complex of temples and shrines on the foothills of Gunung Agung. If you're not planning to venture that way yourself, this tour is a must!

Kintamani

A day tour which travels north to Gunung Batur, an active volcano, and the third highest mountain in Bali. Supposed highlight of the trip is the buffet lunch at Kintamani to view the Gunung Batur and its lake.

Tanah Lot

This is usually an afternoon tour to witness the celebrated sun setting behind the temple. On a good day, the sunset throws the temple into sharp relief and the effect can be enchanting! Having said this, a visit to Tanah Lot on an overcast dreary day is not recommended (see the entry in the chapter on Tabanan.)

Ubud

This tour usually takes half a day, and visits Celuk, Batuan, Mas, Bedulu, and Ubud. Again, if you're not planning to travel to these places, at least take a day tour.

Outlying Attractions

Pura Petitenget

Along the beach, north of the *The Oberoi* hotel, is the temple of Petitenget. Built of white coral, the temple was founded by the famed priest, Nirartha, and shares a common forecourt with the *subak* or irrigation co-operative's temple, Pura Ulan Tanjun.

Ulu Watu

The temple at Ulu Watu is worth visiting particularly for photo opportunities at sunset. But given that the building is perched on a cliff and covered with foliage, the best view is gained by birds. See the section on **Ulu Watu** for more information.

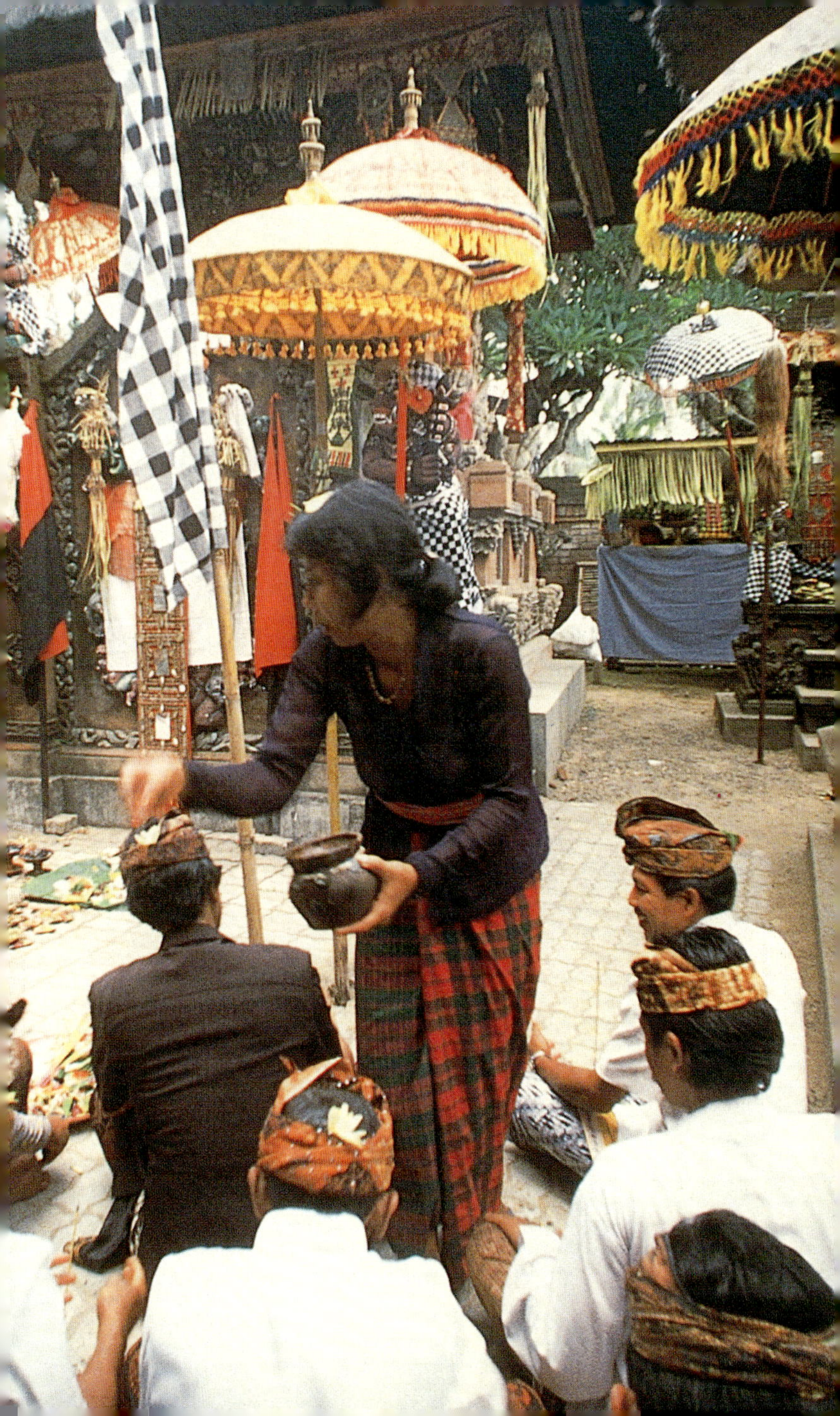

Harvesting rice.

A farmer with his water buffalo.

Bukit Peninsula

"Bukit", literally hill, properly denotes the area south of Nusa Dua; nevertheless, the entire peninsula, from the narrow isthmus of Jimbaran, is limestone. Thousands of years ago the huge barren plateau was probably separated from the mainland, but it is now connected by a narrow isthmus. The rugged white cliffs and austere plains of the peninsula provide a striking contrast to the verdant inland.

The entire area is renowned for its surf breaks and has been attracting surfers for years. The breaks at Padang Padang and Ulu Watu (or Ulu as it's affectionately known) are especially revered for their consistently good but difficult breaks.

Somewhat isolated from the resorts to the north, the Bukit area is poorly covered by public transport, so most people staying in the area either rent a car or hire a driver and car. More information is provided in the relevant sections.

The following description of the Bukit starts at Jimbaran, just south of the airport, and travels anti-clockwise via Ulu Watu to Nusa Dua and Tanjung Benoa.

Jimbaran

On the western side of the Bukit Peninsula, past the airport (along the old airport road), is Jimbaran, an old fishing village. Dependent on Kuta for its prosperity, Jimbaran supplies most of the resort area to its north with tuna, mackerel and baby sharks. You can visit the market, at the northern end of the beach, between 6am-8am.

Jimbaran is far away from the hawkers, shops and traffic, but is only ten minutes drive from the action. Its seemingly untouched environs are perfect for those desperate to escape the madness. Both the five-star Bali-Intercontinental and Four Seasons resorts are located at the southern end of the beach signalling perhaps, that this area is destined to become another resort compound á la Nusa Dua.

From Kuta, driving along Jl. Ulu Watu (the old airport road), you pass a small temple, Pura Ulun Siwi. Built under a holy banyan tree, the typical pura has an ornate split gate and a multi-tiered *meru* tower. A little past the village market, and off to the right, is a group of *kepuh* trees which mark the site of a cemetery used for the internment of bodies before cremation.

The main road that meanders to Nusa Dua, Jl. By-pass Ngurah Rai, by-passes Jimbaran Bay, which is definitely a good thing. White, sandy beaches and **very few people make this a nice quiet retreat.** The bay is protected by a reef, and the surf doesn't break so much as lap. On this island of contrasts, beauty has its counterpoint: on the eastern side of the peninsula is Suwung, an uninviting swampland.

Accommodation

Jimbaran Bay is another area outside of Kuta that is slowly building a name for itself as a "resort" village.

Prices for one night's accommodation are in US$, do not include the tax and service charges, and should be used as a guide only. The telephone code is 0361.

5 star Hotels

All five star hotels have full amenities from restaurants to fitness centres, but it is usually the suites that set the 5 star hotels apart.

Four Seasons Resort, Jimbaran Bay, ph 710 710. Possibly *the* ultimate resort in Bali, the Four Seasons features private villas built in a gently terraced hillside. Each villa has a personal plunge pool, bathing pavilion and private sundeck. Of course, there are several restaurants, swimming pools, saunas, tennis court and more. There's no need to venture beyond the resort, it has it all! Villa $500.

Bali Inter-Continental Resort, Jl. Ulu Watu 45, Jimbaran, ph 755055. A first-class resort-style hotel with all amenities including marine sports centre, games room, gym and spa. Room from $200.

3 star Hotel

Keraton Bali Cottages, Jl. Mrajepati, Jimbaran Bay, ph 753 991. This quaint hotel with all amenities is friendly and comfortable. There are restaurants, a swimming pool, tennis court and water sports galore. The restaurant, with its panoramic views of the bay, is spectacular at sunset — not to be missed if you're in the area! Rooms from $120.

Eating Out

Most of the restaurants and bars are located in the hotels. Right on the beach, *PJ's* in the Four Seasons Resort is fast gaining a reputation for excellent food as well as its live jazz. Menu includes wood-fired pizzas, pasta and a wondrous array of seafood. Also has theme brunches of a Sunday. Expensive, but well worth it. *The Watergarden* restaurant in the Keraton Bali Cottages overlooks the bay and offers some stunning seafood. *Ko Japanese* in the Bali Inter-Continental offers á la carte dining or teppanyaki. It's the best Japanese restaurant on the island.

Nightlife

Again, the night life is mostly confined to the hotels. For some cool jazz and cocktails try *PJ's* in the *Four Seasons*. The *Monkey Forest Pub* in the *Bali-Intercontinental*, ph 755 055, is a sophisticated bar and night club with a resident DJ. Open from 9pm-2am.

From Jimbaran Bay to Ulu Watu

These days it's a relatively easy drive along the sealed road from Jimbaran Bay to Ulu Watu (about 12km). Not so long ago, few bemo would attempt the narrow, pot-holed climb to the famed temple. Travelling south a couple of kilometres along Jl. Ulu Watu the road ascends the limestone plateau to stunning views of southern Bali. Along this route are various limestone quarries, where stone blocks are hewn by hand for the construction of many buildings in southern Bali. Around this area the landscape is noticeably dry and lifeless. Just past Salakan continue south and the next left is the local university, Universitas Udayana, about 2km (1 mile) from the highway. Further south, about 6 km from Jimbaran, is the village of Bakung where the road forks, left for Nusa Dua and right for Ulu Watu.

Continuing to Ulu Watu, a narrow west-bound road leads to the surfing beach at Balangan. Only die-hard surfers take this road which passes by the fishing village of Cengiling, noted for its *subak* sashes woven by the village women. This area of the Bukit is isolated and there are only a few small general stores, one selling petrol. Beyond this point (opposite Cengiling school) is the treacherous track, marked only by red arrows, leading (after 30 or 40 exhausting minutes) to the cave temple of Pura Balangan and the beach.

Back along the Ulu Watu road, the road climbs Gunung Ingas, the highest point on the peninsula at 203m (666ft). The next village is Pecatu, and the road west leads to Ulu Watu.

Ulu Watu

The temple at Ulu Watu forms one of the most magnificent views on the island. During the day, with a brilliant azure sky and waves crashing beneath, the temple is impressive. But as the sun slowly descends, the temple acquires a mystical quality, as the limestone masonry assumes a golden appearance.

The path to the east of the temple provides a good point for photos, but the only way to get a really dramatic photo is from the air.

The sheer cliffs of Ulu Watu are believed to be the petrified ship of Dewi Danu, goddess of the waters. The temple, Pura *Luhar Ulu Watu* or "temple above the stone", is perched on a precipice of 90m (295ft). Originally designed by a Javanese priest, Empu Kutaran, in the 11th century, it was a sanctuary for the Mengwi Dynasty up to 1891. The temple is one of the six most important temples on Bali and is part of the Sad Kahyangan group. The priest, Nirartha, is said to have visited the temple in order to achieve unity with the godhead or *moska*. It is easy to be moved by its beauty and atmosphere.

The temple is carved from Bukit limestone and has three compounds. The **outer courtyard** has a split gate with garuda wings, while the second courtyard has a monstrous image of Siwa flanked by two elephant-looking Ganesha. The sacred **inner courtyard** has a *meru* shrine, but is not open to the public.

The temple complex and the surrounding bush lands are home to a very brazen band of monkeys. Anything shiny, be it sunglasses, reading glasses, jewellery or water, is fair game. Adept at the element of surprise, they have been known to jump over fences and strike visitors in an attempt to steal goods. If you should fall victim, one of the Balinese guides will probably be able to retrieve articles for a fee.

Surfing

Ulu Watu is also **a surfing wonderland of sorts,** and is known to have an almost perfect surfing break all year round and *one of the best left-handers in the world.* The next break down from Ulu (as it is known by surfers) is Padang-Padang. Because of its proximity to a cliff, it is challenging — dangerous is probably a better word.

How to get there

Unfortunately, the only public bemo to Ulu Watu depart from Tegal terminal in Denpasar and don't travel via Kuta.

Those without a car will have to charter a bemo (about Rp60,000 for a round trip) or hire a taxi (Rp35,000) from Legian.

Suluban Beach

For the surfers, just before the Ulu Watu car park is a sign to *Suluban Beach, the* surf beach. Young boys will gladly provide transport by motor bike, for a price, of course. You cross fields for about 2km to a small parking area, and again young boys can be hired to carry boards and gear for the 40-minute walk to the gorge, or motorbikes can traverse the area with great difficulty. There are quite a few *warung* which cater to famished surfers. To reach Padang-Padang, a track continues from Suluban or there's access for bikes.

Nusa Dua

Nusa Dua is far, far from the madding crowd. Although the name means "two islands", Nusa Dua is in fact two small raised headlands connected to the mainland by sand tracts. Once upon a time, the small village called Bualu was a coconut plantation. But the Indonesian government, concerned with the unchecked sprawl of Kuta, had a cunning plan. The idea was to create a prestigious international resort, while minimising the impact on local life. Funded by loans from the World Bank, the government successfully transformed a desolate, isolated area into a burgeoning luxury hotel complex. First came the Bualu Hotel, the forerunner to the School of Tourism, followed by bigger and better hotels.

Nusa Dua is a carefully-crafted paradise. If Kuta is

Nusa Dua

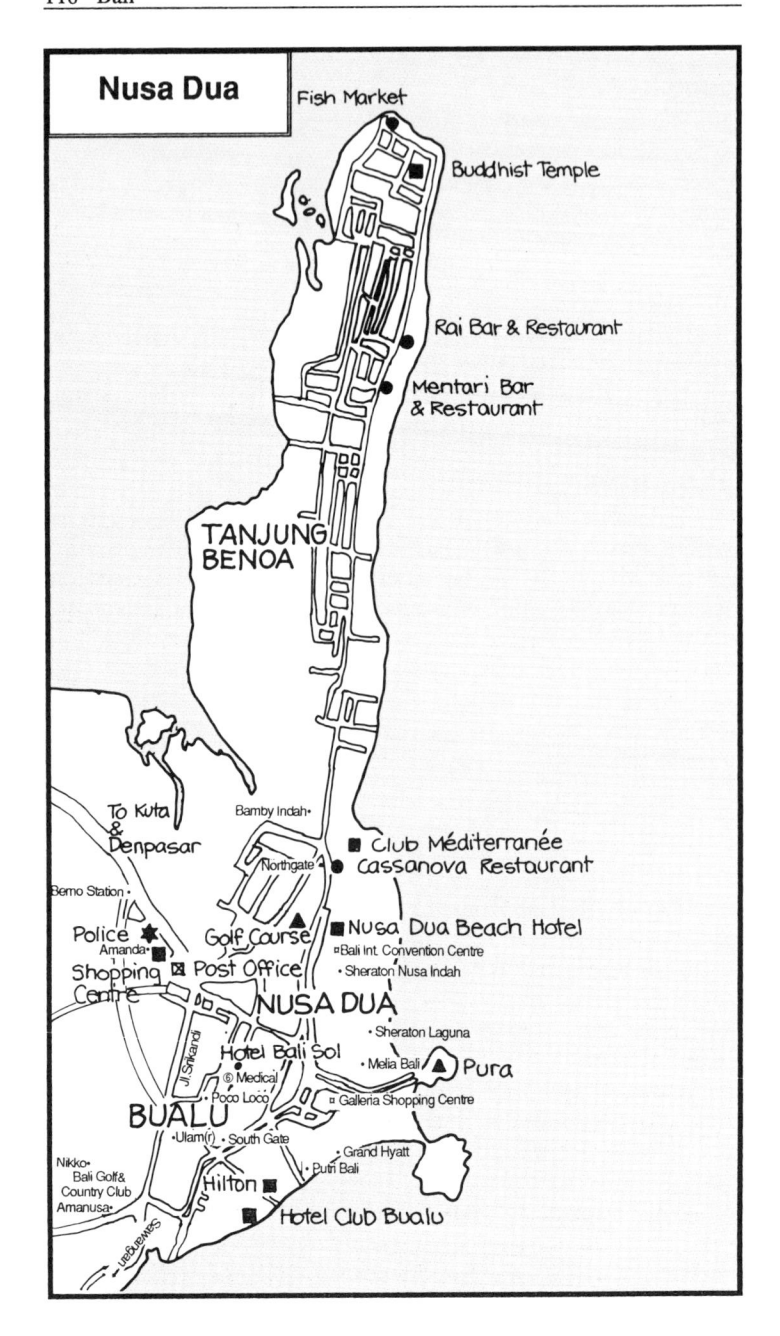

developing out of control, Nusa Dua is growing to plan. There are no losmen nor street vendors nor riffraff and life is grand, if not a little too protected.

How to Get There

If you're staying in one of the resorts and travelling straight from Ngurah Rai airport, your transfer will be arranged for you. If not, you will have to make do with public transport or taxis.

By Taxi

From Ngurah Rai airport, taxi fares can be purchased at the taxi desk for Rp12,000 and the journey takes about 20 minutes. Alternatively, blue and yellow taxis can be hired from outside the airport complex for about half the price: flagfall Rp1500 and Rp500 per kilometre.

By Public Bemo

The dark blue bemo that depart Denpasar's Tegal bemo station ply the routes to Nusa Dua and Benoa via Kuta (Jl. Imam Bonjol), Jimbaran and terminate at Bualu village. They operate sporadically and the journey takes about 35 minutes. Bemo are not permitted in the Nusa Dua resort complex, so if that's your destination, you'll either have to flag a taxi or walk.

Accommodation

Nusa Dua has no less that 15 resorts, all of which are 5 star. Prices in US$ are for one night's accommodation and should be used as a guide only. Rates do not include the 10-15% service charge nor the 10% government tax. **The telephone code is 0361.**
Grand Hyatt, ph 771 234. A modern-day water palace, the Grand Hyatt has its own fabricated lagoon and cascading waterfall. The hotel is typical of the grand resort developments in Nusa Dua. Facilities include 6 restaurants, 3 bars, fun pub, fitness centre, squash and tennis courts, aerobics, 6 swimming pools, a water slide and a children's club. 750 rooms grouped into several four-storey water villages. Rooms from $160.
Sheraton Laguna, ph 771 327. The Lagoon has its own free-form lagoon pool and lucky guests have access from their verandahs. Facilities include 3 restaurants, tennis courts, health club, children's playground and a 24-hour butler service. 276 rooms.

Rooms from $150.
Nusa Dua Beach Hotel, PO Box 1028, Denpasar, ph 771 210. The first hotel in Nusa Dua and Bali's first premier hotel, it is set on the beach amidst landscaped gardens. A traditional Balinese-style hotel, it welcomes guests with a huge split gate or *candi bentar*. Recently refurbished, the hotel offers world-class facilities. This is where the then-president, Ronald Reagan stayed. 380 rooms. Rooms from $140; suites from $350; with private pool $1200.
Hilton Bali, ph 771 102. 540 rooms. Designed to harmonise with the environment and located on the beach, the hotel includes a children's play centre, squash and tennis courts, and complete water sport facilities. Four and five-storey blocks. 537 rooms. Rooms from $180; suites from $450.
Club Mediterranee Nusa Dua, PO Box 7, Denpasar, ph 771 521. 350 rooms. Completely self-contained resort, but accommodation must be booked in advance through Club Med.
Melia Bali, PO Box 1048, Tuban, ph 771 510. 500 rooms. Owned by the Spanish Grupo Sol chain, it was recently renovated to create a more traditional Balinese environment. Facilities include swimming pool, tennis and squash courts, and health club. 500 rooms set in four-storey blocks. Room from $140.
Putri Bali, PO Box 1, Denpasar, ph 71 020. An old-style luxury hotel with cosy cottages as well as rooms. Facilities include 5 restaurants, tennis and squash courts, pool and games room. 391 rooms set in four-storey blocks. Room from $115.

Local Transport

Nusa Dua's resorts stretch over a distance of 6 kilometres so walking from one end of the complex to the other can be a hot and bothersome experience. Thankfully the route is amply covered by a fleet of green and yellow shuttles buses operating services from 8am to 11pm.

Taxi
Taxis are available from all hotels.

Car Rental
Avis Rent-A-Car is located in the Nusa Dua Beach Hotel, ph 771 210 and most resorts offer car rental.

Eating Out

Nusa Dua has over 30 international restaurants from which to choose. All the hotels offer theme nights and dance performances on a regular basis. For Indonesian seafood delights try *Lagoona* in the Bali Hilton, the patio at Sheraton Nusa Indah's *Ikan Restaurant* or *Kolak* at Hotel Bualu. Italian is recommended at *Salsa Verde*, the casual beachfront restaurant in the Grand Hyatt, or *La Cascata* at the Grand Mirage Resort.

There are a multitude of excellent Japanese restaurants including *Genji* at the Bali Hilton, *Hamabe* at Sheraton Nusa Indah, *Inagiku* at the Grand Hyatt, and the *Benkay Japanese Restaurant* in the Hotel Nikko.

The Galleria also has a number of restaurants and cafes worth checking out for lunch and light snacks.

Outside of the hotel complex, a number of independent restaurants are beginning to emerge. Although not within walking distance of the hotels, most restaurants offer free transportation if you give them a call.

Pica Pica, Jl. Pantai Mengiat, 771 886. Spanish tapas bar specialising in tapas, paellas and seafood.

Poco Loco, Jl. Pantai Mengiat, ph 773 923. Just as good as its older sister, this vibrant Santa Fe-style restaurant dishes out excellent Mexican covering all the old favourites with a few Indonesian twists thrown in.

Ulam, Jl. Pantai Mengiat. Strictly Indonesian menu offers some wonderful delights including satays and curries.

Nightlife

Every hotel in Nusa Dua has its own bars and usually a night club. The vibe often depends on the season and the hotel's guests, so check out your own hotel before jumping into a taxi.

Club Tabuh, Nusa Dua Beach Hotel, ph 771 210. Hosts regular parties and theme nights.

Hemmingway's, Grand Mirage, ph 771 636. A sophisticated piano and cocktail bar.

Lila Cita Fun Pub, Grand Hyatt, ph 771 234. Hosts parties regularly, with theme nights, dance shows and live bands. Call for a calendar of events.

Quinn's, Sheraton Lagoon, ph 771 327. Popular up-market nautical-style bar with dance floor hosts dance parties and live bands. Open until 2am (closed Wednesday).

Shopping

A number of clothes boutiques are located out of the hotel complex, as are the typical stock of souvenir shops. Really, nothing compares to Kuta and Legian for shopping.

The *Galleria*, a large air-conditioned shopping mall, is located in the middle of the resort complex (open daily 9am-10pm) and all Nusa Dua hotels offer a free shuttle service to and from the complex. A huge sprawling, landscaped affair, it offers sporting shops, book shops, fashion boutiques, a toy department, duty free outlet and a supermarket ... the list goes on. It is also where you'll find the postal agent, an American Express office, and a Garuda office. The prices in the Galleria outlets are high and there is no bargaining.

The Galleria is an East meets West arena. Every day at sunset a Barong procession marches through the shopping plaza to scare away evil spirits. It also hosts Balinese dance performances (ph 771 662) free of charge, every night from 7.30pm.

Water Sports

Most hotels in Nusa Dua rent out water sports equipment, usually from small stalls on the beach, but you'll find the best range and prices on the beachfront towards Benoa. Windsurfing boards can be hired for around US$8 an hour, canoes US$5 an hour and snorkelling gear for US$3 an hour. Along the beach strip in Benoa you can rent jet-skis or water-skis (US$20 for 15 minutes) or try parasailing (US$10 per trip). Glass-bottomed boats can be hired for US$10 an hour.

Many companies offer cruises around Bali, or its various satellites, on a luxury yacht. *Trade Wind Yacht Charter* (PT Tourdevco) offers numerous organised tours or devise your own itinerary (PO Box 1081, Tuban, Denpasar, ph 231 591). Trips to Nusa Penida on the catamaran Quicksilver can be arranged at Benoa in the Beluga complex, ph 771 969.

Tanjung Benoa

North of Nusa Dua along a peninsula, the village of Tanjung Benoa was formerly the port for Denpasar. Now it's a mooring for visiting yachts and is gaining favour with water sports enthusiasts (see the Nusa Dua entry for a listing). In terms of accommodation and restaurants, Benoa tends to cater to the middle to lower budget end—the market spurned by Nusa Dua.

Although a small village, a Bugis mosque and a Chinese Klenteng temple bear testimony to the variety of peoples who have made Benoa their home.

How to get There

By Taxi
From Ngurah Rai airport, taxi fares can be purchased at the taxi desk for Rp12,000 and the journey takes about 20 minutes.

By Public Bemo
The dark blue bemo that depart Denpasar's Tegal bemo station ply the routes to Nusa Dua and Benoa via Kuta (Jl. Imam Bonjol), Jimbaran and terminate at Bualu village. They operate sporadically and the journey takes about 35 minutes.

Accommodation

Benoa is becoming home to more and more hotels catering to middle to lower range budgets. There are also quite a few losmen, but always inspect these establishments before committing to a night's stay.

Prices in US$ are for one night's accommodation and should be used as a guide only. Rates do not include the 15.5% tax and service charge.

The telephone code is 0361.

Grand Mirage Hotel, ph 771 888. Although the hotel is really a 4 star property, it represents excellent value, and has all amenities. It's also home to Bali's Thalasso Therapy Centre which specialises in body and facial rejuvenation. Built in a three-storey block, all rooms have open-plan bathrooms. Room $110.

Bali Tropic Palace, ph 772130. Some of the largest rooms in Bali, the Tropic Palace is not like the usual hotel-block accommodation. This hotel caters for families. Room $80.

Ocean Blue Resort Nusa Dua. Located on the beachfront in what's commonly known as North Nusa Dua, the Ocean Blue caters more to couples and families. Room $65.

Local Transport

Green bemo run frequently between the Tragia Supermarket in Bualu and the Chinese temple at the northern tip of Benoa.

Eating Out

The myriad of *warung* along Jl. Pratama and the beachfront serve excellent Indonesian dishes. For restaurants try the *Rai Seafood Restaurant* which has a cocktail bar and superb seafood, and right next door is the *Mentari Ming Garden,* whose bar is also amply stocked, and the food comparable. They both look out to Serangan Island which makes a great backdrop.

Of course, there are numerous first class restaurants in the hotels in Nusa Dua, and while their standards are very high, so are the prices.

Sanur

Sanur Beach, with its shimmering sands and crystal-clear waters is idyllic, so it's little wonder that a cosmopolitan and luxurious village resort has blossomed. Surrounded by lush tropical gardens, Sanur has managed to retain its serene beauty. Affluent tourists stroll leisurely along the beach; or swan about at the various soirees offered by the hotels. Although many young people stay in Sanur, typically the tourists tend to be older and richer — those who find Kuta a bit hectic.

On Badung's east coast, Sanur has developed around Bali's largest traditional village and is still administered by a priestly caste. Juxtaposed with the highly religious atmosphere is the whisper of black magic. But ask a local and they just clam up.

Sanur was Bali's first international resort, and the Grand Bali Beach Hotel (formerly the Bali Beach Hotel) was built in 1966 with reparations from the Japanese. President Sukarno hailed it as a symbol of modern Indonesia, but the Bali Beach Hotel is more like a monument to monstrosity. It spawned a statute preventing the erection of buildings taller than palm trees.

How to Get There

By Taxi
From the airport take a taxi. Fares are fixed (Rp12,000), and tickets can be purchased from the taxi desk outside customs.

Alternatively, hire a blue and yellow taxi from outside the compound and it will cost you half the price: flagfall Rp1500 and about Rp500 per kilometre.

By Public Bemo
There are two bemo stops in Sanur, one north of the village opposite the Grand Bali Beach Hotel, the other south on the main street near the By-pass road. Bemo do not run from Sanur to Kuta, so you must change in Denpasar.

By Hiring a Bemo
Bemo can be chartered from anywhere on the island to any destination, for a price. What that price will be, is largely determined by inexplicable factors. Shop around and bargain.

By Car
Sanur is 7km (4 miles) from Denpasar; 8km (5 miles) from Kuta; and 28km (17 miles) from Ubud.

Tourist Information
Sanur has no official tourist bureau, but the Tourist Information Centre, Jl. Danau Tamblingan 85, ph 286 531 (daily from 8am-6pm) can provide information on local transport and upcoming events.

Accommodation
Although Sanur is no longer *the* place to stay for five-star accommodation (Nusa Dua has usurped that title) there are still many first-class hotels. Prices for one night's accommodation are in US$ and do not include the 10-15% service charge nor the 10%

126 Bali

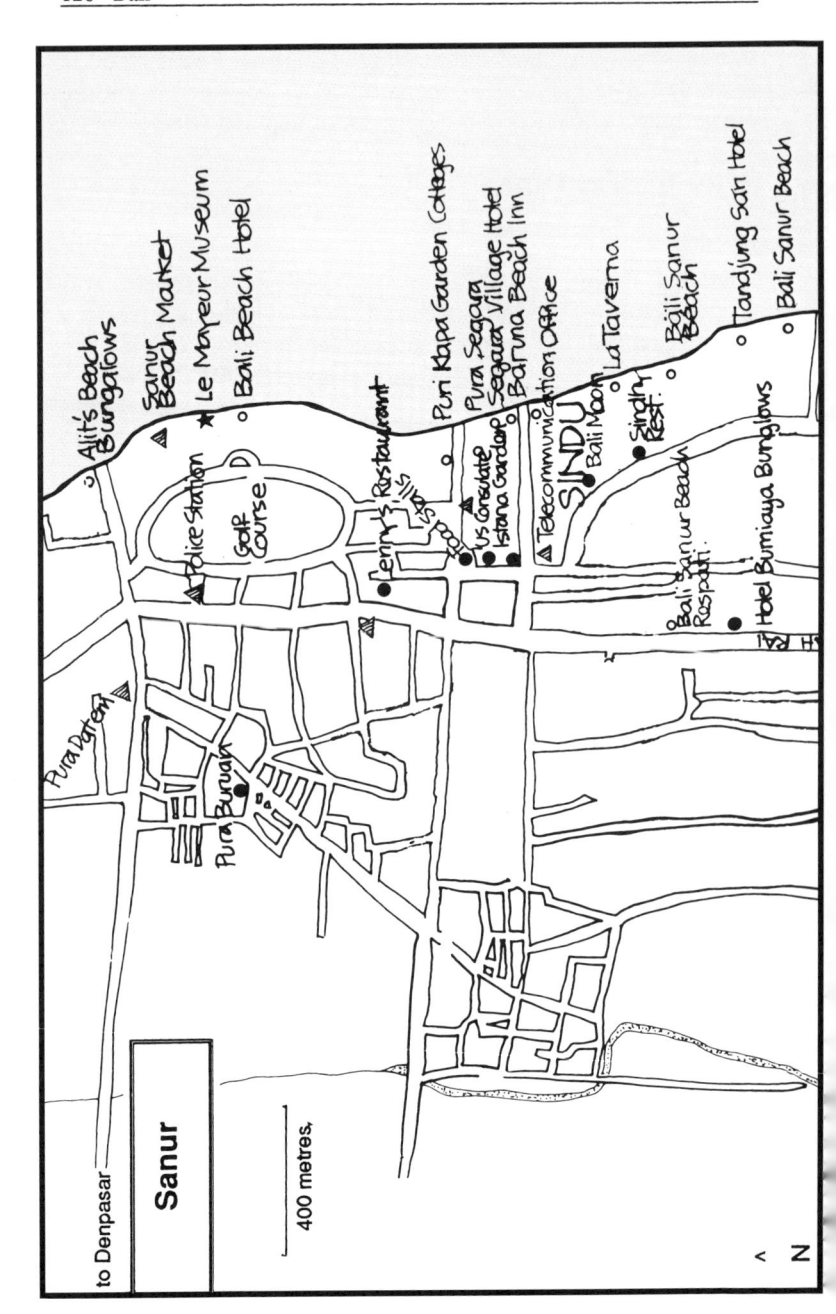

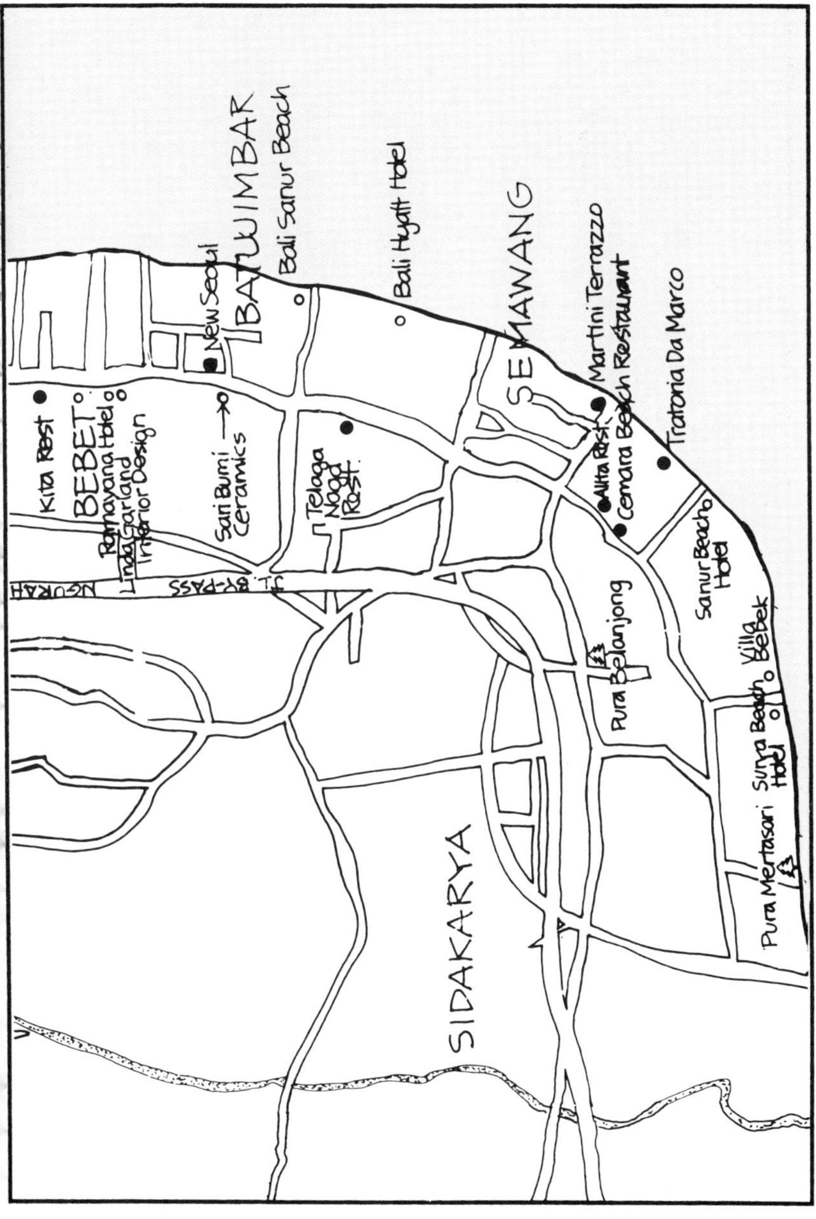
Kita Rest
BEBET
Ramayana Hotel
Linda Garland Interior Design
Sari Bumi Ceramics
New Seoul
BATUJIMBAR
Bali Sanur Beach
Bali Hyatt Hotel
Telaga Naga Rest.
SEMAWANG
Martini Terrazzo
Alita Rest.
Cemara Beach Restaurant
Tratoria Da Marco
Sanur Beach Hotel
Villa Bebek
Pura Belanjong
Surya Beach Hotel
Pura Mertasari
SIDAKARYA
JL. BY-PASS

government tax, and should be used as a guide only.
The telephone code is 0361.

5 star Hotels

These hotels are on the beach and include facilities such as bars, restaurants, shops, swimming pool, sporting centres and all rooms have a TV, telephone, air-conditioning, hot water, a fridge and complete room service. All major credit cards are accepted.

Bali Hyatt, Jl. Semawang, ph 288 271. Built on 15 hectares (36 acres) it boasts five restaurants, four bars, a mini-golf course, tennis court, sauna, gymnasium, disco, and 15 shops. One of the pools even has a replica of Goa Gajah. Rooms from $136.

Grand Bali Beach Hotel, Jl. Hang Tuah, ph 288 511. Formerly the *Hotel Bali Beach*, it was Bali's first big hotel and has a history of catering to famous international guests. The resort was substantially remodelled following a fire in 1992. At the northern end of Sanur Beach, its 600 rooms are in a ten-storey tower. With a nine-hole golf course, ten-pin bowling alley, football field, children's playground, theatres, seven restaurants, six bars, a supper club, a cafe, local banks, shops, galleries and airline offices — it has just about everything. Rooms from $115.

Hotel Sanur Aerowisata, Jl. Semawang, ph 288 011. The former *Hotel Sanur Beach* has four restaurants, two swimming pools, playground, tennis court, badminton, windsurfing, snorkelling, and a comprehensive fitness centre. Rooms from $110.

4 star Hotels

These hotels are on the beach and include facilities such as bars, restaurants, shops, swimming pool and all rooms have a TV, telephone, air-conditioning, hot water, a fridge and complete room service. All major credit cards are accepted.

La Taverna, Jl. Danau Tamblingan, ph 288 357. Old-world charm with all the modern-day comforts. One of the nicest beach-front hotels with semi-detached bungalows or family units. Rooms from $90.

Tandjung Sari Hotel, Jl. Danau Tamblingan 41, ph 288 441. This hotel is one of Sanur's oldest and most elegant hotels and many jetsetters stop here. An intimate hideaway right in the middle of Sanur. Rooms from $210.

Sanur Bali Travelodge, Jl. Mertasari, ph 288 833. Formerly the *Surya Beach Hotel*, it is located at the southern end of the beach so it's very quiet and is ideal for families. Amenities include 2 swimming pools, children's pool, tennis courts, restaurants and bar. Rooms are built in groups of two or four. Rooms from $90.

3 star Hotels

The 3 star hotels are located on the beach but they do not have the sporting facilities or services offered by the 4 star hotels. All rooms have TV, telephone, mini-bar and 24-hour room service.

Besakih Beach Resort, Jl. Raya Sanur, ph 288 425. Formerly the *Bali Sanur Beach Bungalows*, it's on the beach front and offers many water sports. Amenities include two swimming pools, two restaurants and each room has a balcony. Rooms from $60.
Santrian Beach Resort, ph 288 009. On the quiet southern end of Sanur beach, it has several swimming pools, a tennis court and regular entertainment. Rooms from $70.
Santrian Bali Beach Cottages, Jl. Danau Tamblingan 10, ph 288 181. This beachfront property has suites, cottages and standard rooms with private terrace or balcony. Rooms from $60.
Segara Village Hotel, Jl. Segara Ayu, ph 288 407. Located on the beach, and has 2 swimming pools, jacuzzi, recreation centre and kids club. Offers motel room or bungalow-style accommodation organised in clusters of different villages. Families welcome. Rooms from $80.

1-2 star Hotels

Most 2 star hotels are a walk from the beach, and some rooms do not have air-conditioning, otherwise they all have a restaurant, bar and pool. Prices include the tax and service charges.

Alit's Beach Bungalows, ph 288 576. Close to shops and restaurants, this is a charming family-run property whose rooms do have air-conditioning. Rooms from $30.
Baruna Beach Inn, Jl. Sindhu, ph 288 546. Pretty bungalows with courtyard and water views. Breakfast, tax and service charges are included. Rooms from $40.
Bumi Ayu Bungalows, Jl. Bumi Ayu, ph 587 517. Ten minutes' walk to the beach, it's characterised by friendly service. Room facilities by request. Rooms from $30.

Janur Garden Hotel, Jl. By-pass Ngurah Rai, ph 288 155. As it's on the highway, few tourists stay. Rooms from $35.
Puri Kelapa Garden Cottages, Jl. Segara, ph 288 999. Set away from the beach the cottages are built around gardens and a pool. Rooms from $35.
Swastika Bungalows, Jl. Danau Tamblingan 128, ph 286 487. In the heart of Sanur, Swastika Bungalows offers excellent budget accommodation with pools and restaurant. Choose from either cottages or motel-style rooms. Rooms from $30.

Local Transport

By Public Bemo
There are numerous public bemo that wend their way around Sanur, from dawn to dusk, and most journeys cost about Rp200.

By Hiring a Bemo
Prices differ depending on the season, the tourist, and the mood of the driver. In the low season, US$5 should get you to Denpasar; in the high season probably double the price.

By Taxi
Praja Taxi, Jl. By-pass Ngurah Rai, Sanur, ph 289090, 289191, services the Sanur area to any other destination on the island. Taxis can be hired from most hotels for Rp1000, then Rp1500 flagfall and about Rp500 per kilometre.

By Car
Renting a car is probably the best way to see Bali, and ditto for Sanur. The following are a few of the rental agents in Sanur:
Avis, Bali Hyatt Hotel, Jl. Bali Hyatt, ph 288 271.
Bali Car Rental, Jl. By-pass Ngurah Rai, ph 288 539.
Holidays Company, Jl. Sanur Beach, ph 288 328.
Samudra Car Rental, Jl Sanur Beach, ph 288 471.

Eating Out
There are numerous restaurants in Sanur. The restaurants in the *Bali Hyatt, Grand Bali Beach* and *Hotel Sanur Aerowisata* are all quite good but serve mainly European food or Indonesian-style food modified for Western taste buds.

The *Tandjung Sari Hotel* is renowned for its *rijstaffel*, a Dutch buffet of assorted goodies, and on Saturday nights there's a *legong* performance.

Or the *Sari Karya Bar and Restaurant* offers Italian, Chinese, Indonesian and International cuisine with different dance shows and live music (Jl. Bali Hyatt, ph 288 376).

Here is a list of restaurants you might care to try and most will organise transport:

Chinese

Lenny's, Jl. By-pass Ngurah Rai 70, ph 288 572. The first Chinese restaurant in Sanur, it has a good selection of Cantonese as well as Indonesian food, and has expanded its menu to include a selection of seafood dishes.

Telaga Naga (across from its proprietor, the Bali Hyatt). Mainly Szechuan food in a relaxed atmosphere by the lotus pond.

European

Cafe Batu Jimbar, Jl. Danau Tamblingan, central Sanur. Slightly up-market, Italian and Mexican are the focus of the menu, with fresh bread and cakes thrown in. Moderately priced.

La Lagune, Jl. Danau Tamblingan, south Sanur. Popular for its European breakfast with good breads, croissants and cappuccinos, and other coffees.

La Taverna, just off Jl. Tandjung Sari, in the La Taverna Hotel. Typical selection of pastas, but the pizzas straight from the brick oven are good and the view is great.

Le Pirate, on the beach in north Sanur. Next to Segara Village, Le Pirate has a large menu from European to Asian, and is moderately priced.

Indonesian

Kul Kul, Jl. Bali Hyatt, ph 288 038. Reasonably-priced Indonesian food and some Western dishes set in a series of Balinese bale.

Sanur Beach Market, Jl. Segara. Right on the beach, the spartan furnishings belie the rich and tasty menu. The market is actually organised by a collective and the profits are used for the community. Dances are held on Wednesday and Saturday nights. Inexpensive.

Sita, just off Jl. Ngurah Rai By Pass 41. Always busy, seafood is the specialty and the menu is extensive. *Legong* performances

nightly. Reasonably priced.
Warung Jawa Barat, Jl. Kesumasari 2, cnr Jl. Danau Tamblingan. Popular warung-style eatery prides itself on its authentic Javanese fare. Inexpensive.

Japanese
Kita, Jl. Tandjung Sari, ph 288 158. For a nice change from pasta and Chinese you can try sukiyaki, tempura, yakitori and others. A little more expensive than most.
Ryoshi, Jl. Danau Tamblingan, 150, ph 288 473. Sushi, tempura, robata and soba in simple Japanese surrounds. Moderately priced.

Seafood
Resto Ming, Jl. Mertasari 2, ph 286 250. Specialises in seafood from Western-style lobster thermidor to tangy Indonesian. Seafood lovers won't be disappointed. Moderately priced.

Nightlife
As with any of the resorts, the night life can change with season and the types of visitors. Many hotels have discos and bars worth checking out before jumping into a taxi. Those looking for a '90s-style club scene will be disappointed, but there are plenty of dance floors and bars where you can while away the hours.

Bali Hai Restaurant and Bar, rooftop of *Grand Bali Beach Hotel*, ph 288 511. Old-time dance band and stunning views draw a mature crowd to wine, dine and dance.
Banjar, Jl. Duyung, central Sanur (next to the Hyatt). On the beach and reminiscent of the 1950s beach parties, Banjar draws a young crowd with current mainstream dance music mingled with reggae.
Cockatoo Bar, Jl. Danau Tamblingan, central Sanur. Small open-air bar draws a mixed crowd. Happy hour daily from 5pm to 7pm.
Grantang Bar, *Bali Hyatt*, ph 288 271. A sophisticated cocktail bar serving up live jazz every night except Wednesday from 8pm-1am.
Koki, Jl. By-pass Ngurah 9, Blanjong, ph 287 503. A casual pub atmosphere complete with pool tables, draught beer and pub

food. Closed Monday. Transport available.
No 1 Club, Jl. Danau Tamblingan 138, central Sanur. Sanur's favourite pick-up joint catering to the 30s-50s set. This is reflected in the expensive beer prices. Takes off 'round midnight.
Subec Club, Jl. Danau Tamblingan 21, central Sanur, ph 288 888. A cavernous black and chrome discotheque complete with mirror ball and frequented by a mix of Denpasar's yuppies, local expatriates and tourists.
The Trophy, Trophy Pub Centre, Jl. Danau Tamblingan 49, south Sanur. Ex-pat pub with pool table and satellite TV. Live music (covers, of course) nightly.

Entertainment

Dance Performances
There are two popular performances held out of Sanur, and tickets can be purchased from hawkers or any of the many tour "agencies". For around Rp30,000 you'll receive a ticket and return fare, or you can make your own way there and pay the Rp6000 admission. The **Barong** is performed at the Pura Puseh in Batubulan from 9.30-10.30am. (You can make your own way there via a Batubulan-bound bemo from Kereneng terminal.) The **Kecak** is performed at the *Werdhi Budaya Cultural Centre* on Jl. Nusa Indah nightly from 6.30pm and is not to be missed. (Take the dark green Sanur-Kereneng bemo, although you'll have to take a taxi or charter a bemo home.)

Many of the hotels have dance performances as do the restaurants, but you must dine to take advantage of the shows.

The **Frog dance** at the *Penjor Restaurant* on a Sunday night at 7pm, ph 288 226; regularly at *Oka's Restaurant*, Jl. Danau Tamblingan, south Sanur and at the *Sanur Beach* every Sunday, ph 288 011.
The **Legong** is performed nightly at the *Legong Restaurant*, Jl. Danau Tamblingan, south Sanur; regularly at the *Penjor*, Jl. Danau Tamblingan, central Sanur; and every Monday at the *Grand Bali Beach* in north Sanur, ph 288 511 and at the *Sanur Beach*, ph 288 011.
The **Prembon** dance is performed at the *Grand Bali Beach* in north Sanur every Wednesday, ph 288 511.

The **Ramayana Ballet**, is performed at the *Sanur Beach*, ph 288 011, every Wednesday, and at the *Grand Bali Beach*, ph 288 511 every Friday.

Wayang Kulit or shadow puppet play is at the *Laghawa Beach Inn Restaurant*, Jl. Danau Tamblingan 51, central Sanur, at 7pm every Monday, Wednesday and Saturday. You can phone 288 494 for free transport.

Shopping

Like all the tourist centres in Bali, Sanur is filled with shops. Most of the boutiques are located along Jl. Danau Tamblingan and its side streets. In Kuta there's a better selection of shops and the prices are generally cheaper, however, Sanur tends to have more ceramic and antique shops which rival the best on the island.

Art Markets
Pasar Seni, Jl. Danau Tamblingan, central Sanur. Hone your bargaining skills. Stalls selling every kind of art, craft, jewellery and such associated with Bali.

Books
Kika Bookshop, Jl Danau Tamblingan. Decent range of general interest Indonesian and Balinese titles and some international periodicals, all substantially cheaper than the book shops in the big hotels.

Pottery
Keramik Jenggala at Batu Jimbar is well known and has some interesting and original works.
Sari Bumi, Jl. Hyatt. Brent Hesselyn, a New Zealander, has been creating ceramic goods for Bali's hotels and restaurants for many years. Worth a visit.

Supermarket
Gelael Supermarket, Jl. By-pass Ngurah Rai. Well-stocked grocer.

Textiles
Many of the chain stores you see around Kuta and Ubud are also in Sanur, especially in the big hotels.

Nogo Ikat, Jl. Danau Tamblingan 98 and 208. Designer wear using traditional *ikat* and *endek* fabrics. Purchase from the rack or have clothes made to order; and watch the weaving.
Putra Batik, Jl. Sindhu 5, central Sanur. Specialises in rayon batik-dyed sarongs for Rp10,000.

Linda Garland
Linda Garland has won international acclaim as an interior designer. Her showroom, on Jl. Hyatt, has a wide selection of home furnishings. Fashionable but expensive.

Sightseeing

Prasasti Belanjong
At Belanjong village, in the temple past the Sanur Hotel, is an inscribed stone pillar shaded by a lotus. It is Bali's earliest dated artefact. Only partially deciphered, the inscriptions suggest that it was erected in 914AD, by Sri Kesari Varma, a Javanese king. Reference is made to a military invasion against eastern Indonesia.

Coral Pyramid
At the end of Jl. Segara, is a small temple with a coral pyramid that is thought to date back to pre-Hindu times.

Le Mayeur Museum
The former home of the Belgian painter, Le Mayeur (1880-1958), who arrived in Bali in 1932 at the age of 52. He lived on the outskirts of Denpasar until captivated by the young *Legong* dancer, Ni Polok. Said to be stunningly beautiful, she regularly posed for the artist and they later married and moved to the residence in Sanur. The house has been maintained as a museum by the Indonesian Government since Ni Polok's death in 1985.

Built on the beachfront, much of the original 1935 dwelling remains. The low-roofed wooden house is quite impressively decorated with ornate carvings, gold and red doors, and window shutters displaying carved scenes from the *Ramayana*.

Most of Le Mayeur's work was undertaken in the tiny garden courtyard which is littered with statuary and shrines. Many of his works are displayed inside, but there's a surprising dearth of his Balinese paintings. Le Mayeur often worked in oils but there are also charcoal and photographic portraits. Two of the most outstanding portraits are of Ni Polok, but from the displays, it's obvious she was not his sole inspiration.

Located behind the Grand Bali Beach Hotel. Open Tuesday to Thursday from 8am-4pm; Friday 8am-1.30pm; Sunday 8am-4pm; Closed on Monday and Saturday. Admission Rp200.

Water Sports and Other Activities

Sanur attracts water-sporting enthusiasts from all over the island. If you'd like to do more than take a dip, say for instance, water-ski, jet-ski, dive, parasail, windsurf or simply snorkel, try the big hotels.

While many people come to Sanur for the diving, the reefs on the east coast around Candi Dasa, are gaining in popularity. Having said that, if you want to dive in Sanur try the *Bali Marine Sports Dive Centre*, Jl. Kesuma Sari, Semawang, ph 288 776 or Jl. By-pass Ngurah Rai, ph 289 308; *Bali Diving Perdanda*, Jl. Duyung 10, Semawang, ph 288 871; or *Dive and Dives*, Jl. By-pass Ngurah Rai 23, ph 288 052.

Fishing trips are another organised sport. Boats usually leave from Tanjung Benoa (for more information see that section).

Surfers should consult the surfing section in the Travel **Information** chapter.

Sanur also has its fair share of indoor and outdoor sports, and most of the larger hotels are happy for non-guests to use the facilities for a fee. The *Grand Bali Beach*, ph 288 511, has a nine-hole golf course offering shoes and clubs for hire.

Serangan Island

Turtle Island, as Serangan Island is sometimes known, was once famed for its turtles. Less than 300 metres off the coast of Sanur, at the entrance to Benoa Harbour, it has an area of 73 hectares (180 acres) of mostly scrub-like vegetation. Many of Sanur's snorkelling trips are destined for Serangan Island, but its charms extend well beyond its reef. Although not as picturesque as you'd expect, the lack of cars and roads, and the sweet pink coral temples and dwellings make a visit to Serangan Island an attractive proposition.

Serangan Island was the centre of Bali's lucrative turtle market until hunting was outlawed in 1990 in an attempt to save the species. There are only 70,000 or so females turtles worldwide, and despite the Jakarta-endorsed turtle-raising project, farming has dropped considerably. The only evidence of the Government's initiative is the pathetic captives in the fetid pond by the Pojok jetties. Avoid them and the hawkers imploring you to visit them.

Turtle meat has always been considered a ceremonial delicacy and turtles caught for ceremonial purposes are considered fair game. Furthermore, the market price for each animal is Rp150,000, so it's probable that poaching still continues. Meat is not the only commodity the turtle provides and international trade in tortoiseshell has been banned under the Convention of International Trade in Endangered Species since 1992. Thus travellers returning from Bali bearing tortoiseshell goods will have them impounded by Customs.

Serangan Island also has a special temple, *Pura Sakenan*. Situated on the north-west coast of the island, the temple dates back to the 16th century and is associated with the wandering priest Nirartha. An almost ziggurat-like structure, the complex, in fact, houses two temples or *pura*: the first has only a single obelisk (the throne of Dewi Sri, the goddess of agriculture); while the second, the larger *pura*, is typically Balinese. While not as impressive as the Tanah Lot and Ulu Watu temples, Pura Sakenan is a public temple and attracts vast crowds during the Galungan festival.

How To Get There

The *jukung* fishing boats that line Sanur Beach will ferry tourists to Serangan Island and return, for Rp20,000. Motorised *prahu* can be hired for Rp40,000 an hour to sail around the lagoon, but are a bad deal for tourists.

The trip from swampy Suwung, directly opposite the island, is much cheaper (Rp3000) and quicker. Suwung is about 2km from Sanur, just off Jl. By-pass Ngurah Rai (the turn-off is well sign-posted), so a car is recommended.

Coming from Denpasar take a grey bemo (destination Pesanggaran) from the Suci terminal in the city.

There is only one losmen on Serangan Island, the six-room *Homestay Santap Sari*, which is located between the east coast and *Pura Dalem*.

To Nusa Lembongan and Nusa Penida

Across from Sanur are the outlines of two islands that actually shadow Serangan Island. *Prahu* can be hired to take you from Sanur to Nusa Lembongan, the smaller of the two islands, and the fare will depend on the number of people travelling, as well as the cost of the petrol which will vary with the tide, the current and the wind.

For more information see the section on **Klungkung**, which is the regency to which these islands belong.

Gianyar

Gianyar lies in the cultural and geographical heart of Bali. Separated from the regency of Badung by the Ayung river, the regency of Gianyar extends south to the coastline, north to the mountains a few kilometres below Gunung Batur, and shares its eastern border with Bangli. Although the town of Gianyar is the regency's capital, most travellers make a beeline for Ubud.

Gianyar is the second most populated regency after Badung, and derives most of its income from tourism. Ever since the German artist Walter Spies set foot in Ubud in 1928, the area has attracted artists and travellers from all over the world.

But Gianyar isn't simply known for its cultural attractions. It has some of Bali's earliest relics and important archeological sites. The Pejeng-Bedulu region, which lies between the locally revered rivers, the Pakrisan and the Petanu, bears testimony to Gianyar's ancient past. A brass drum, known as the "Moon of Pejeng", is one of the oldest antiquities on the island and is probably more than 2000 years old. The hermitage of Goa Gajah at Bedulu (the Elephant Cave), dates back to the 10th century, as do the holy springs at Tirta Empul. In any historical summary of things Balinese, fact is blurred with fiction: the people prefer to believe that the "Moon of Pejeng" was a wheel from the moon god's chariot that fell to earth; and that the giant, Kebo Iwa, carved the architectural stone masterpieces with his thumb nail.

History

The regency of Gianyar was established as a separate realm in the 17th century by Dewa Manggis. Following successful alliances and wily political manouvres, he invaded the borders of Klunkung, Badung, Bangli and Mengwi, declared himself the Raja of Gianyar, and built a court in what is now Gianyar town. Despite initial incursions from the Dewa's vengeful neighbours, the regency grew into a wealthy and powerful territory.

Towards the end of the 18th century power waned. The new Raja of Gianyar requested that the regency become a Dutch protectorate. In 1900, in return for many concessions, the Dutch agreed. Whilst the rest of southern Bali suffered from Dutch invasions coupled with power-broking between regencies, Gianyar prospered.

On the Road to Ubud

The 13-kilometre stretch of road from Denpasar to Ubud, dubbed the "handicraft highway", is a chain of villages specialising in various arts and crafts.
Batubulan is known for its paras and sandstone carvings;
Celuk for its silver work;
Sukawati for Wayang Kulit shadow puppets;
Batuan for its paintings; and
Mas for its woodcarvings.

Some words of advice to those planning a shopping spree in the area. Many tour agencies organise trips to Ubud via the "handicraft highway" and that's how most visitors come to this area. The classic tour guide's cant: "I know the best place to buy silver, woodcarvings, paintings, etc" should translate as "I know a place where I'll make a cut". That's how most Balinese trade is made — tour agents bring in customers and make a commission on tourist purchases.

Batubulan

A bridge over the Biaung River marks the border separating the regency of Badung from the regency of Gianyar. The first village after the border is Batubulan (the name means "moon stone"), and it is famed throughout Bali for its guardian statues carved from soft volcanic stone or *paras*. Visitors are more than welcome to visit shops and may observe the artists at work. Originally, stone works were found only in temples and palaces, but now the art can be seen everywhere. Fantastic mythological and religious figures are posted at intersections, and bas-reliefs with

Western themes are carved on facades of buildings. Many images are inspired by the Hindu epics of the *Ramayana* and *Mahabharata*, but the elephant god Ganesha and temple guardian Garuda are probably the most popular figures.

There are plenty of workshops along the main road and interested buyers should exercise restraint first, comparing prices and quality before they buy. Interspersed with the stonemasons are a number of woodcarving outlets specialising in antique-style furniture. Once again, caution is recommended. At the southern end of the village are a number of emporia catering to bus-loads of tourists. Their wares are usually expensive and tacky, and the shops are well-worth avoiding.

The *Pura Puseh*, Batubulan's main temple (follow the signs to the Barong stage), has some astounding ornamentation. Besides the unusual five-tiered gateway and Buddhist motifs, the remaining embellishments are characteristically and ostentatiously Balinese. The figure of the god Siwa adorned in skulls is particularly awesome for its detail.

Batubulan is also known for its various interpretations of the *Barong* dance. The Barong is performed daily from 9.30am-10.30pm next to the *Pura Puseh*, and also by various other companies in temples along the main road.

Celuk

The village of Batubulan ends at the intersection marking the turn-off east to Celuk. Renowned for its intricate, filigree silver, Celuk is definitely the best place to watch silversmiths at work. Many artists have extended their homes to allow for workshops and salesrooms, and the shops are worth visiting. Rings, chains, bracelets, earrings and ornaments abound, and pieces can be commissioned or chosen from the displays. Disappointingly, imitation is rife, many pieces are old-fashioned and prices are more competitive in Kuta and Legian.

Sukawati

Sukawati is located midway between Denpasar and Ubud, and was once the residence of the 18th century raja, Dalem Sukawati.

These days, Sukawati is known for its *pasar seni* (art market). Located in the heart of the village, the market trades daily from dusk to dawn. People gather from miles around to buy supplies that are generally cheaper than anywhere else on the island. Rows and rows of stalls selling baskets, fabrics, artefacts, sarongs, parasols, chimes and fans are crammed together. Bargaining is essential.

The village is also known for its puppet masters, the *dalang*, who not only make the puppets, but also write the plays and perform them. Many of the puppet masters travel around the island performing with their troupes; or they can be commissioned to write plays or make a special set of puppets. About a kilometre west from the *pasar seni* intersection in the village of Puaya, are astonishing leather puppets and accomplished *dalang*. Sukawati is also known for its wind chimes. Take a walk down the main road, you'll probably hear them before you see them.

Batuan

For centuries, Batuan has been a hive of artistic activity, thanks to the prevalence of *Brahman* families, and their support of the arts. Dancers, musicians, carvers, painters, and even foreign artists work in Batuan, and travellers are free to browse through their studios.

Batuan is probably best known for its painters. There are two styles of painting associated with Batuan. Under the tutelage of Spies and Bonnet, artists adopted a "realistic" rather than "stylised" attitude to the human form. The paintings are intricately drawn and details are shaded by a technique called *sigar mangsi*, literally "ink fragments", using sombre reds, browns and blacks. The second style of painting was developed by Dewa Ketut Baru, who worked with black ink on a white background. The Puri Lukisan Museum at Ubud has an excellent exhibition of paintings in the Batuan styles. Wooden panels, screens, statues and *Topeng* masks, all carved by Batuan artists, are the best buys in Bali.

There are many galleries churning out uninspiring pastel geometric paintings. In Bali, once a fashion or genre is born, it's exploited to its fullest potential. On the western edge of the village, though, are a number of artists' homes and galleries and you'll find their works original and much more satisfying, if not more expensive.

Batuan dancers are known for the *Topeng* (mask) dance, as well as the exquisite, court dance called the *Gambuh*. Only two troupes in Bali still perform the ancient *Gambuh* dance, and visitors can see the performances daily.

Mas

Although Mas means "gold", the village is a centre for woodcarving. Traditionally, woodcarvers were Brahman priests who sculpted scenes from the *Ramayana* and *Mahabharata* epics, to adorn temples.

During the 1930s, under the influence of Walter Spies and the Pita Maha arts group, secular activities and themes were incorporated into designs and a more realistic style developed.

Typical *Mas* carving is highly polished and made of superior wood. Walk into any studio and watch young apprentices chiselling gnarled pieces of wood into elegant figurines. The entire village spans 5 kilometres, so unless you have your own transport it's difficult to see everything.

The village of Mas is supposedly where the priest Nirartha built a hermitage, and the temple, *Pura Taman Pule*, is built on the site of Nirartha's former residence.

Teges

The village of Teges is divided into two communities: to the east is Teges Kanginan, famous for its dancers and musicians; and to the west is Teges Kawan, whose villagers are woodcarvers. The sculptors of Teges Kawan are lauded for their interesting fruit arrangements — you may have noticed one or two in Kuta.

Peliatan

Although Teges and Peliatan are distinct artistic communities, they are really the same village. Peliatan is best known for its graceful *Legong* dance, and a group of Peliatan dancers was the first to perform abroad at the Paris Colonial Exhibition in 1931. Today, a number of accomplished dance groups perform the *Legong* for visitors on a weekly basis. The Ubud Tourist Information Centre sells tickets (Rp7000) and transport to all the Peliatan performances.

The village is very much at the forefront of dance, and

classical and modern styles develop concurrently. A dance troupe performs the *Barong Nandini* "ballet", which combines modern choreography with traditional theatrical techniques.

Peliatan has more than 15 *gamelan* groups, and has one of the few women's *gamelan* in Bali. They perform every Sunday at 7.30pm (tickets Rp7000), and transport and tickets can be arranged at the Ubud Tourist Information Centre. The Smar Pegulingan Gong orchestra has travelled the world, and performs in Peliatan weekly (ask at the tourist office in Ubud).

Don't miss the exceptional gallery (daily 9am-6pm) of former painter Agung Rai, at the southern end of Peliatan. The gallery boasts works from some of Ubud's renowned foreign artists including Hofker, Le Mayeur, Bonnet and Blanco, as well as many of Ubud's young artists and Pengosekan traditionalists.

Peliatan is a 20-minute walk from Ubud along Jl. Tebasaya (south from Jl. Raya Ubud) or a short bemo ride (Rp100).

Pengosekan

Until recently, Pengosekan was almost isolated from the surrounding villages, enabling its painters to develop a unique character to their work. Under the direction of I Dewa Nyoman Batuan and his brother I Dewa Putuh Mokoh, the village artists pooled their resources for supplies, exhibition costs and purchases, and in 1969, the group formed a co-operative, calling themselves the Pengosekan Community of Artists. Famous for their paintings of whimsical animals, the community's works were exhibited overseas and for some time the group experienced relative prosperity. The co-operative no longer exists, but their legacy is the Pengosekan Community of Artists gallery on the main road east of the river. There are a few in the community who still continue to create works in the inimitable Pengosekan style, others participate in the mass-production of painted tissue boxes, fruits and frames for the tourist market.

To get there, walk down the Monkey Forest Road from Jl. Raya Ubud, following the road as it swerves to the left past the forest. Turn right to Pengosekan (which is signposted) or left to Peliatan.

Ubud

Hidden in green forests and protected by lush valleys, Ubud is often touted as the cultural heart of Bali. Many people flee the south in search of the **real Bali** and some never venture past Ubud. While the village has many cultural attractions, it is not a typical Balinese village and doesn't really deserve the tag the "real Bali". But those wishing to escape from the commercialism and pace of the south won't be disappointed. Although boutiques and souvenir shops abound, there are also many opportunities to explore the local environs on foot and to venture into nearby villages and artisans' workshops. Despite the increase in tourism in the last ten years, Ubud retains its cultural integrity and remains a forum for the marriage of Eastern and Western traditions.

Apart from Ubud's cultural attractions, it also boasts some excellent restaurants and hotels. Like the artistic tradition, locals and expatriates are successfully mixing Eastern and Western influences. Restaurants like *Casa Luna*, *Miro's* and the pavilion restaurant in *The Chedi* hotel are blending traditional Balinese and Indonesian ingredients and techniques with those from Australia and Europe. And the results are lauded well beyond the island. Likewise, hotels such as The Amandari, The Chedi again, and the Waka Di Ume, to name a few, are blending contemporary design with traditional Balinese architecture, and always in idyllic settings.

Given that Ubud is geographically central, and surrounded by cultural and artistic activities, it is little wonder that travellers head straight to Ubud with little thought for the south.

History

Ubud dates back to the 8th century, when a Hindu priest, Rsi Markandeya, and his disciples discovered the intersection of two rivers — a favourable omen for Hindus — and built a temple at the site. The temple is called *Pura Gunung Lebah*; and the village, Campuhan, means the "meeting of two rivers". Further up the mountains, Ubud became the home of the priest's disciples.

A royal court was established in Ubud in the 19th century by Cokorda Gede Sukawati who was made a nobleman after

146 Bali

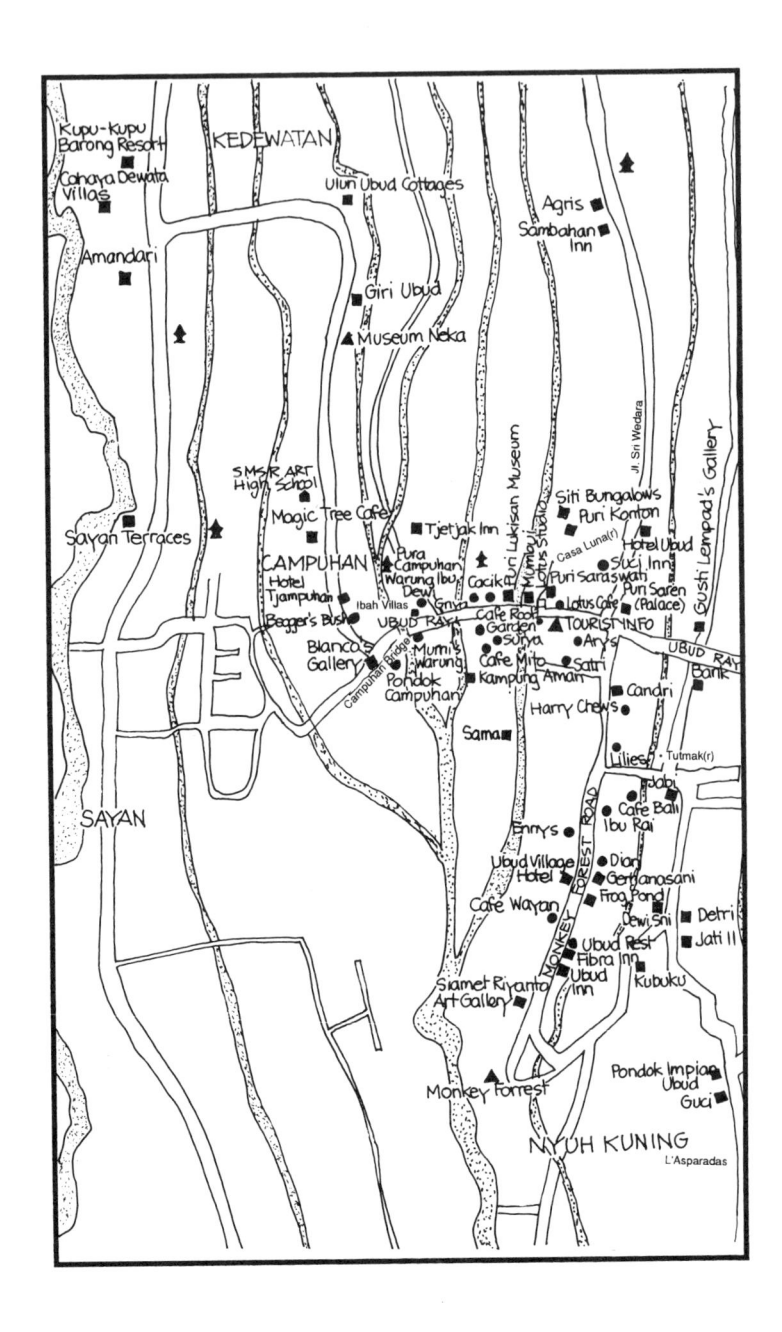

Ubud Area

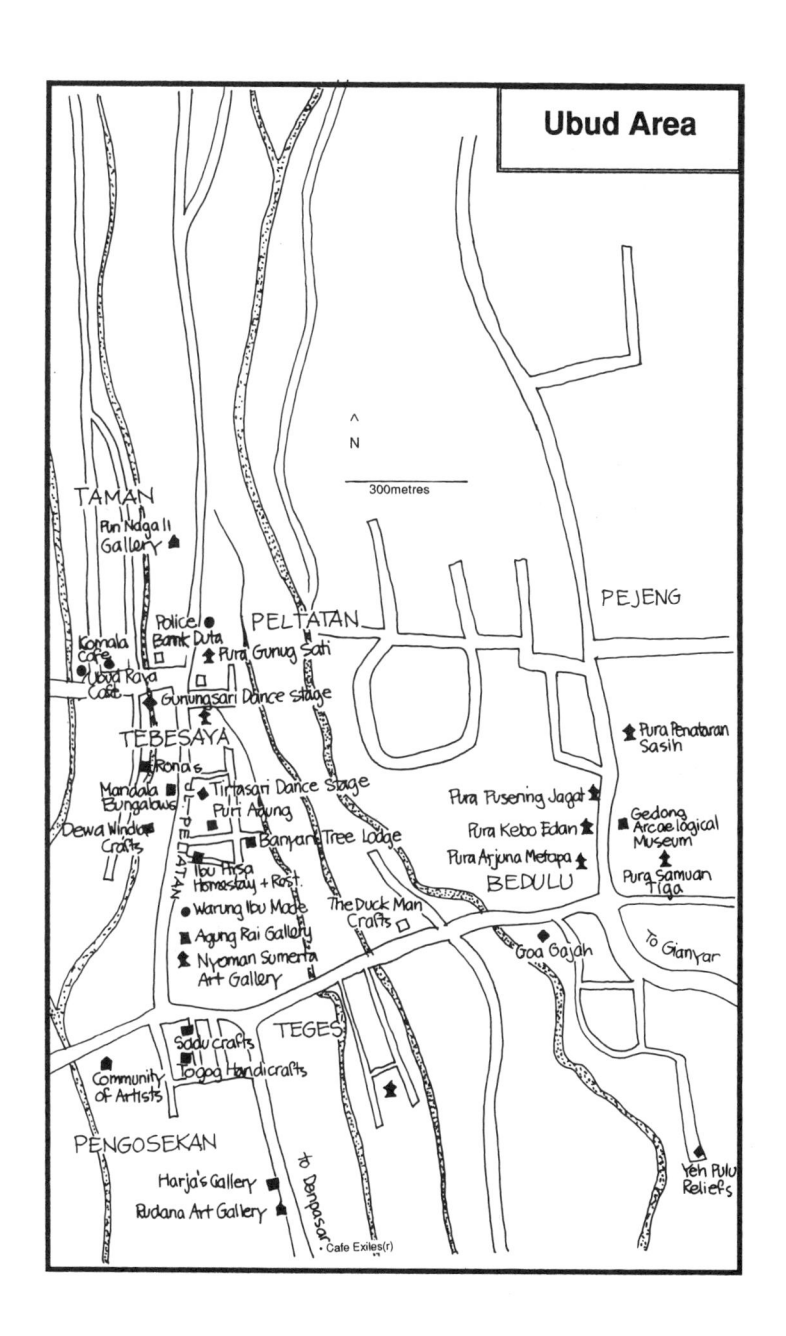

distinguishing himself in battle. He chose Ubud as the location for his court, and amassed enough power and wealth to protect his kingdom from warring enemies. When the royal family of Gianyar was struggling to win back its territories in 1893, it was Sukawati who was instrumental in its success, ensuring Ubud's prosperity continued.

A few years later the Raja of Gianyar requested that the kingdom be protected by the Dutch, and in 1900 a deal was struck. While the rest of Bali suffered under the harsh policies of the Dutch and incursions from warring neighbours, Gianyar and its ally Ubud, flourished. With its safety ensured, the court at Ubud could focus on secular and religious activities, and Cokorda Gede Sukawati befriended young artists and enticed them to live in the village. The young sculptor I Gusti Nyoman Lempad, an enemy of the Raja of Bedulu, was invited to assist in the creation of the *Puri Saren* palace and the adjacent temple. Cokorda Gede Agung Sukawati (1910-1978) continued his father's cultural tradition and encouraged young and foreign artists to settle in Ubud. The German artist, Walter Spies, accepted an invitation to make Ubud his home, locating in Campuhan on the site of what is now the Hotel Tjampuhan. Miguel Covarrubias was enchanted by pictures of Bali, and Rudolf Bonnet heard about the island on the grapevine.

In 1936, Spies and Bonnet founded the Pita Maha society for artists, under the auspices of Cokorda Gede Agung Sukawati. Although the group disbanded at the outbreak of war, an artistic collective-consciousness had evolved which was to augment and direct the village's cultural heritage. In 1953, Cokorda Gede Agung Sukawati and Bonnet founded the Puri Lukisan Museum — a monument to the fine arts in Bali.

During the 1950s, Arie Smit, a Dutch painter, founded the Naive School of Painters in Penestanan. The group was dedicated to drawing and painting subjects ignoring conventional dictates. Han Snel, another Dutch artist, still lives in Ubud, as does Antonio Blanco.

Ubud is not only a concentration of Balinese talents, it is also a happy marriage between East and West. No doubt Bali will change as tourism increases but the Balinese resilience and willingness to utilise foreign influences will hopefully enable the continuation of a rich cultural heritage.

How to Get There

By Public Bemo
In Denpasar, bemo depart from Kereneng terminal for Ubud and cost Rp1000.

By Taxi
A fixed-price taxi from the airport costs around Rp35,000 and tickets can be purchased outside customs. Alternatively, outside of the airport compound, blue and yellow metered taxis can be hired for Rp1500 for flagfall and about Rp500 for each kilometre. A metered taxi from the airport to Ubud costs about Rp21,500.

By Car
Ubud is 25km (16 miles) from Denpasar and takes about 45 minutes by car. From Kuta, the distance is about 34km(21 miles).

Tourist Information

The Bina Wisata Tourist Office (daily 10am-8pm), on Jl. Raya Ubud, near the main crossroads, will supply information and tickets for festivals and dance performances, as well as tours to destinations all over Bali. They are also rental agents for cars, motorbikes and bicycles.

Accommodation

The range of accommodation in Ubud has expanded considerably in recent years, catering to all budgets. You can be sure that most have lush surroundings with an outlook to appreciate them.

Most of the more expensive hotels are located in villages on the outskirts of Ubud, but all provide regular shuttle services back into the village.

Lower-priced accommodation is concentrated along the Monkey Forest Rd, but the area tends to be noisy and congested.

Prices are in US$ for one night's accommodation, do not include tax and service charges, and should be used as a guide only. Telephone code is 0361.

5 star Hotels

All 4 and 5 star hotels have a swimming pool, restaurant, bar, IDD in each room, 24 hour room service, minibar and free shuttle service to Ubud. All rates are in US$ and are subject to a 10-15% service charge and a 10% government tax.

Amandari, Kedewatan, Ubud, ph 975 333 (for reservations call 771 267). In the village of Kedewatan and overlooking the Ayung River, the Amandari has lavish, spacious suites, each with its own private garden, an outdoor sunken marble bath and most have a private plunge pool. The main swimming pool is designed to blend with the surrounding rice terraces. The *Verandah Restaurant* rivals the best in Ubud, although it's expensive. This is a first-class resort with all amenities. Rooms from $400.

Banyan Tree Kamandalu, just off Jl. Tegalalang, Nagi, ph 975 825. About four kilometres out of Ubud and built into the hillside above the Petanu River, this first-class property has a swimming pool, children's pool, tennis court, restaurant, bar and gallery. Each suite is a traditional Balinese-style accommodation with private courtyard, raised pavilion to enjoy the view, and a sunken bath. Rooms from $220.

The Chedi, Desa Melinggih Kelod, Payangan, ph 975 963. Recently opened, The Chedi is a secluded mountain retreat perched high above the Ayung River. This self-contained sanctuary melds contemporary design with traditional Balinese architecture. There's even a health spa offering aromatherapy massage, fresh herbal scrubs, volcanic mud masks and soothing spring-water baths. The restaurant affords stunning views of the valley and exquisite modern Balinese or Western cuisine, and is highly recommended even if you don't stay in the hotel. Room from $210.

Kupu Kupu Barong Resort, Kedewatan, Ubud, ph 975 478. High above the Sayan Valley, each luxury bungalow has stunning views of the valley and all amenities. The restaurant is expensive and outdated, but the views are nice. Does not cater for children under 12, and as there are many steps may not be suitable for people with walking disabilities. Rooms from $320.

4 star Hotels

Ibah Luxury Villas, Jl. Raya Ubud, Campuhan, Ubud, ph 974 466.

On the Ubud side of the Campuhan bridge, the Ibah is another example of the new-age luxury accommodation. The ten villas are located above the Tjampuhan River with views of rice terraces and ravines. There's a salt-water swimming pool and health spa and beauty centre for your complete indulgence. Rooms from $195.

Pita Maha, Jl. Sanggingan, Campuhan, Ubud, ph 974 330. Designed and owned by members of the Ubud royal family, the Pita Maha overlooks the Oos River close to where it meets the Tjampuhan River. The architecture is stunning combining simplicity with traditional Balinese styles. Rooms from $300.

Waka Di Ume, Jl. Sueta, Ubud, ph 96 178. The House in the Rice Fields is a modern resort with an emphasis on relaxation. Each gorgeous room has a balcony or terrace with views of rice paddies, and is furnished with dressed slate tiles, smooth unpainted wood and homespun fabrics. Meditation room and massage centre aid the relaxation process. Rooms from $160.

3 star Hotels

Hotel Tjampuhan, Jl. Raya Campuhan, ph 975 368. Once an artists' colony headed by Walter Spies (Spies' house forms part of the hotel), it overlooks the Campuhan River. The bungalows are set in the hillside with verandahs. Amenities include 2 swimming pools, tennis court, restaurant and bar. Rooms from $70.

Siti Bungalows, Jl. Kajeng, ph 975 699. Owned by painting personality, Hans Snel, the charming bungalows are in the centre of Ubud, but tucked away in a side-street behind the Lotus Cafe. Book in advance. Rooms from $50.

Puri Bunga Village Hotel, Kedewatan Village, ph 975 488. About 10 minutes' drive from Ubud, this property is set above the Ayung River and the four-storey accommodation has spectacular views of the valley. Has swimming pools, restaurant and bar. Rooms from $65.

Ulun Ubud Cottages, Sanggingan, Ubud, ph 975 024. On the outskirts of Ubud (the turn-off is just past the Neka Museum), this property overlooks the Campuhan River. All rooms are open-air and have good views, and there's a swimming pool, restaurant and bar. There's a steep descent to the restaurant which is not suitable for less mobile people. Room $50.

2 star Hotels

Ananda Cottages, Jl. Campuhan, ph 975 376. Located about a kilometre out of Ubud, this small hotel is set in rice fields and is surrounded by tropical gardens. Hotel has swimming pool, restaurant, coffee shop and bar. Rooms from $40.

Dewi Sri Bungalows, Jl. Hanuman, Padang Tegal, Ubud. Quiet location with pool and restaurant. Room $35.

Fibra Inn, Monkey Forest Road, ph 975 451. Small rooms set in gardens and has a swimming pool. Room $30.

Pondok Impian Ubud, Jl. Raya Pengosekan, ph 975 253. Fifteen minutes' walk from the centre of Ubud, this hotel has a restaurant and swimming pool. Room $35.

Ubud Village Hotel, Monkey Forest Road, ph 975 069. In the middle of Ubud, this standard hotel has a swimming pool with sunken bar as well as a restaurant. Rooms have private courtyard. Rooms from $45.

Budget

Losmen are everywhere in Ubud. Rooms are available for as little as US$5 — they're spartan but clean, and families are welcome. Try along Monkey Forest Road or Jl. Hanuman.

Local Transport

Ubud is easily explored on foot. The main road is Jl. Raya Ubud, and the heart of Ubud is the junction of the Monkey Forest Road and Jl. Raya Ubud (in front of the *Puri Saren* palace). To the east is the Peliatan T-intersection; to the west is Campuhan and the suspension bridge.

By Bemo

Bemo can be hired along Jl. Raya Ubud, particularly near the Ubud Palace, and all along the Monkey Forest Road. These touts are much easier to bargain with than those in the southern areas, and as taxis are rare, they really are the best option for transport. After dark, they're probably the only option. For example, from Ubud Palace to the Campuhan Bridge area expect to pay Rp3000, from the palace to Peliatan about Rp5000.

By Public Bemo

Public bemo depart from the "terminal" in front of the market (to the east of the palace), from dawn to dusk, and can be stopped at any point along their route. Fares are usually about Rp100 per kilometre. To get to Campuhan, the Neka Museum or Kedewatan, flag down the turquoise bemo heading west for Payang. For Pengosekan or Peliatan board the brown Batubulan-bound bemo, or the orange bemo for Petulu.

By Taxi

There are only ever a few taxis in Ubud, most of which congregate outside the rank near Casa Luna. Most of these have come from other destinations on the island and cannot be relied on for regular use. Flagfall is Rp1500 and about Rp500 per kilometre. The bemo touts hanging around Ubud Palace are a much better option and easier to deal with than their counterparts in the south.

Renting Transport

Motorbikes (100cc) cost about Rp10,000 per day, and bicycles can be rented for about Rp3000. Suzuki Jimneys can be rented for about Rp45,000 daily, and cheaper for a month. Try Ngurah Agung at *Bayu Putra Car Rental*, Jl. Campuhan (opposite Ananda Cottages), ph 974 334; *Three Brothers*, Jl. Hanuman, ph 975 525; or inquire at the Ubud Tourist Information Centre.

Eating Out

With literally a few hundred restaurants spread across a few kilometres, the only problem you'll have is deciding where to dine. Ubud doesn't have fast food outlets, thank the gods! What is does have is an exciting array of restaurants many of which are successfully blending Eastern and Western ingredients and techniques. Alternatively, those restaurants concentrating on Indonesian and Balinese cuisine are offering some of the most authentic meals on the island. The tourist fare of jaffles, sandwiches and steaks is also in ample supply.

The restaurant in *The Chedi* hotel offers both Balinese and Western dishes all of which are sublime. Not to mention the astonishing view. For moderately priced European and

Indonesian fare *Casa Luna* is a must, or for inexpensive, Indonesian and Balinese meals try *Nomad Bar & Restaurant*.

Main Road - Jl. Raya Ubud

Nomad Bar & Restaurant, ph 975 721. Offers some of the cheapest and freshest fish specials in town. Excellent and extensive range of Indonesian meals. Highly recommended and inexpensive.

Han Snel, Kajeng Lane. Intimate and romantic atmosphere. The service is very good and the mini-rijstaffel is a local legend. Moderate to expensive.

Ary's Warung, ph 975 053. Chic cafe and restaurant decorated with photographs and relics of a by-gone Bali. Extensive menu is international. Moderate to expensive.

Cafe Lotus. Eat breakfast, lunch or dinner in front of a sea of lotus flowers. A long-established Ubud institution, it was once *the* place to be seen. Still worth visiting, though. Curries, pasta, veal, jaffles, Moët and lots more. Moderately priced.

Casa Luna, Jl. Raya Ubud, ph 96 283. Overlooking the river, this restaurant and bakery has become a cultural centre of sorts. Films are sometimes shown or acoustic entertainment, and there's a gallery as well. The chef, Janet De Neefe, an ex-Melburnian, holds cooking classes on the premises. The menu is extensive with an excellent selection of Indonesian curries, salads and satays, some subtle, some spicy and some with a modern Australian twist. There are also pastas and the breads and foccacia are made on the premises. Wine by the glass. Moderately priced.

Mumbul's Garden Terrace Cafe, Jl. Raya Ubud, ph 975 364. Modern-style cafe complete with statues and niches, overlooks a pretty gully. Extensive Indonesian menu including a Saturday night three-course meal featuring Bebek Tutu (smoked duck) (Rp12,000). Also has many and varied vegetarian meals. Next door is their ice-cream parlour.

Miro's Garden Restaurant, Jl. Raya Ubud, ph 96 314. Set in a private garden above street-level, Miro's offers a diverse range of cuisine from Balinese and Indonesian meals, to pizzettas, empañadas, fish and excellent smoked duck. Moderately priced.

Murni's Warung, Jl. Raya Ubud, ph 975 233. On the main road near the suspension bridge, and overlooking the Campuhan river, Murni's is one of Ubud's oldest tourist establishments.

Standard fare includes soups, sandwiches, jaffles, curries and home-made Balinese cakes. Sells wine by the glass. Inexpensive to moderately priced. Lounge bar downstairs opens at 5pm.

Beggar's Bush, Campuhan, ph 975 009. **The** pub in Ubud. Across the Campuhan Bridge, this is the closest joint Bali has to an English pub, and the atmosphere can be great. The food, however, is average. The publican, Victor Mason, is a bird expert and local personality.

Pita Maha Terrace Restaurant, Pita Maha Hotel, Jl. Sanggingan, ph 974 330. Split on two levels, there's pavilion or alfresco dining with spectacular views of the Oos valley. Both Western and Oriental specialties and an excellent cellar to complement the meal. Very expensive.

Monkey Forest Road

Ibu Rai II, Monkey Forest Road 72, ph 975 066. Warung-style cafe with a fashioned waterfall backdrop offering standard tourist fare as well as good curries. Inexpensive.

Cafe Wayan. Delicious cakes and breads, as well as European, Thai and Indonesian meals served in a Balinese pavilion, with low tables and cushions. Moderately priced.

Lotus Lane, ph 975 357. Gorgeous cafe with lotus pond vista offers home-made pastas and yummy wood-fired pizzas. Moderately priced.

Jl. Dewi Sita (between Monkey Forest Road & Jl. Hanuman)

Tutmak, ph 975 754. Expensive warung offering superb coffees, salads, sandwiches, jaffles and desserts. Live music.

Jl. Hanuman

Bebek Bengil or the Dirty Duck Diner, ph 975 489. Cool, breezy restaurant set in the rice fields in Padang Tegal specialises in duck. In fact, it's one of the few places you can walk into without having to pre-order. The duck is good, and so are the home-made desserts, with chocolate cake, apple crisp and cheesecake, to name a few.

Sayan, Kedewatan and Payangan

The Chedi Restaurant, The Chedi Hotel, Payangan, ph 975 963. A large grand pavilion restaurant blending Balinese architecture with modern simplicity. The menu is divided between modern

European and Indonesian, with both menus offering sumptuous delights. The chef hails from Paris, Boston and New York and gives some wonderful interpretations particularly to the Indonesian menu. Expensive.

Kupu Kupu Barong Resort Restaurant. Acclaimed for many years as the best restaurant in Ubud, it is now outdated although the bus loads of Japanese tourists don't seem to mind. Surf'n'Turf, Lobster Thermidor, and many old favourites. The view is spectacular. Exorbitant.

Nightlife

Ubud's night life is very different from that offered at the beach resorts, tending to be focused in the restaurants and cafes. Most people catch a cultural performance at the Ubud Palace around 7.30pm before heading off to dinner. However, there are a few venues offering live music.

The *Sai Sai Bar*, about half-way along the Monkey Forest Road, has live music nightly. Although mostly cover bands, they often attract a lively crowd and the vibe can be good. *Tutmak*, ph 975 754 also has live music, usually acoustic, a couple of nights a week. The newly-opened *Mai Restaurant & Bar* also has live bands nightly.

South in Pengosekan, *L'Asparagus*, Jl. Pengosekan, and *Cafe Exiles*, east of the former, both have live music nightly.

For those just interested in a drink, try the *Beggar's Bush Pub*, just past the Campuhan bridge; *Casa Luna* or *Ary's Warung* which stay open until about 1am; or *Nomad* which finishes serving after midnight.

Entertainment

The Ubud Tourist Information Office has information on dance performances in Ubud and the surrounding villages. Most performances cost Rp7000 or higher where transportation is included. Tickets and transport for the following performances can be arranged through the Ubud Tourist Information Office.

Sunday

Kecak Fire and Trance Dance at Bona 7pm, or at Padang Tegal at 7pm. Padang Tegal is much closer, and both performances are very good. The *Women's Gamelan* plays at Peliatan Village at 7.30pm. The *Wayang Kulit* shadow puppet at Oka Kartini, 8pm.

Monday
Kecak at Bona, 7pm. *Legong* at Puri Saren palace, 7.30pm. Ciwa Ratri Dance with the *Classical Gamelan Gebyug* at Pura Dalem Puri, 7.30pm.

Tuesday
Ramayana Ballet at Ubud Palace, at 7.30pm, presented by the Bina Remaja troupe of Ubud. Dramatic excerpts from the *Mahabharata* in Banjar Teges, 7.30pm.

Wednesday
Wayang Kulit shadow-puppets at Oka Kartini, Jl. Raya Ubud, at 8pm. *Kecak* at Bona, 7pm. *Legong and Barong Dances* at Ubud Palace, presented by Panca Arta, 7.30pm

Thursday
Gabor dance from the *Mahabharata* at Ubud Palace, 7.30pm. *Kecak* at Puri Agung, Peliatan, 7.30pm. Calon Arang Dance at Mawang Village, 7pm.

Friday
Barong at Ubud Palace, 6.30pm. *Kecak* at Bona, 7pm. *Legong* at Peliatan at 7.30pm.

Saturday
Legong at Ubud Palace, 7.30pm. *Calon Arang* Dance at Mawang Village, 7pm.

Shopping

Art Galleries
Agung Rai Fine Art Gallery, Jl. Peliatan. Mostly commercial establishment also has a permanent collection. Highly respected gallery with all Balinese styles represented and prices starting from around US$45.

Komaneka, Monkey Forest Road, ph 976 090. New spacious and grand gallery is an excellent showcase for new works. The gallery is worth a look even if you don't intend to buy, and there is also a huge range of fine art books available.

Munut's Gallery, Jl. Raya Ubud (eastern end past the Neka Gallery). Well-known and respected dealer. Prices from US$40.

Neka Gallery, Jl. Raya Ubud (opposite the Post Office). Owned by Wayan Suteja Neka, founder of the Neka Museum. Huge maze-like collection of recent works by the Young Artists and well-known foreigners. Prices range from about US$100 for a small canvas up to thousands.

Rumah Seni, Jl. Raya Ubud, ph 976 319. Modern Balinese paintings, wooden and stone sculptures and fabrics. A really exciting range of works that deviates radically from traditional genres. All unique pieces and reasonably priced.

Seniwati Gallery for Women, Jl. Sri Wedari. The only gallery in Bali that exclusively sells work by women. Some really interesting works spanning traditional and modern genres.

Sika Studio and Gallery. Houses mostly modern and abstract works by Bali's young artists. Well worth a visit.

Books

Both *Ary's Bookshop* and *Ganesha Bookshop* (along Jl. Raya Ubud) have good collections on Bali and Indonesia, as well as maps.

Cloth

Argasoka Gallery, Monkey Forest Road, ph 96 231. Exquisite batik and ikat cloth in original designs.

Kamar Sutra, Monkey Forest Road. Batik designs on expensive silk, crepe, and chiffon.

Wora, Monkey Forest Road. Gorgeous *ikat* designs from Sumbawa from around Rp40,000.

Curios

Pondok Seni Jl. Pengosekan. A hotch-potch of curios and relics, some interesting, some garish.

Murni's Collection, Jl. Raya Ubud (before the Campuhan bridge) has an array of antiques, clothes, silver, pottery and cloth.

Casa Lina Homewares, Jl. Raya Ubud. A wondrous array of table cloths, candelabras, knick-knacks, jewellery boxes, decorations, etc, but quite expensive.

Silver

There seems to be fewer silver shops as time passes. Kuta is still the best place to buy jewellery, but if you fall for a piece buy it, you may never find one like it again. Although fixed-prices are the order of the day, often-times bargaining is permissible if you buy a few pieces.

Suarti, on the Monkey Forest Road, is one of a chain of silver stores throughout the island. Prices are the same in each store.

Markets

In the centre of town, in a two-storey cement eyesore are the markets; fabrics, clothes, baskets, carvings, and food galore.

Miscellaneous

For **24-hour medical attention** call *Ubud Clinic*, Jl. Raya Ubud 36 (west just before the suspension bridge), ph 484 833.

Police Station is located on Jl. Tegalalang (north of the Peliatan T-intersection) opposite the **Kantor Telcom** (the telecommunications office). **Chemist** (*apotik*), Ubud Farma, Jl. Raya Ubud, (daily 8am-9pm).

Bank Duta, Jl. Raya Ubud (near the T-intersection to Peliatan), and **BCA Bank**, Jl. Raya Ubud (down from Nomad's). If you simply need to change money there are various money changers along Jl. Raya Ubud and the Monkey Forest Road offering competitive rates.

The **Post Office** is on Jl. Raya Ubud, east towards the Peliatan T-intersection, and post restante services are available. (Open from 8am-2pm Monday to Saturday). More conveniently, there are a number of postal agents along Jl. Raya Ubud and Monkey Forest Road who are just as reliable.

Museums and Galleries

Lempad Gallery

The former home of the revered painter and Pita Maha member, I Gusti Nyoman Lempad is on the main street, Jl. Raya Ubud. Said to be quite a traditionalist, he was also known for his risqué and humorous interpretations. However, the best collection of his work is housed in the Neka Museum. Most of the works contained in his home are those of young Balinese artists, but the *bale* at the back of the compound does have some memorabilia. Open daily from 8am-6pm; free.

Puri Lukisan Museum

The Puri Lukisan or "Palace of Paintings" was opened in 1953 by Cokorda Gede Agung Sukawati and Rudolf Bonnet both of whom helped establish the esteemed Pita Maha art society in the 1930s. The society's aim was to encourage painting and the museum marked the deliberate separation of painting from religious life.

The museum has three buildings set amidst landscaped gardens and a lotus pond.

Much-needed renovations are almost complete. Many paintings have been dusted-off, re-framed, placed under glare-free plexiglass, and the lighting redesigned to aid vision. Works are now arranged according to schools of art and are appropriately labeled.

The curator is very enthusiastic and helpful. The two main buildings house the permanent exhibitions, while the third is for visiting collections. Open from 8am-4pm; admission Rp500.

Neka Museum

About a kilometre past the Campuhan suspension bridge is the most comprehensive collection of artistic works on the island. Founded in 1976 by Wayan Suteja Neka, a former art teacher, Ubud collector and art patron, the museum is a series of purpose-built pavilions and halls, arranged to take the visitors on a historical journey through Bali's artistic life. Incidentally, Fine Arts students at Udayana University must be familiar with the works in the Neka Museum in order to graduate.

The first room of the first pavilion, past the entrance, focuses on Balinese painting. Classical *Wayang* (shadow-puppet) paintings show stylised two-dimensional figures in narratives from the Indian *Ramayana* and *Mahabharata* epics. This is known as the Kamasan style after the village where most of the artists lived. In the next two rooms, following the historical route, are works in the Ubud style dating from the 1930s. The works illustrate the influence of Walter Spies, Rudolf Bonnet and the Pita Maha collective on light and perspective. Subject matter is also extended from religious and courtly topics to secular activities. Market places, festivals and daily chores have lent themselves to inspiration. Alternatively, the Batuan style of the same time shows little experimentation with light and perspective. Instead, sombre dark colours and densely-packed canvasses were used to parody political and daily situations.

The second building, the Arie Smit Pavilion houses paintings by the Dutch-born artist on the top level and the so-called Young Artists whom he inspired on the bottom level. In the 1960s Smit encouraged a group of teenage artists to express themselves beyond the confines of traditional styles. Their works were naive, characterised by lack of perspective, bold colours and expressionless subjects.

The third pavilion houses a collection of photographs by American Robert Coke documenting ceremonies and personalities in the Bali of the 1920s and 1930s.

The fourth building is entirely devoted to the works of I Gusti Nyoman Lempad, Bali's most esteemed artist. His works are characterised by a mixture of traditional styles and a sense of humour, although there is little evidence of Western influences.

Modern works by other Indonesian artists are displayed in two separate buildings. Styles range from realism to abstraction.

The lower floor of the sixth pavilion continues the display of modern Indonesian artists, while the upper floor exhibits works by foreign artists. The likes of Bonnet, Donald Friend, Theo Meier, Paul Nagano, Chang Fee Ming and Willem Gerard Hofker are represented. The final pavilion is for temporary exhibitions to promote new and established artists. Open daily from 9am-5pm, admission Rp2500.

Seniwati Gallery of Art by Women

If you've visited the Neka Museum or Puri Lukisan, you may have noticed the dearth of paintings by women. To make amends, British-born Mary Northmore set up the Association of Women Artists in Bali, out of which grew the Seniwati Gallery of Art by Women. Committed to fostering the development of women artists, both native and foreign, it promotes and displays their works, with over 40 artists represented in the permanent exhibition. The group is also committed to teaching young girls and holds classes over the road.

All styles are covered from Kamasan to modern and abstract, and information sheets and guides are very informative. Well worth a visit. Jl. Sriwedari (off Raya Ubud). Open daily from 10am-5pm; free.

Antonio Blanco's Gallery

Past the suspension bridge on the left, the gallery is declared with a grandiose and curly sign, "Antonio Blanco", and underneath, "The Blanco Dynasty". The one-man PR machine, who dubbed himself Bali's Dali is at best eccentric and at worst pretentious. His exhibition features erotic and fantasy drawings of his Balinese muse and wife, Ni Ronji, as well as several multimedia pieces illustrating his bent sense of humour. The arrangement of works is flamboyant, if not slightly camp, with a huge easel in the middle of one room to set the scene. You might run into the bereted Blanco mincing about his parlour — it'll make your day. See the **Shopping** section for more galleries.

Sightseeing

Puri Saren (Ubud Palace)

In the heart of Ubud, opposite *pasar seni* (the market) and the Jl. Raya Ubud-Monkey Forest Road intersection, is the palace of the Sukawati family. Rebuilt in 1917 after an earthquake, the district of Ubud was ruled from this palace complex, until the 1940s.

The palace is similar in design to the traditional family compound, if not on a much grander scale. Today, the complex accommodates a hotel, but many of the original features remain intact. The main pavilion still showcases the guardian statues of elephants and lions, and the smaller *bale* nearby is decorated with stone carvings and wooden reliefs by Lempad.

Next door is the royal family's temple, *Pura Pamerajaan Sari Cokorda Agung* or *Pura Saraswati*.

Puri Saraswati

Behind the lotus pond and *Puri Saren* is *Pura Saraswati*, one of I Gusti Nyoman Lempad's greatest achievements. Set in a water garden, this enchanting temple was dedicated to Saraswati, a sacred Hindu river and the goddess of learning.

Entrance is either through the gate on Raya Ubud or through Cafe Lotus and both lead to the gateway visually blocked by an *aling-aling*. This unusual device is built into all temples to prevent evil spirits from entering the inner chambers. Turn left or right past the *aling-aling* (which incidentally, is the back of a demonic-looking Rakasa guardian) and a *bale* protects barong costumes to ward-off evil spirits. The main lotus throne is a disordered rambling of figures juxtaposed with the floral details on the tower.

Pura Gunung Lebah

Across from Antonio Blanco's gallery, *Pura Gunung Lebah* or *Pura Campuhan*, is perched at the crossing of the Wos Barat and Wos Timor rivers, a sacred site since the 10th century. Although the temple is none too exciting, it's a great vantage point to the rivers, and walks either east or west along the rivers are pretty.

The Monkey Forest Temple

At the bottom of Monkey Forest Road is the Monkey Forest, and yes, it's the residence of a very bold band of monkeys. Admission is Rp1000 and a scarf must be worn around the waist to enter the temple further afield.

Everything you've been told about these monkeys is probably true. They will steal your sunglasses, jewellery or wallet, and they can be quite aggressive, especially face-to-face. Make sure all your valuables are out-of-sight and reach, and be wary. Apart from that advice, the grounds themselves are without note and hardly worth the effort.

Walking past the ticket gate turn left before the forked path and up a slight incline to the *Pura Dalem Agung Padang Tegal*. This is the temple for the dead for the community of Padang Tegal. There's a *Pura Dalem* for every community and they are generally inhabited by malevolent spirits. You'll notice the various figures of Rangda the evil witch, she of the long stringy hair, pendulous breasts and awesome fangs. One of her favourite past-times is eating children.

As in most temples, tourists are not permitted into the inner courtyard, but the kulkul drum tower is worth a peek for its garuda guardian. *Kulkul* are used to herald community gatherings including cremations and festivals. Further south, before the village of Nyukhuning, is the *Blue Yogi Cafe*.

Pejeng - The Holy Rock Route

Pejeng, designated as the area between the Pakrisan or "Kris River" and the Petanu or "Cursed River", includes the majority of Bali's antiquities. One could easily spend an entire day travelling around this rather small area which is only 7 kilometres from Ubud.

Goa Gajah

In Bedulu, about 2km (1 mile) from the T-intersection at Ubud, is the Elephant Cave or Goa Gajah. According to myth, Dalem Bedulu, the King of Bedulu, was a devout Buddhist given to decapitating himself before meditating. One day, the courtiers who were instructed to mind the King's head, lost it, and quickly replaced it with that of a pig. The king, understandably ashamed of his appearance, concealed himself in a tower and forbade visitors to view the grotesque sight. News of the king's condition reached Java, and the prime minister of the Majapahit Empire, Gajah Mada, was ordered to meet the king of Bedulu and verify the tale. Of course, Gajah Mada found the pig-headed king, so to speak, and caused Bedulu's ruination. The cave at Goa Gajah, was the real head of the King of Bedulu, which eventually fell back to earth. Another myth is that Bedulu's minister, the giant Kebo Iwa, carved the rock-face with his thumbnail.

Goa Gajah, called the Elephant Cave because archaeologists thought it looked like the head of an elephant, was once a Buddhist monastery. Situated above the Petanu River, the complex of temples and baths is testament to the influence of Buddhism before the arrival of Hinduism. The entrance to the cave is over 2m (6ft) high and features the whimsical carving of a man with huge eyebrows and moustache — his mouth is the opening. Inside is a dimly lit T-shaped chamber, with niches carved in the wall (don't forget to take a torch). At each end of the "T" is a statue of Ganesha, Siwa's son. Of course, Ganesha is a Hindu god, but there are statues of Buddhist figurines in the pavilion adjacent to the cave, and down the 50 or so steps behind the compound are statues of Buddha. A confusion of motifs, the Buddhist Balinese established the compound first, and as Hindu influences filtered through, Hindu religious figures were added.

Admission is Rp500 and visitors should be sartorially resplendent in sash and sarong (or long pants). As is the custom, temple gear is for hire.

Yeh Pulu

About a kilometre from Goa Gajah is a 14th century life-size frieze, depicting scenes of rural life. Unfortunately, few tourists visit the site as it entails a walk through rice fields, but it's easy to find and the walk isn't difficult. Between Goa Gajah and the Bedulu crossroads, follow the cobblestone road on the right (south), past *warung* to the rice fields. From there it is a walk to the site. (Open during daylight hours and admission is Rp1500.)

Carved into the side of a rock, the relief (25m x 2m - 82ft x 6.5ft) is either a series of isolated vignettes on daily life or a story. The carvings are very different from any others found either on Bali or Java; the scenes are naturalistic, and do not conform to the traditional styles found elsewhere.

Framed by a leave motif, the impressions include hunters attacking a boar; a farmer hoeing a field; a woman furtively peeking behind a door; a woman pulling a horses tail; culminating in a relief of Ganesha, Siwa's elephant-headed son. Interestingly, towards the end of the frieze, smaller animal scenes seem to parody the human scenes, for instance, a frog stabs a snake and a monkey steers another monkey by pulling its tail. The carving was "discovered" in the 1920s by the Dutch artist, Nieuwenkamp, although the Balinese had known about it for years. Legend has it the carvings are the handiwork of the giant, Kebo Iwo, who etched them with his thumbnail.

Bedulu

The village of Bedulu was once the abode of the Pejeng kingdom, the last bastion of Buddhism on the island following the arrival of the Majapahit empire. Bedulu has two main temples, to the west *Pura Arjuna Metapa* and to the east, *Pura Samuan Tiga*, which is associated with the wandering priest Empu Kuturan.

Pejeng

Travelling north from the Bedulu crossroads is the village of

Pejeng. Inhabited since the bronze age, when it was first considered a holy site, it has proffered many of the area's antiquities which have since been despatched to Jakarta, Denpasar, and of course, parts of the Netherlands.

Pejeng's three main temples are located on the Bedulu-Tampaksiring road, north of Bedulu. The most famous being the "temple of the moon", *Pura Panataran Sasih* which enshrines the monumental drum, the "moon of Pejeng".

Cast in a single piece, it is the largest drum of its kind found anywhere in Asia. It probably dates back to the bronze age, around 300BC, but no one knows for sure. And whether it was made on the island or was a gift from other lands is a total mystery. But, archaeologists have excavated at least one stone mould, so it's known that drums were cast on Bali.

The drum, which looks more like a gong with a waist, is decorated with geometric patterns and stars, and four garish faces. Fable has it that the drum was one of the wheels of the moon god's chariots which dropped to the earth. Other fables tell that it was a moon that dropped to the earth and when discovered by a thief, he urinated on it, causing the moon to explode. One of the fragments dropped to the earth in the form of the drum. Still another myth has it as the earring of the giant, Kebo Iwa. Although the temple is almost in ruins, it was the most important *pura* in the area. The gong no doubt had the same use as the modern *kulkul*, to herald festivals and community gatherings.

The drum is truly enigmatic, and will remain so, for it is perched high in a shrine and very difficult to see — take binoculars. Admission is by donation and as the drum is in a temple, a sash is mandatory.

The second temple, *Pura Pusering Jagat*, or "temple of the navel of the world", stands south of the main temple (admission Rp 1000; sash compulsory). Most notable is the metre-high vessel for storing holy water which has been hewn from a single block of sandstone. The vessel's exterior is detailed with the Hindu myth, the Churning of the Ocean, which recounts the battle between the gods and the demons to obtain the elixir of immortal life. Just before the holy vessel are two important fertility icons, the metre-high phallic *lingam* and it's female counterpart, the *yoni*.

The third temple, *Pura Kebo Edan* is the "mad buffalo temple". Inside the compound is a 4m (13ft) high statue, probably of Bima, one of the brothers from the Pandawa family in the epic poem *Mahabharata*. The awesome figure, complete with horns and fangs, has a huge (one hesitates at saying realistic) set of the male genitalia, with four pins pierced through it (apparently, a custom of the time). Snakes are entwined about its feet and wrists, and it stomps on a dead body. Notice that the cadaver's eyes are open.

Museum Gedong Arca

Given the wealth of antiquities in the area, this museum is very disappointing. Four pavilions house a haphazard and poorly-labelled assortment of artefacts ranging from Neolithic stone axe heads and adzes, to bronze jewellery, Chinese ceramics, as well as Hindu relics. At the back of the complex, are a dozen sarcophagi dating back to 200BC. These massive coffins are hewn from two sections of hollowed stone ranging in size from one metre to three. Some are simple affairs, while others are elaborately detailed monuments commissioned for wealthy community members.

Open Mon-Thurs 7am-2pm, Fri 7am-11am, Sat 7am-12pm; admission by donation.

Gunung Kawi

Just north of Tampaksiring's bemo terminal are the monumental royal tombs and hermitage of Gunung Kawi, the "Mountain of the Poet". Built in the 11th century, the tombs are thought to have been built by Anak Wangsa, the ruler of Bali, for himself and his concubines, as well as his brother King Erlangga of Java. The tombs are hewn from the rock-face of the gorge of the sacred Pakrisan river.

Walk past the customary souvenir vendors and up a steep path of stairs for a view of the magnificent gorge. The blackened tombs set amidst the lichen-covered ravine and cool waterfalls make this an austere place. As one enters the site, the four concubines' tombs are on the left, and across the Pakrisan River are the five royal tombs and adjacent hermitage.

The tombs are carved niches or *candi* and have no interior compartments, they are merely sombre facades. These monuments were probably testament to the fact that the correct and full ceremonial rituals had been completed.

The Queens' tombs are four huge tiered reliefs, chiselled from the cliff face to resemble temple facades. Originally the facades would have had plaster carvings, but these have long been eroded by the elements. Each *candi* has three sections symbolising hell, earth and heaven.

Across the Pakrisan River is the Gunung Kawi temple complex, comprising several caves and a particularly deeply-hewn chamber with windows and a skylight. This was probably a hermitage for the priests who attended the tombs. At the back of the complex are the five royal tombs, with their false doors and facades still visibly intact. The tomb at the far left end is thought to be that of Anak Wangsa as it is higher than the others. The tenth tomb is back across the river, past the exit signs, along the slippery path adjacent to the rice paddies. Thought to be erected in memory of a political personage, it stands alone, its facade eroded by water.

Pura Pedarman

South-east of Bedulu, in the village of Kutri, is the *Pura Pedarman* temple. Enshrined in the temple is a 2m (6.5ft) high statue of Durga, the goddess of death. The six-armed goddess was the wife of Siwa, although many believe that the statue was crafted after the evil Mahendratta (wife of Udayana and mother of Erlangga), known in myths as Rangda the witch.

Tirta Empul

A couple of kilometres out of Tampaksiring lies the spring of Tirta Empul (it's well-signposted). Open during daylight hours, admission is Rp1500 and a sash is compulsory.

Legend tells of a demon king named Maya Danawa who believed that he was the supreme ruler. Siwa, the supreme god, was maddened by the mortal's delusions of grandeur, and sent an army of heavenly warriors, commanded by Indra, to defeat the fraud. During the battle, the dastardly demon king murdered Indra's warriors by poisoning their drinking water. So Indra shot his magic arrow into the ground to tap the earth's "elixir of life" (*amerta*), and presto! the sacred Pakrisan gushed forth. Maya Danawa attempted to escape by changing into a rock in the stream, but the warriors found him and murdered him — his blood became the cursed Petanu River. So cursed, the Balinese refused to use the river, even for irrigation purposes, until the 1920s.

The supposed curative and cleansing powers of the spring of Tirta Empul make it one of the most revered sites on Bali. Behind the outer courtyard, and shaded by a magnificent banyan tree, are two pools, one for men, one for women. The spring flows from the inner sanctum of the temple which is protected by a wall lest it be defiled. The complex was restored in 1969 and is meticulously maintained.

Surrounded by these beautiful stone carvings and cleansing waters, one can't help noticing the huge concrete monstrosity on the hill. Istana Negara was built by the late President Sukarno in the 1950s as a weekend retreat, supposedly so he could be near the sacred grounds, an area revered by his Balinese mother. But rumour has it, it was so he could spy on the beautiful young women who bathed in the springs. Visitors are allowed in the grounds (open during daylight) but not in the palace, which is now used to accommodate visiting Indonesian dignitaries. Entrance is from the main Tampaksiring road, and not the stairs from the springs.

Gianyar Town

Gianyar town is the capital and administrative centre of the regency of Gianyar. Devoid of the tourist rush, visitors invariably pause here before heading east. The coast south of Gianyar town is also noticeably absent of tourists as the beaches are known to be perilous to swimmers and the sands black. Even so, from the coast the panorama back to the inland is picturesque with vistas of terraced paddies contrasted with the dramatic Gunung Agung or "mother mountain". Far out to sea, the outlines of Nusa Penida and Nusa Lembongan are visible on a clear day.

With Ubud so close, there's really no need to stay in Gianyar, and besides the accommodation on offer is not of a high standard. The Government Tourist Office of Gianyar is located on Jl. Ngurah Rai (Mon-Fri 8am-5pm) but the staff are not particularly helpful. There are no money changers in Gianyar, but Bank Rakyat Indonesia is central.

Gianyar town is famed for its *babi guling* (roasted duck) and you'll see it being served at the various *warung* lining the streets. However, it doesn't seem to fare well in the heat and is usually swarming with flies, so most delicate Western stomachs should avoid the temptation.

Gianyar is also known for its fine endek (Balinese cloth in which the weft (lengthwise) threads are dyed before the cloth is woven). Along the main road are various textile shops where women can be seen working the huge wooden looms. On the outskirts of the town are several emporia and the prices, starting at about Rp13,000 per metre, are competitive with the southern tourist centres.

On the main road, Jl. Barata, is Gianyar's market, a huge modern complex of two three-storey high buildings. One has stalls lined with fruit, vegetables and other assorted foodstuffs, while the second is for clothes and household goods.

In the heart of the town of Gianyar is one of the few remaining traditional Balinese palaces. It is presently inhabited by the family of Anak Agung Gede Agung, former Foreign Minister and heir to the throne of Gianyar, and as such visitors are not permitted in the grounds. The *puri* was originally built in 1771 by Dewa Manggis IV, but was completely rebuilt following an earthquake in 1917.

Originally built on the site of a priest's home, "Gianyar" is an abbreviated form of "new priest's home".

Next to the palace is the royal family's temple, the *Pura Langon* or "temple of beauty".

Klungkung

The tiny, prosperous regency of Klungkung is nestled between the regencies of Gianyar to the west, Bangli to the north and Karangasem to the east, and includes the islands of Nusa Penida and Nusa Lembongan. The smallest regency on the island, Klungkung was the abode of the illustrious Gelgel royal family.

History

Gaja Mada, the Javanese general, conquered Bali in 1343, and claimed the island as part of the Majapahit Empire, establishing a court at Samprangan, near modern Klungkung. As the empire in Java buckled under the pressure from the Islamic Mataram Empire, the Majapahit entourage, led by the emperor's son, fled to Bali.

In 1515, the emperor's son established a court at Gelgel, near modern Klungkung, and bestowed upon himself the title of Dewa Agung, the "Lord of Lords". He empowered the noble *Brahmana* and *Satrya* to divide and administer the island, and slowly extended the Empire to East Java, Lombok and Sumbawa. And with power, wealth and prestige, the Gelgel Empire witnessed a cultural renaissance — Bali's "Golden Age".

Nothing lasts forever, and successive generations watched the power and wealth dwindle. In 1868, an ambitious general, Maruti, conquered the Raja of Gelgel and proclaimed himself Raja. But, in 1705, assisted by the Rajas of Badung and Buleleng, the next generation recovered the throne. In 1710, believing that Gelgel was cursed, the Raja shifted the royal residence to Klungkung. The gods must have been displeased. By the 1860s, political power in Bali was focused in the regency of Buleleng, and the Dewa Agung was the supreme ruler in name only. By 1908, the Dutch controlled most of Bali, and their final "acquisition" was to be Klungkung, the residence of the Dewa

172 Bali

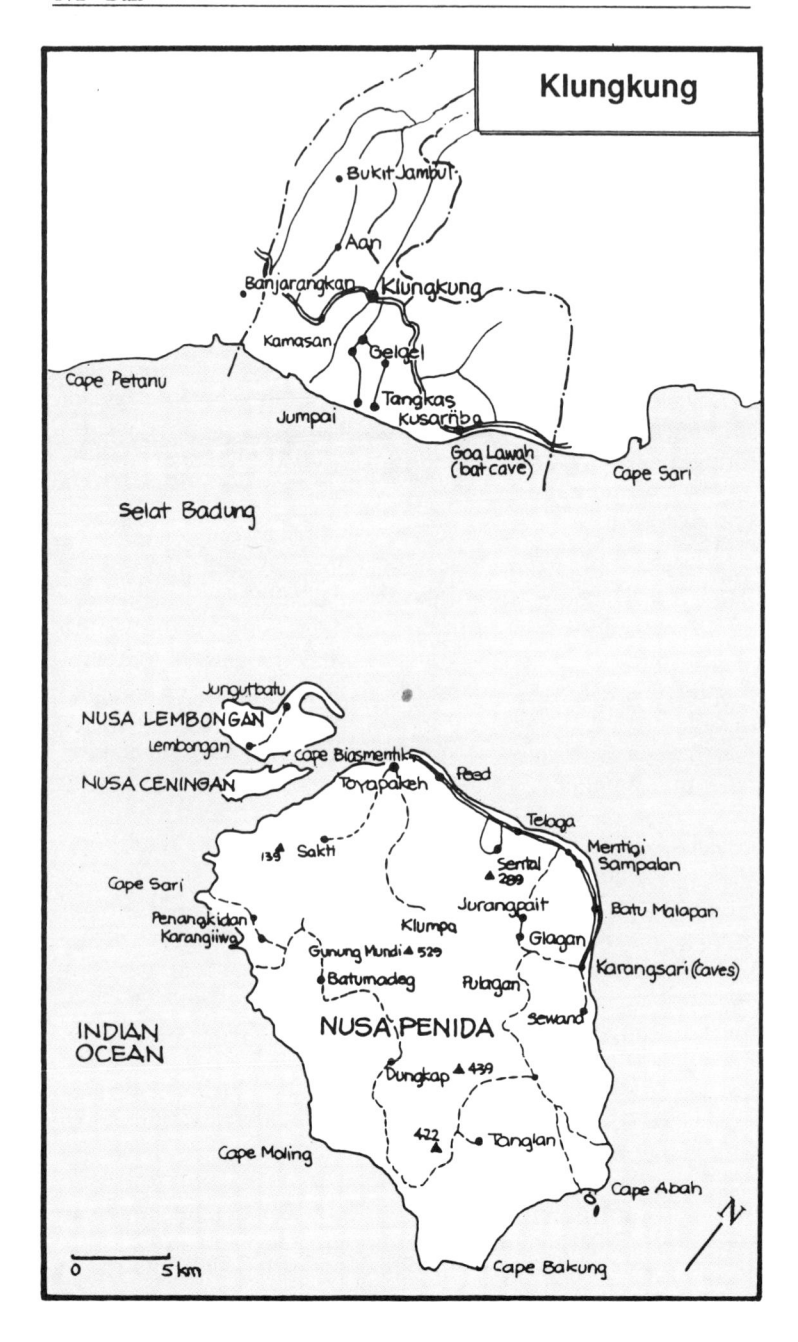

Agung. Rather than relinquish power, the Dewa Agung and his retinue chose ritual suicide *(puputan)*.

Most Balinese royal families claim descent from the Gelgel dynasty and today the Gelgel royal family is the most respected family on the island. Alas, little remains of their past glories, as most buildings were razed by the Dutch during the 1908 invasion.

Klungkung is somewhat removed from the tourist rush but has some interesting antiquities. Kerta Gosa, the Court of Justice, located in the former palace at Klungkung, and Goa Lawah, the bat cave temple, are two often-visited attractions.

In the village of **Kamasan**, not far from the town of Klungkung, is a commune of artists who still practise the traditional *Wayang* style of painting, derived from the shadow puppets *(Wayang kulit)*. The village is definitely worth a visit.

Klungkung Town

Klungkung town is the capital of Klungkung, the regency, but despite its historical attractions it does not cater to visitors. The few losmen, mainly frequented by businessmen, are not worth mentioning. There are a few restaurants, but the night market, *Pasar Senggol* (at the bemo station), has a good variety of food, and is highly recommended.

Pasar Klungkung, the day market, is one of the best on the island, because the harbour nearby is a major port of call between Java and Lombok. The market is located on the main road (Jl. Diponegoro), and is held every three days, falling on the Balinese day known as *pasah*. The market, as well as the souvenir stalls nearby, often sell fabrics and crafts not available elsewhere in Bali. Fine embroidered *songket*, cheaper than anywhere else on the island, is definitely worth purchasing. The Handicraft Promotion Centre, opposite the Kerta Gosa, also sells crafts. There are quite a few antique shops on the main road, but they mostly sell reproductions.

How to Get There
The bemo station at Klungkung is a major stop for buses

travelling to Besakih (21km - 13 miles), Penelokan (40km - 25 miles), Padangbai, and Candi Dasa (24km - 15 miles).

Bemo to Besakih and points east, cost Rp800, but tourist prices are gaining favour; and most bemo do not run after 4pm. Klungkung town is situated 40km (24 miles) from Denpasar and 13km (9 miles) east of Gianyar.

Sightseeing

The Palace Complex

Kerta Gosa, the royal **Court of Justice**, was built under the watchful eye of the Dewa Agung, Gusti Sideman. An ornate *bale* (open pavilion), it lies in the far-eastern corner of the complex, almost on top of the town's main intersection. Perhaps it served as a warning to passers-by. The elaborately painted ceiling of the Kerta Gosa has traditional *Wayang*-style murals in red, gold and black. The scenes depict the heinous punishment of criminals, for instance: an unfaithful woman has her offending parts burnt; a bachelor is attacked by a wild boar; miscreants are boiled to death; and a childless woman is forced to suckle a monstrous caterpillar. Then there are scenes of the afterlife, with the virtuous reigning in the heavens. Indeed, the scenes tell a multitude of stories focusing on fate and divine intervention. The roof of the Kerta Gosa is meticulously maintained, and was last repainted in the 1960s.

The Court of Justice heard only important cases, such as murder or treason, and three *Pedanda* presided over the hearings. The judges probably sat in the *bale* in gilt chairs, looking towards the ceiling for inspiration. The court was active until the 1950s when the assembly was moved.

The *Bale Kambang*, or **Floating Pavilion**, was originally used as a reception hall for visitors, and was completely reconstructed in the 1940s. The *bale* "floats" on a moat, surrounded by stone carvings of figures from the *Mahabharata*. The ceiling also has illustrations, some from Balinese astrology, others depicting Balinese myths. One such story called *Sang Sutasoma*, tells of the trials and tribulations of a family of eighteen children, while the story of *Pan Bryut*, espouses the virtues of the wise man, Pan. Beyond the pavilion is the ornate gateway to the former palace.

Outlying Attractions

Kamasan

A few kilometres south of Klungkung lies the village of Kamasan, renowned for its co-operative of artists who still practise the traditional *Wayang* style of painting. Known as the Kamasan style, the figures are stylised, with faces drawn in three-quarters, rather than frontal or profile. There is no perspective, as such, and subjects of importance are painted in the centre, with gods at the top, and evil spirits at the bottom. The ceiling of the Kerta Gosa is a typical *Wayang* depiction. Originally, the paintings were drawn on cotton, wood or paper, with a palm-leaf quill filled with soot; then, natural dyes were applied with bamboo brushes to colour the figures. These days, most painters use acrylics and ink on canvas. Although Western conventions demand a single artist, painting was, and in many cases still is, a joint effort. The master painter plans the themes and layout of the painting, and then directs the apprentices in the colouring of the figures. Finally, the master outlines the figures in ink, occasionally enhancing details with gold paint.

Although wealthy Indonesians and Westerners commission paintings, sadly, most painters are impoverished, and the government fears that this traditional style may die out. The artists in Kamasan are all willing to demonstrate their techniques and appreciate Western patronage.

Gelgel

About four kilometres (2.5 miles) south of Klungkung is the former Court of Gelgel, the once magnificent and powerful capital of the Gelgel kingdom. The first Raja built the palace in 1515, and it remained the political centre until the courtly retinue moved to Klungkung. The only vestiges of past glory can be found in the ruins of the sacred *Pura Jero Agung* or "Great Palace Temple", and the remnants of the second largest palace in Gelgel, *Pura Jero Kapal*. To the east, is *Pura Dasar*, a state temple built as an adjunct to the "Mother Temple" at Besakih.

Goa Lawah

The celebrated "Bat Cave", as its name implies, almost pulsates with thousands of flapping, squealing, fruit bats. A temple guards the entrance to the sacred cave from malign spirits and intruders, but even the most intrepid or stupid would not dare enter, for the cavern and everything nearby is covered by a blanket of excrement. The cave was found by the priest Empu Kuturan, and supposedly extends to *Pura Goa*, the "cave temple", at the Besakih complex. Legend has it that a huge snake, Naga Basuki, resides in the cavity, living on a infinite supply of bats. Admission Rp500 and temple dress is required.

Nusa Penida

Few tourists venture to Nusa Penida. An arid, limestone island it was, until recently bereft of vegetation, except for the odd cactus. Once thought to be inhabited by malign spirits, the Balinese still believe that all diseases hail from Nusa Penida. The home of Jero Gede Macaling, the mythical giant, Nusa Penida became the last abode of criminals, and seditious subjects banished from Gelgel. Today, it seems a sinister ambience still haunts the island.

Thanks to government grants, limited cultivation is possible, and irrigation systems utilise the rainfall that previously seeped into underground caverns. Apart from cassava, corn, coconuts, peanuts and soybeans, little is grown, and rice has to be imported. The economy is largely funded by seaweed farming, and dried seaweed is exported to Hong Kong, Singapore, Japan and France, for the manufacture of cosmetics, as well as agar-agar, a thickening agent for cooking.

This is definitely not a tourist resort — few people speak English, the roads are treacherous, and tourist accommodation is almost non-existent. But Nusa Penida and the surrounding islands offer swimming, surfing, snorkelling, and scuba diving.

Located in Badung Strait between Bali and Lombok, the island is 20km by 16km (12 miles x 10 miles) rising to a height of 529m (1735ft) at Bukit Mundi. Nusa Penida along with the satellite islands of Nusa Lembongan and Nusa Ceningan make up Bali's three "sister islands". A counterpoint to the lush mainland, Nusa Penida is more like the Bukit Peninsula which is also a limestone formation. Exotic fauna abound — some surprisingly reminiscent of Australian wildlife — including the rare Rothschild's mynah bird.

How to Get There

Transport to the three islands is available from Padangbai and Kusamba in the east, or from Sanur and Benoa in the south. Most boats leave at 7am, and the choppy straits and severe winds can make for an arduous journey — cover all valuables with plastic as most boats are open. Different boats travel to different destinations, but bemo on the islands meet all of them, so it doesn't really matter where you disembark.

The easiest way to arrange transport to the islands is through travel agents, but here's how to do it yourself.

From Kusamba

About 200m from the market, outriggers carry passengers to either Jungutbatu on Nusa Lembongan, or to Toyapakeh on Nusa Penida. Another port in Kusamba, down Jl. Pair Putih (towards Amlapura), has bigger boats. The crossing is about 14km (9 miles) from Kusamba to Nusa Lembongan, and the journey from either point takes about two to three hours (Rp5000 one way). Boats leave when they are full so departure times vary. Boats can be chartered from both harbours — a round trip starts from Rp50,000 (depending on the boat size).

From Padangbai

The best alternative is to take a "speed" boat and they leave at about 7am. The fare is slightly higher than from Kusamba, but the journey is considerably faster — about 50 minutes. The boat arrives at Buyuk, which is close to Samalan.

From Sanur

Traditional outriggers (*prahu*) can be hired from near the Natour Grand Bali Beach Hotel. There is no regular service and the price is negotiable. The journey takes over two hours (less on the return journey). If intending a day trip, leave early in the morning because the skippers do not like travelling through Badung Strait in the late afternoon.

From Benoa
The most pleasurable means of travelling to Nusa Lembongan is by hiring a yacht from Benoa. Tour Devco (ph 31 591) has day trips, and will organise transport to and from your hotel.

Accommodation
The main village on the island is Sampalan. The only accommodation is the very cheap losmen-style, *Bungalows Pemda*, which are at the eastern end of the village. Of course there is no restaurant, but there are a few *warung*.

Local Transport
In Nusa Penida the boats arrive at Buyuk or Toyapakeh. Bemo run from both ports to Sampalan, and run irregularly between villages. Charter a bemo around the island for Rp20,000 an hour.

Sightseeing
Tourism has not reached Nusa Penida and everywhere are authentic unspoiled sights. Temples, as on the mainland, are ubiquitous, but tend to be simpler in design.

Goa Karangsari
You'll probably have to hitch a ride on a goods truck and most carry passengers for a fee. Take the coast road east from Sampalan. The cave is past Karangsari but before Sewena.

Disembark at the *warung* and hire a guide (about Rp6000). Although the guide will have a kerosene lamp, take a strong torch to see the shrine and bats. The entrance is small but the cave itself is huge and side passages lead nowhere. The cave emerges at the other side of the hill.

Pura Peed
From Sampalan, take the road west for a ten-minute journey to the village of Peed. On the right side of the road is the limestone temple dedicated to the malicious giant, Jero Gede Macaling. The temple's architecture features monstrous and hideous statues, and nearby a gruesome mouth gapes from the trunk of a gnarled tree. Worshippers come here to placate the awesome

figure, who they believe responsible for unleashing evil forces.

Nusa Lembongan

Most travellers that visit this small island arrive with surfboard in tow. But Nusa Lembongan is simply a quiet retreat. There are no bemo, and in fact, no traffic. However, there are a few restaurants and a selection of losmen. Like Nusa Penida, the island derives its main source of income from seaweed farming. Bird watchers (of the feathered kind) will be fascinated with the exotic bird life. There are also great views of south Bali, especially at night.

Marine Sports
The surfing is fabulous.
A perfect right breaks over a coral encrusted shipwreck — the "wreck". "Lacerations" and the "playground" are also much lauded breaks, and an outrigger can be hired to travel between them. See **Surfing** in the **"Travel Information"** section.

The small channel between Nusa Lembongan and Nusa Ceningan is a very good spot for snorkelling — the water is crystal clear and visibility is very good. Snorkelling gear can be hired on the island for Rp8000 per day, but scuba gear has to be hired in Sanur. For information on **"How to get There"** see the same in the section on Nusa Penida.

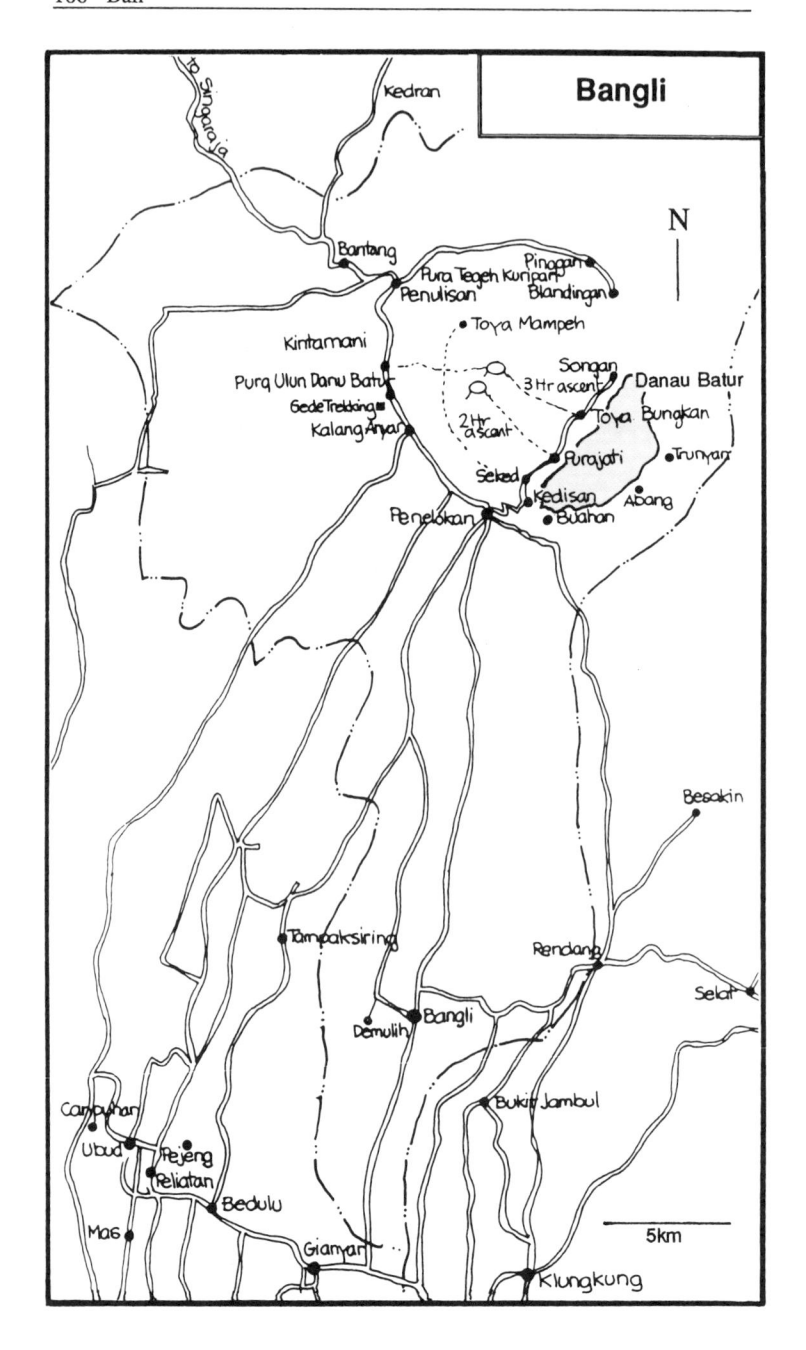

Bangli

Bangli

The land-locked and mountainous regency of Bangli includes some of the most magnificent scenery on the island. Luminous green rice fields cover the undulating land, and the revered Gunung Batur (1717m - 5633ft), a still active volcano, dominates the landscape. The placid Lake Batur rests in a huge crater, overshadowed by Batur, and the lesser-known but higher, Gunung Abang (2152m - 7060ft). In the morning, tourists visit the towns of Kintamani and Penelokan to observe the imposing Batur before clouds descend to obscure the mountain. The afternoon panorama is as splendid as the morning, enhanced by the eerie atmosphere of mysterious clouds. Little wonder that locals speak in hushed tones of black magic.

The main road through the regency of Bangli starts east of Gianyar, passes through the town of Bangli, and climbs to Penelokan, then Kintamani. Past the town of Bangli, the road ascends and the picturesque rice fields diminish, replaced by ashen, volcanic terrain. Vegetation is sparse, it's much cooler, and you know the altitude is high because your ears have popped. The route from Penelokan to Kintamani follows the mountainous crater of an ancient, extinct volcano that surrounds Gunung Batur.

Bangli Town

The capital of the regency, Bangli is a sleepy little village. About 40km (25 miles) from Denpasar, via Gianyar, Bangli was once the site of a royal court. It is said that the Dewa Agung of Klungkung ordered his son to find the "auspicious red forest". The prince did, and "Bangli", which means the "red forest", became his kingdom. For a time, Bangli was annexed by the king of Karangasem, and later in 1849, it was colonised by the Dutch.

Bangli is home to the only psychiatric hospital on the island, the source of much mirth to those from other regencies. Bangli is also known for its "black" and "white" magic, and many trance healers, known as *balian*, are sought by Balinese from all over the island. There are eight royal palaces spread around the town. The most notable is the Puri Denpasar palace. Fully restored, it also operates as a hotel, managed by the late king's grandson.

Pura Kehen
Pura Kehen, the beautiful state temple of Bangli, lies north-east of the centre of town. Three copper pillars indicate that the temple was built in the 11th century, and the animistic motifs incorporated in the carvings suggest pre-Majapahit architecture. There are 8 courtyards and 43 altars climbing to the sacred inner *jeroan*, which houses an 11-tiered *meru* tower. A sprawling complex of temples and shrines, the site resembles the impressive network found at the "Mother Temple" in Besakih. A huge staircase lined with dancing *wayang* figures leads to a gateway known ominously as the "Great Exit". Notice the customary *kulkul* drum perched in a *banyan* tree, and the not so customary Chinese porcelain which adorns the walls of the outer courtyard. If in Bali at the time of the *Pura Kehen*'s anniversary festival (*Odalan*), be sure not to miss the unrivalled spectacle. As the year is 210 days, the date of the festival differs each year. The tourist offices in Kuta and Denpasar will happily supply a calendar of events for the month.

Not far from *Pura Kehen* is the **Wisata Budaya Art Centre**. One of the biggest art centres on Bali, it houses an excellent exhibition which surpasses displays found elsewhere. The centre also hosts several different local *Barong* performances.

Gunung Batur and Lake Batur

Penelokan
Driving up to Gunung Batur on the Bangli road, Penelokan is the first village on the crater rim. Penelokan, which means "lookout" has spectacular views — stay awhile and contemplate the serene majesty of this mountain. Effectively, what you're admiring is the cavernous remains of a massive volcano,

probably bigger than Agung, that erupted thousands of years ago, bursting the entire cone and leaving only the hollow rim on which you're standing.

A quick word about Penelokan, the hawkers are insufferable. The minute you open the door of your car, mobs of men, women and children will bombard you with the usual garish garuda and tawdry temple-sashes. Eat lunch, enjoy the view, then scoot.

Gunung Batur

In the crater of a once gargantuan volcano stands the blackened cone of Gunung Batur. This sacred volcano, second only to Gunung Agung, is still active. Batur erupted in 1917, again in 1927, when it completely destroyed the village of Batur, and further activity occurred when Agung erupted in 1963. Batur has two craters and its slopes are blemished from lava flows, particularly on the eastern side adjacent to the lake. The cone is 1717m (5633ft) high, and the crater in which it sits is 11km (7 miles) in diameter and 183m (600ft) deep.

The Ascent of Batur

Guides can be contacted at Gede's Trekking, just near the market at Kintamani; alternatively, many of the losmen organise treks. Although most climbs take about three hours up and less than two hours down, make an early start (around 6am) as the afternoon heat can be exhausting. Don't even think about climbing during the wet season.

There are **two tracks** favoured by visitors: one starts from Toya Bungkah (a three-hour climb to the second crater); and the other begins at Purajati (a two-hour climb to the first crater). Both paths are well signposted and are frequented by young locals selling drinks.

Public bemo run from Penelokan to Kedisan for around Rp700, then to Purajati for Rp400. The walk from Penelokan to Kedisan takes about 45 minutes.

Lake Batur

Danau Batur is the biggest lake in Bali. Set in the monstrous crater next to Batur, the lake is over 7.5km (5 miles) long, 2.5km (1.5 miles) wide, 70m (230ft) deep, and lies 1031m (3383ft) above sea level. To the west of the lake is desolate lava rock and to the east are the lush slopes of Gunung Abang (2152m - 7060ft), the second highest mountain in Bali.

Around the Lake

From Penelokan, take the road that zigzags down the crater to the lakeside village of Kedisan. At the bottom of the road, turn right to hire boats across the lake; or turn left to the villages of Toya Bungkah and Songan (this road also meanders to the bubbling hot springs known as Air Panas).

Trunyan

This famous Bali Aga village can be reached by boat from Kedisan. The arts and customs of the people of Trunyan predate Hindu times and their social tenets are unique. The one thing for which they're famous is that their dead are not cremated but are left to decompose beneath a tree.

Those adventurous enough to hire a boat to Trunyan are in for a real treat. The moment happy travellers disembark, locals besiege them to pay money for simply stepping on land! Then, a guide must be purchased as an escort to the temple, fending off beggars and ignoring the scowls of villagers along the way, to farewell a couple of thousand rupiah to walk around the temple — few are permitted entrance — and told that the biggest statue on the island, the 4m (13ft) high, Dewa Ratu Gede Pancering Jagat ("god who is the centre of the world"), the statue you've paid rupiah to see, is hidden in a shrine. Lots more rupiah will be handed over by intrepid statue viewers, but they'll die wondering if it is indeed 4m high. Then it's in the boat again to view (without fear or favour) the long-awaited cemetery. All this to see a rotten skull or two. There's not a putrefying body in sight! Naturally, the villagers conceal the real cemetery from intruders. Then it's back to the boat for an argument with the licensed bandit with a boat, because he's increased the price of the fare and you've already paid! Why bother?

Batur

The original village and temple of Batur were built on the lake's shore, but following the eruption in 1917, the entire village was devastated and a thousand lives were lost. Surprisingly, the lava flows ceased at the gate of the temple and the Balinese felt that they should rebuild the village due to the propitious omen. When Batur erupted again, in 1926, the temple was also devastated, but the *meru* shrine to the goddess of the lake survived. The people finally gave up, and the entire village moved to the rim of the crater, just before Kintamani. The temple was dismantled and relocated on the rim. The temple, *Pura Ulun Danur Batur*, is a complex of nine temples which are slowly increasing in number. Here, deference is paid to Dewi Ulun Danu, goddess of the lake, and her shrine, an 11-tiered *meru* tower, is in the main temple.

Kintamani

Most visitors take a day tour to Kintamani, spending time in one of the various restaurants that are huddled on the outer rim of an ancient volcano. The food buffet-style is invariably lukewarm, but all establishments have superb vantage points.

A tiny market village, Kintamani is 1500m (4921ft) above sea level. Palm-leaf *(lontar)* and stone inscriptions suggest that the village precedes the Majapahit empire. Many of the surrounding villages claim to be "Bali Aga" or indigenous Balinese.

How to Get There

By Bemo
From Denpasar's Kereneng terminal, take a bemo to Bangli (Rp1000) via Klunkung, then to Penelokan (Rp600).

From Ubud, take a bemo to Sakah (Rp400) where you change for Gianyar (Rp800), then change again for Penelokan (Rp1000).

From Singaraja a minibus costs Rp1500.

By Car
Kintamani is 68km (42 miles) from Denpasar; 75 km (47 miles) from Kuta; 41km (25 miles) from Gianyar; and 52km (32 miles) from Singaraja.

Tours

Tours can be arranged at Kuta, Sanur, Ubud, Candi Dasa and other places. Prices differ according to the number of passengers and the route taken — shop around to get the best price for what you want to see. From the south, the route generally taken is via Ubud and Tampaksiring, stopping at Goa Gajah and Tirta Empul. A less-frequented route (the road is narrow and pot-holed) passes through Ubud and the villages of Tegalalang, Sebatu and Pujung.

Accommodation

Prices range from around US$4 a night to US$20. At night it gets quite cold so take a blanket and a jumper. The accommodation is more or less losmen-style, which means it's very spartan, but cheap. Most hotels have great views, but lack hot water. There are no telephones nor air-conditioning.

Two hotels recommended are:
Hotel Puri Astina. Kintamani, north of the market. Four of the rooms are quite big and have great views. Room $20.
Lakeview Restaurant and Homestay. Penelokan. Very basic but fabulous views. Rooms for around $11.

Eating Out

Many of the losmen have *warung* attached. There are a few *warung* in Kintamani, but most of the larger restaurants cater to the tour crowds and serve buffets — avoid them.
Lakeview. Penelokan. Open for lunch and dinner, and offers a variety of dishes.
Batur Garden Restaurant. Chinese and Indonesian dishes. Open for lunch only.
Rumah Makan Cahaya. North Kintamani. One of the nicest *warung* in Kintamani. Good food and nice atmosphere.

Karangasem

The regency of Karangasem is unrivalled in beauty. The diversity of Bali's landscape offers wonders to behold, but in Karangasem, the contrasts are intensified. In the highlands, impeccably terraced hills affording views to the sea are set against black rivers of volcanic ash, and large, stupa-like rocks. Such scenery could only be dwarfed by the colossal presence of Gunung Agung. On the slopes of this, Bali's sacred mountain, lies the sprawling complex of temples, the "Mother Temple".

Karangasem has not experienced the whirlwind developments of the other regencies, and has changed little. For instance, the "language of courtesies" is still prevalent, and many old dances and rituals have persisted unchanged. **Candi Dasa**, the only resort in the regency, is sedate compared to its counterparts in the south. Indeed, who could blame such conservatism, when plainly, one imagines the gods must sit upon Gunung Agung, watching every move the people make.

History

When the Majapahit descendant, Dewa Agung of Klungkung, divided Bali in the 16th century, he ruled the regency of Karangasem through a regent. But, as time passed, the regency claimed more independence, until in the early 18th century Karangasem attained enough power to colonise Lombok and Sumbawa. Alas, in 1894, the tables turned and the Dutch "removed" the Balinese rulers from Lombok and soon after invaded Karangasem. The Raja, Agung Anglurah Ketut, retained limited power, and managed to commission several lavish, even ostentatious, palaces.

Amlapura, a bustling little village, is the capital. The regency derives much of its economy from farming rice, coffee and cloves, as well as fishing and salt-panning.

188 Bali

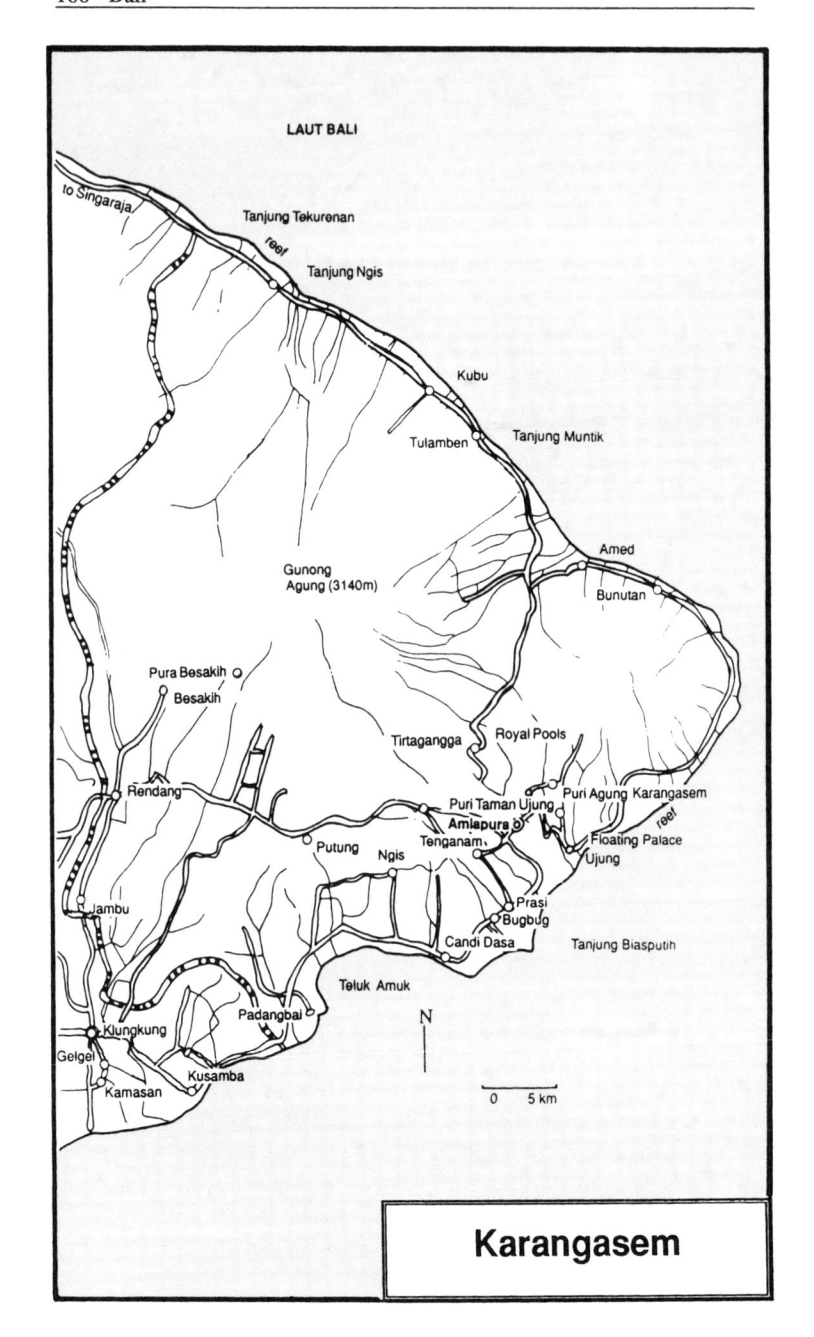

Padangbai

Nestled in a small cove, this tiny village is Bali's eastern-most port, where cruisers and yachts moor and from where the ferry to Lombok departs three times a day. (The trip takes three hours and costs from Rp8000-Rp12000).

Cornelius De Houtman stopped here and was so enamoured of the land that he called it "Young Holland". "Padangbai", however, derives from the Balinese *padang* for grass, and the Dutch *bai* for "bay". This quiet little village has become a stopover for those wishing to snorkel and has a number of cheaper, losmen-style accommodations. There's a tourist information centre on the main road, and a number of *warung* for inexpensive dining.

Tenganan

Before you reach Candi Dasa, a road branching off to the left (it's well sign-posted) leads to the village of Tenganan, the home of the *Bali Aga*, the "original Balinese". An ordered and prosperous village, it is the antithesis of Trunyan, the "Bali Aga" village at Lake Batur. The descendants of Tenganan settled in Bali long before the Hindu Majapahit Empire called Bali home, and the village traces its origins to a holy chronicle known as the *Usana Bali*. According to the text, the ancestors of the Tengananese where chosen by their creator, Batara Indra, to perpetuate the rituals and ceremonies passed to them from the gods. Furthermore, the sacred lands granted to the ancestors were to be administered by the people of Tenganan, and kept free from impurity. Life in this exclusive and cloistered village is devoted to maintaining the divine order, and to following the traditional law (*adat*) to the letter.

Tenganan is possibly the only village on the island that still maintains a co-operative where all homes and property are owned by the village. The rice fields are tended by exiles (who live outside the compound) or by neighbouring villagers who receive half the yield in payment. Consequently, the village is quite wealthy and its residents have much time to dedicate to the arts.

The people of Tenganan are famed for their expertise in

creating *geringsing* cloth, by the technique known as double *ikat*. The *ikat* method involves selectively dyeing threads prior to weaving by binding them in groups, so that the threads will not absorb colour when dipped in a dye bath. The process is repeated, adding different colours to the thread. In south Bali, only the weft is bound, but the double *ikat* process dyes both the warp and the weft. This makes weaving the threads extremely difficult, as the tension of the threads must be exact so that the patterns on both threads match. It is said that *Geringsing* was taught to the Tengananese by Batara Indra, and that the cloth protects the wearer from malign spirits.

Before Candi Dasa became a burgeoning resort, Tenganan was inaccessible and virtually isolated; now a sealed road connects the village with the outside world. Protected by natural boundaries and walls, the immaculate village is 500m by 250m (1640ft x 820ft), and has four impressive gateways located at the cardinal points. Three parallel roads run downhill, north to south, aligned with Gunung Agung and the sea, and the dwellings are set in parallel rows of nearly identical brick and mortar boxes. The village is a microcosm of 13th century, pre-Hindu life — except for the odd television antenna impaled on a thatched roof and the occasional blasting from a stereo.

Tenganan is also famous for its three-day *Udaba Sambah* festival, which is held every six months. The unmarried girls of the village, ceremonially adorned, participate in a ritual to unite the earth with the heavens. They sit atop a huge wooden frame, not unlike a Ferris wheel, displaying their charms. The young men engage in a man-to-man combat ritual, armed with spiky pandanus leaves, to the accompaniment of the haunting tones of the ancient *gamelan*. Tenganan has its own *gamelan*, the *gong selunding*, which is unique to the village.

Candi Dasa

A developing, yet relatively unspoiled tourist resort, Candi Dasa (pronounced "chandy"), is the perfect place to stop for a while to explore the environs. A nice escape from the south, the restaurants and hotels are good, although the night life is a little subdued. The locals are also more relaxed, with few soliciting travellers to buy, buy, buy. In fact, Candi Dasa has some of Kuta's virtues, without all the vices.

Candi Dasa means "ten temples" and although there are not ten temples, the village shrine has a ten-tiered gateway, one of the few shrines to use even-numbered symbolism. Perched high above the palm-fringed lagoon, the temple offers superb views of the beach.

The white coral sand beaches, calm water and colourful sea-life make Candi Dasa a lovely sea resort. The problem is that the sea is fast encroaching on the beach, which at high tide is barely visible. A huge wall has been built between the main road and the coast to enable the construction of tourist facilities, and huge cement breakwaters attempt to combat erosion. Popular opinion though, holds that rather than stopping the erosion, they are actually aggravating it.

How to Get There

By Bemo
Bemo depart from Denpasar's Kereneng terminal for Candi Dasa and cost Rp3000 (although tourist prices are becoming popular). From Klunkung and Amlapura, bemo leave frequently and the fare is Rp500.

By Taxi
While it is possible to charter a bemo to the east coast, it is probably cheaper and easier to hire a blue and yellow metered taxi. For instance from Kuta to Candi Dasa by taxi costs about Rp40,000 for the 78-kilometre journey. Flagfall is Rp1500 and then about Rp500 per kilometre.

By Car
Candi Dasa is 13km (8 miles) south-west of Amlapura; 25km (16 miles) from Klunkung; 38km (24 miles) from Gianyar; 69km (43 miles) from Denpasar; and 78km (48 miles) from Kuta.

Accommodation
Although Candi Dasa is small, it has a good selection of hotels. Prices based on one night's accommodation are in US$, do not include the 10-15% service charge nor the 10% government tax,

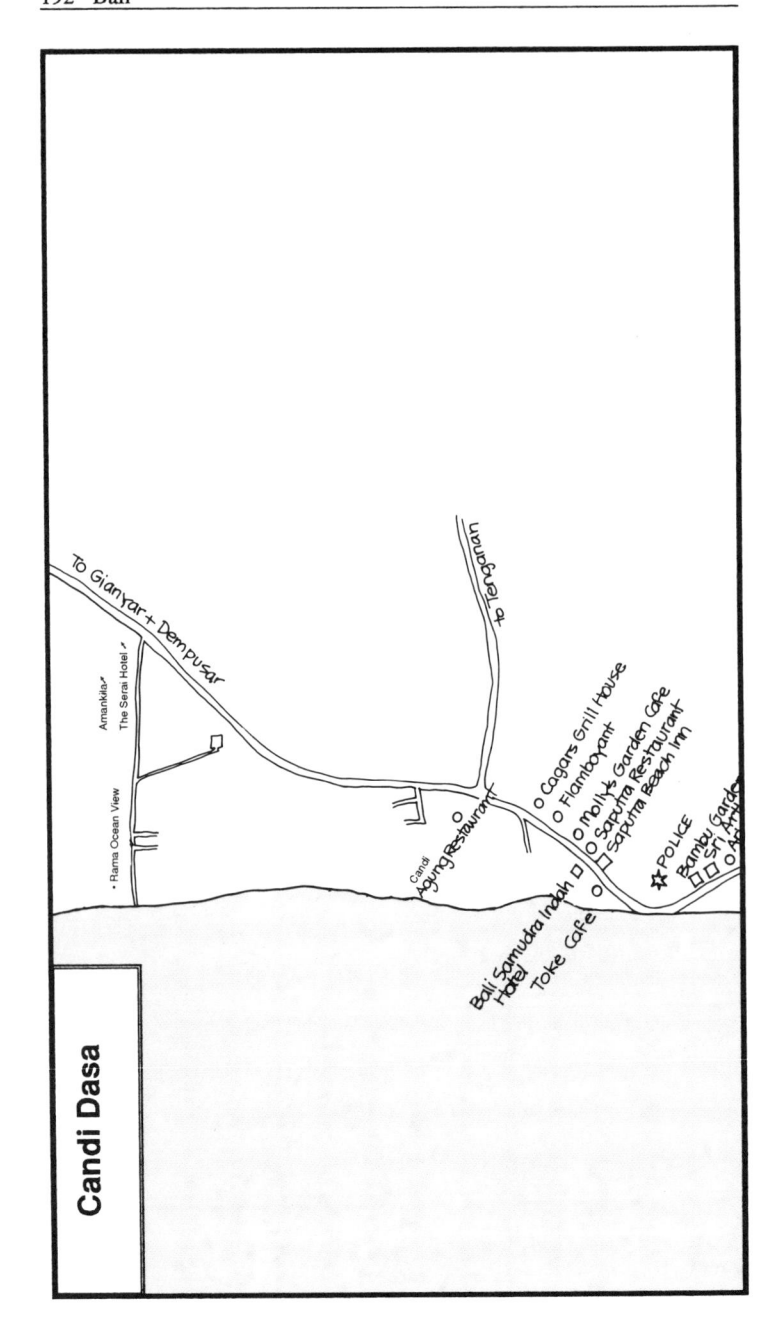

Candi Dasa

- To Gianyar + Denpasar
- To Tenganan
- Amankila
- The Serai Hotel
- Rama Ocean View
- Candi Agung Restaurant
- Cogars Grill House
- Flamboyant
- Molly's Garden Cafe
- Saputra Restaurant
- Saputra Beach Inn
- Bali Samudra Indah Hotel
- Toke Cafe
- POLICE
- Bambu Garden
- Sri Artha

Karangasem

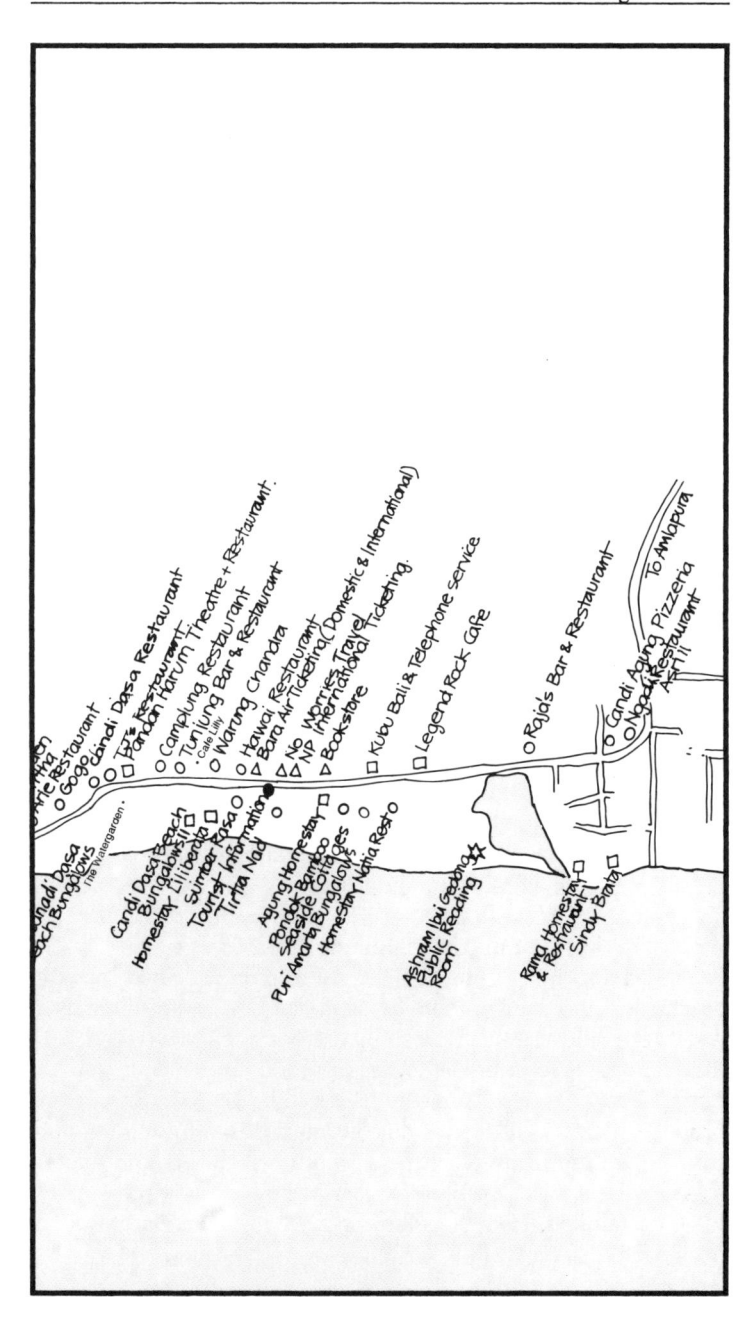

Map of Candidasa area showing:

- Candi Dasa Beach Bungalows
- The Watergarden
- Ggg Candi Dasa Restaurant
- Pandan Harum Theatre + Restaurant
- TJ's Restaurant
- Campung Restaurant
- Tunjung Restaurant
- Cafe Lilly
- Warung Chandra
- Hawai Restaurant
- Bara Air & Restaurant
- No Worries Restaurant (Domestic & International)
- NP International Travel Ticketing
- Bookstore
- Kubu Bali & Telephone Service
- Legend Rock Cafe
- Raja's Bar & Restaurant
- Candi Agung Pizzeria
- Napoli Restaurant
- Asrili
- To Amlapura
- Candi Dasa Beach Bungalows
- Homestay Liliberata
- Sumber Rasa
- Tourist Information
- Tirta Nadi
- Agung Homestay
- Pondok Bamboo Seaside Cottages
- Puri Amarta Bungalows
- Homestay Natia Rest
- Ashram Ibu Gedong Public Reading Room
- Rama Homestay & Restaurant
- Sindy Brata

and should be used as a guide only. All rooms have air-conditioning unless fan-cooled is specified.
The telephone code is 0363.
Amankila, Manggis, ph 41 333. Perched on the hillside, the Amankila was created as a celebration of the sea. Each suite is a spacious pavilion with an outdoor terrace and some have their own swimming pool. Price depends on the views. The beach club, Amankila's daytime haunt, is located on the beachfront amidst a coconut grove. Both the restaurant and bar have stunning views to Nusa Penida and Lembongan and the offerings are sublime (with prices to match). Rooms from $360.

The Serai Hotel, Buitan, Manggis, Ph 41 011. Nestled on a secluded beach in a coconut grove, The Serai is gaining a reputation for affordable luxury. Traditional Balinese-style pavilions blend with 90s sophisticated simplicity and boldly-coloured furnishings. Rooms are set in two-storey accommodation with either a terrace or balcony outlook to the handsome pool and beach. Seven or so kilometres out of Candi Dasa, there is a shuttle service for those wishing to escape. Few do though, being more content to luxuriate by the pool and indulge in the restaurant's fine offerings. In fact the restaurant alone is reason enough to stay here. Very modern and perfect for the climate, both the dinner and pool-side menus offer Mediterranean, modern Australian and Asian. This three-star hotel is reasonably priced with rooms from $120.

The Watergarden, ph 41 540. 12 rooms. Across the road from the beach, these charming thatch-roofed cottages are set amidst beautiful gardens and lily ponds. The salt-water pool is perfect for cooling-off and the popular TJ's restaurant offers full room service. Rooms are fan-cooled. Rooms from $55.

Bali Samudra Hotel, Ph 41 795. 56 rooms. Located on the beachfront and surrounded by lush gardens, Samudra has a restaurant and cafe, as well as a pool with a sunken bar. Excellent value for money. Rooms from $55.

Candi Beach Cottages, Mendire Beach, Ph 41 111. Beachfront property about 3 kilometres out of Candi Dasa offering a tennis court, swimming pool, fitness centre, games room, small basketball court, as well as a restaurant and swimming pool. Ideal for families. Has free shuttle service to Candi Dasa. Rooms from $55.

Hotel Rama Candi Dasa, Ph 41 974. Located about a kilometre out of town, but on the beach, this hotel has a swimming pool, tennis court, games room, restaurant and bar. Rooms from $40.

Nirwana Cottages, Candi Dasa Beach, Sengkidu, ph 41 136. Located on the beach, these bungalow cottages are set in landscaped gardens and all have small terraces. There's a restaurant and swimming pool with a sunken bar. Reasonably priced. Rooms from $40.

Candi Dasa Beach Bungalows II, Ph 35 536. Set in the centre of Candi Dasa, with a beachfront position. Rooms are set in a two-storey building and have either a balcony or verandah. Has a swimming pool and restaurant. Rooms from $35.

Eating Out

Cafe Lily. Pretty cafe offering a small but delightful menu from smoked salmon and poached asparagus to foccacia, profiterole and gorgeous cheesecake.

Candi Agung Pizzeria. Large and generous pizzas, as well as Indonesian dishes.

Kubu Bali. Huge tanks of seafood, the open kitchen and a large blackboard menu seduce passing trade. Reasonable seafood, as well as the typical offering of Indonesian dishes, but the service is poor. Avoid sitting under the stuffed rat in the back left-hand corner. Moderately priced.

Lotus Seafood. Large beachfront restaurant dotted with bright candles makes a pretty dinner setting. Menu is extensive including a range of excellent seafood dishes, as well as the usual Indo-Chinese offerings.

Pandan Restaurant. On the beach, renowned for its Indonesian and Chinese fare, as well as the excellent chilli crab.

Pondok Bamboo. Beachfront restaurant offering excellent fish, prawns, lobster and crab cooked to your liking.

Tirta Nadi Restaurant & Bar. Lots of good seafood and surprisingly good steaks. Stays open till late.

TJ's Cafe, Watergarden Hotel. Romantic and relaxed atmosphere is complemented by the pretty pond and miniature falls. The menu includes Indonesian and European dishes with a spicy Mexican 'special' thrown in. A little more expensive than most.

Toke Cafe. Small seafront cafe offers pizzas, pastas, seafood and

Indonesian meals in a relaxed and friendly environment.

Entertainment

The night life in Candi Dasa is fairly quiet, although it picks up a little in peak season. The *Beer Garden Disco* has occasional live bands playing covers, or a DJ spins hits for those wanting to strut their stuff on the small dance floor. The *Legend Rock Cafe* also has live bands depending on the season. Those desperate for a game of pool should head to the *Candi Bagus Pub*, or *Flamboyant* towards the Tenganan end of the resort.

Shopping

Candi Dasa is not a shopper's paradise, in fact if you're after clothing, jewellery, or carvings, forget it.

The Bookstore, on the main road, has a wide range of titles on Bali and Indonesia, and also sells good maps.

For general merchandise, Asri Shop has two stores (in the middle of town, and also out of town towards Amlapura).

Miscellaneous

Doctors

Two doctors are available at limited times. Inquire at the Candi Dasa Beach Bungalows II.

Money Changers

There are several money changers although the rate is not comparable with Kuta. Shop around.

Police

The Police are located at the Tenganan end of town, a few doors before Perama Travel.

Postal Agents and Telephones

There is a postal agent and *wartel* next to Kubu Bali.

Tours

Perama Travel organises day tours taking in various destinations, as do a number of the tourist offices located on the main street. Tours start at about Rp25,000 for one person.

Water Activities

Candi Dasa beach is great for snorkelling and diving, but not for surfing. A couple of hundred metres from the shore, near the breakers, is a snorkelling wonderland. A dazzling selection of multi-coloured fish darting in and out of labyrinths of coral, will entertain you for hours.

Most of the hotels rent snorkelling gear. For scuba gear see the Stingray Dive Centre at the Bali Samudra Indah Hotel or the Bali Dive Centre in the Candi Dasa Beach Bungalows II. Both offer diving in various places around the island.

Outlying Attractions

Amlapura

In times past, Amlapura was the capital of an affluent kingdom — now it is a weary little village. Once called Karangasem, its name was changed, according to local legend, to confuse malevolent spirits who orchestrated the eruptions of Gunung Agung — the bane of Karangasem. But to no avail, for in 1963, the town was again devastated by an outburst from the volcano. Lava never reached the town, but the attendant earthquakes and whirlwinds resulted in its isolation for three years. A huge lava flow is evident when entering the town from the south.

The last Raja of Karangasem, Agung Anglurah Ketut, built several water palaces worth visiting for their eccentric grandeur.

Puri Kangin

The famous residence of the late raja was built early this century. Slowly decaying, the palace is a whimsical mishmash of Balinese, Chinese and European architectural designs. Through the red-brick pagoda gateway, the main building is the Maskerdam (a corruption of "Amsterdam"), built as a tribute to the Dutch. Queen Wilhelmina donated much of the furniture and it's decorated with her family's crest. Visitors are not allowed in the building, so you'll have to peep through the windows. The *bale kambang*, surrounded by a small moat, was where the royal family hosted dance performances; and the two smaller *bale* were used for religious ceremonies. The palace is still inhabited by some of the raja's wives and his descendants, but visitors are welcome to wander around the compound. Admission Rp500; open daily from 8am-5pm.

Ujung Water Palace

Three kilometres out of Karangasem is the first of the Raja's water palaces. Built in the early 1920s, the magnificent and stately residence was set amidst green terraces and placid ponds. But alas no more. All that remains after the eruption of Gunung Agung in 1963 is a huge pool and a few statues and portals — woeful vestiges of a once great palace.

Ujung is 4km (2 miles) south of Amlapura and a bemo to Ujung from the Amlapura terminal costs about Rp500.

Tirta Gangga

On the slopes of Gunung Agung lies the second water palace, Tirta Gangga. The name means "water of the Ganges" and commemorates the Hindu's sacred river. Built in 1947, on the site of a natural spring, the landscape and fountains make this a fine place to enjoy the salubrious pools. Although the palace was damaged in the 1963 eruption of Gunung Agung and an earthquake in 1979, it has been restored and is an impressive arrangement of pools, fountains and channels in landscaped gardens. Enjoy lunch or stay overnight in the *Tirta Ayu Restaurant & Homestay*, which is set in the hillside of the complex. About 6km (4 miles) north-west of Amlapura, a bemo costs Rp700. Admission is Rp550, and Rp2000 to use the higher, deeper pool or Rp1000 to use the shallow pool.

The Mother Temple

The most sacred temple in all of Bali, *Pura Besakih* or the "Mother temple", graces the slopes of the venerated Gunung Agung. The temple is considered the essence of divine powers on Bali, and is visited by thousands upon thousands of pilgrims annually. Gunung Agung is the tallest mountain on Bali (3014m -9888ft), and the temple is nearly 1000m (3280ft) above sea level. Arrive before 9am, because Gunung Agung is often veiled in clouds by mid morning.

The name, "Mother Temple", is misleading as there is not a single temple, but a complex of 22 temples meandering up the mountainside. In prehistoric times, the auspicious Gunung

Agung was probably the site of a terraced sanctuary where animistic cults worshipped the god of the volcano. When the Majapahit Empire established itself at Gelgel, the Dewa Agung appropriated the sanctuary transforming it into a Hindu temple for the entire island. *Pura Besakih* retained the distinction even when the court shifted from Gelgel to Klungkung, and since those times, the complex has gradually increased.

At first sight, the temple complex appears a confusion of shrines. Nonetheless, the complex has a tripartite design which venerates the holy trinity of Siwa, Brahma and Wisnu. Additional shrines are located throughout the compound, representing all the regencies, as well as the entire pantheon of Hindu gods and ancestral deities. *Pura Penataran Agung*, "the Great Temple of State" is the symbolic centre of the Besakih complex and is a shrine to Siwa. *Pura Kiduling Kreteg*, the "temple south of the bridge" honours Brahma, while *Pura Batu Madeg*, the "temple of the standing stone" is dedicated to Wisnu. The longitudinal axis of these temples faces *kaja* (north), to the peak of the great Agung.

Pura Penataran Agung

At the top of some 50 steps is the split gate, or *candi bentar*, which opens onto the main courtyard. The courtyard has over 50 shrines half of which represent deities. A forest of *meru* towers (the more tiers, the higher the god), is impressive, but unlike most Balinese shrines, those in the Besakih complex are bereft of colour and ornate carvings.

The lotus throne or *padmasana* dates from the 17th century, and is the symbolic centre of the entire complex. The three seats of the temple are dedicated to Wisnu (left), Siwa (centre) and Brahma (right). During festivals, the seats are enshrined with cloth: black for Wisnu, white for Siwa and red for Brahma. Most of the structures in the temple were built after the earthquake of 1917. Unfortunately, visitors are not permitted in this temple, but a climb above the courtyards enables views of the many shrines and statuary, as well as the coastline.

Festivals
Bhatara Turun Kabeh

An annual festival, celebrated on the full moon of the tenth lunar month (in March or April) is the time when the "gods descend together", a basic translation of the name of the month-long festival. Conducted by Brahman priests, it is the most important ritual in the Balinese calendar.

There are, in fact, over 70 rituals held each year, most of which are conducted by Besakih's own priests.

Eka Dasa Rudra

The most important ritual celebration in Bali, the Eka Dasa Rudra is celebrated every hundred years to purify the cosmos and placate Rudra, the merciless manifestation of Siwa.

In 1963, amidst political turmoil, Bali prepared itself for the most important ritual of the century. President Sukarno had invited many international guests, and although smoke and steam were issuing from the mountain during February, the government continued with preparations despite warnings from religious leaders. On March 12, Gunung Agung exploded. The mountain erupted with such force that much of the temple complex was destroyed. Fatalities reached 1600, crops were destroyed, over 50 villages were ruined, and huge ominous, black clouds covered east Java. Thousands of people were evacuated to Sulawesi. Today, there is little evidence of the destruction except for the blackened countryside north-east of Klungkung.

Eka Dasa Rudra was held again in 1979 on a propitious date, and the mother mountain was serene throughout.

Maintenance of the Complex

Originally, the Dewa Agung was responsible for the temple through vassal princes, and even when the Dutch took over, the arrangement continued. The only regency that has not been designated temples to maintain is Tabanan, because it has its own state temple, *Pura Luhur*. Since 1979, and the successful *Eka Dasa Rudra*, Besakih is considered to be **the** Hindu temple in Indonesia, and consequently is partly funded by the Indonesian government. Admission is by donation and is recorded in a log.

Suspiciously, there are no donations under a couple of thousand rupiah — one suspects that a nought is added here or there. But, given that all donations fund the temple, and this is Bali's temple, a couple of dollars is little price to pay for hours spent wandering through the maze of Hindu shrines. After paying admission, visitors are besieged by tour guides offering their services — you'd be wise to take a guide, but negotiate the price before leaving. The complex is huge, and three hours can easily pass walking amongst these wondrous shrines. And remember to wear sensible walking shoes.

Gunung Agung

All roads lead to Gunung Agung — so it is said. The most sacred of mountains, it is also an active volcano. The Balinese regard the "Great Mountain" as the "navel of the world" and the basis of the *kaja - kelod* axis. Everything that is holy faces towards the mountain or *kaja*, while everything that is evil points towards the sea or *kelod*. The construction of temples and houses obeys this principle, and indeed many people sleep with their heads towards Gunung Agung. The cone of the volcano has an elevation of 3014m (9888ft), and rose to 3142m (10308ft) before the eruption in 1963.

If you want to climb Gunung Agung, a guide is essential, as there are many tracks and it is easy to get lost. Guides wander around the complex at Besakih and are not apprehensive about approaching tourists. The climb is much more difficult than that of Gunung Batur, and takes an entire day. In fact, most leave prepared to camp overnight. The trek should start very early, before 3am on a night with a full-ish moon. **Never attempt the climb in the wet season.**

Tulamben

Some of Bali's most interesting diving is found at Tulamben, where the shallow wreck of WWII US cargo ship is now festooned with colourful corals and schools of tropical fish. It is also one of the few places one can stay on the east coast, north of Candi Dasa. The beach, although pebbled, is quite pretty and the water is clear and good for snorkelling. There are a number of losmen and *warung* along the main beach, and it can get quite busy here on the weekends, and throughout June and July.

The wreck of the *Liberty* is the most popular dive site on Bali. It was torpedoed by a Japanese submarine about 15km south-west of Lombok on 11 January 1942. Two US destroyers tried to tow it to Singaraja, but it started to take in water and was beached at Tulamben. The crew were evacuated, but its cargo of raw rubber and railway parts were never retrieved. It sat on the beach until 1963, when the eruption of Gunung Agung caused it to slip into deeper water where it broke into two pieces.

It lies only 50 metres offshore, parallel with the coast, and its bow is only metres from the surface. There are over 400 species of reef fish, mostly accustomed to divers, and they will often eat out of your hand. The wreck can be visited by up to 40 divers at a time, especially between 11.30am and 4pm, so avoid the site at that time.

There are a couple of dive centres along the beach which offer dives, and the going price is about US$50 for two dives.

How to Get There

Tulamben is 104km from Denpasar, and about 40km from Candi Dasa. From Candi Dasa by car, the two main routes are either the coastal road from Ujung to Amed, or through the foothills of Gunung Agung. The latter is probably the quickest and easiest route to take. For those travelling by bemo, Tulamben is a stop on the main route from Amlapura to Singaraja.

Accommodation

There are a number of small hotels like the *Paradise Palm Beach Bungalows* on the beachfront (rooms from $25) or the *Ganda Mayu* (rooms from $25) which is the closest to the wreck. The nicest hotel is probably the *Mimpi Resort*. Set in landscaped gardens, these charming cottages have standard rooms, garden villas or suites. The restaurant offers Indonesian and European delights and the pool is by the sea. Mimpi is fully equipped for qualified divers, or for novices wishing to qualify for their PADI certificate. Rooms from $30. Inquiries to the booking office on (0361) 701 070 or direct on 21 642.

Buleleng

The regency of Buleleng is a narrow band of land across the top of the island of Bali. To the north is the Bali Sea, and to the south, Buleleng shares borders with every regency except Gianyar and Klungkung. The largest regency, it covers an area of 1370 sq km and is isolated from the rest of the island by a chain of volcanoes stretching across the island east to west.

The climate is drier than in south Bali, and wet-rice cultivation is not as extensive; instead, the region is known for its fruit, coffee and clove plantations. In the dry season, the parched red earth splits, the grass withers, and doe-eyed cattle roam amongst fruit trees. Famed for its black sand beaches, natural springs and waterfalls, Buleleng is very different to the south, and that's half the attraction.

Cultural Character

But Buleleng isn't just geographically different to the south. Its physical isolation from the south, coupled with its proximity to the Java Sea and foreign influences, have enabled the regency to develop a distinct cultural character. The regency's intricate style of carving adorns many temples and palaces, and is some of the most stunning sculpture to be found on the island. Many of the dances are more aggressive than those found in the south; the strenuous and frenetic *Kebyar* dance originated in Buleleng, as did the suggestive, *Joged*. The jazzy *Gong Kebyar* orchestra was also an innovation of the north, and styles are now featured in the programs of dance performances in the south.

History

During the 17th century, Buleleng reached its political zenith under Gusti Panji Sakti, founder of the regency, who extended his realm by conquering East Java and Karangasem. But power waned under Sakti's grandsons, who were caught off guard when the Raja of Karangasem embarked on a crusade to acquire the throne. In 1823, Buleleng successfully rebelled against Karangasem's authority, but its freedom was fleeting.

The Dutch were also interested in northern Bali, and between 1846 and 1848, made three assaults on Buleleng. The first two proved unsuccessful, but the third saw the largest assembled force ever used in the Archipelago. The Raja of Buleleng, assisted by his brother the Balinese hero Djilantik, fought valiantly against the Dutch, but was defeated and died in battle.

In 1849, the raja's family signed an agreement with the Dutch to relinquish power in all but name. The Dutch ruled through a family member, but it wasn't until 1882 that they officially controlled northern Bali. Indeed, the Dutch dominated the north decades before the south, and Dutch influences are more prevalent in Buleleng than anywhere else on the island. Ironically, during colonisation, Singaraja was the capital of Bali, and the gateway to the rest of the world.

Today, many travellers seem to shun Buleleng, unaware of its manifold charms, and the hospitality of its people.

Singaraja

Singaraja has experienced successive historical transformations; first as a regal court centre, then as the capital of Dutch commerce and administration in Asia, and finally as a district capital. Although it's a modern, bustling city, Singaraja also marks time. Horse-drawn dokar still saunter along the tree-lined streets. Old Chinese shops and markets reflect a colonial age.

Before the first surfaced roads connecting the north with the south were built, the northern regency was exposed to more international than southern influences. Bugis traders from Sulawesi frequented the northern port, Chinese and Muslim traders made Singaraja their home, and then there were the Dutch. Many of the buildings in Singaraja attest to the various international influences it has experienced through the centuries; and the Chinese Temple, mosques and Christian churches bear testimony to the diversity.

"Singaraja" means "lion king", and the huge winged lion statue at the intersection of Jl. Veteran and Jl. Ngurah Rai, built as a monument to Indonesian Independence, represents the heroic spirit of the people of Buleleng. The pentagonal plinth symbolises the *panca sila* (the five creeds of Indonesia), the lion's wings each have 17 feathers, the cob of corn he holds has eight leaves, and with the 45 grains of corn they represent August 17, 1945: the day of Indonesian Independence.

How to Get There

By Public Bemo
A regular express bus departs from Ubung terminal in Denpasar, to Singaraja's Banyusari terminal in the west. The journey takes two hours, travels via Bedugul, and the fare is Rp2500. From Kereneng terminal in Denpasar, the bemo travels along the eastern coast road, via Gianyar, Klungkung and Amlapura, to Singaraja's eastern terminal, Kampung Tinggi. The journey takes five hours and costs Rp2500.

Bemo also run from the terminals in Klungkung and Amlapura and cost Rp2000.

Bemo to and from Gilimanuk cost Rp2100, and arrive and depart from the Banyusari terminal in Singaraja.

By Car
There are many ways to reach Singaraja from Denpasar, and the roads are sealed. The most direct route is 78km (48 miles) and takes about two to three hours, via Mengwi, Baturityi and Bedugul. Or, the eastern coast road passes through Gianyar, Klungkung, Amlapura, Tirta Gangga, Kubu, then on to Singaraja. This route takes about five hours but the views are stunning; Gunung Agung on one side, the sea on the other.

Tourist Information
The Buleleng Government Tourism Office is located at Jl. Veteran 23, ph 61 141 (open Mon-Fri 8am-5pm).

Accommodation
Few travellers stay in Singaraja, as Lovina is only 10km (6 miles)

away and has many fine hotels with the accustomed comforts. Most of Singaraja's hotels are located on Jl. Jen Achmad Yani, and are simple losmen-style accommodation not familiar with the tourist trade.

Hotel Duta Karya, Jl. Jen Achmad Yani 59, ph 21 467. Simple and clean fan-cooled rooms from $15.

Tresna Homestay, Jl. Gajah Mada 95, ph 21 816. Antique shop and guesthouse has nice rooms with shared bathrooms from $8.

Telephone code is 0362.

Local Transport

By Public Bemo

Singaraja has two bemo terminals: Kampung Tinggi on the eastern side (Jl. Surapati) and Banyusari on the western side (Jl. Yen Achmad Yani). Bemo run frequently between these stations using the main roads, and dokar ply the back roads.

Bemo around the city cost Rp150, and a bemo to Lovina costs Rp400 (although "tourist fares" are popular).

By Car

Travelling around Singaraja by car is much easier than negotiating the streets of Denpasar. And finding a park is not impossible. There are two petrol stations in Singaraja and one at Seririt. Jl. Yen Achmad Yani, near the Banyusari bemo station, Jl. Patih Jelantik Gingsir and Jl. W. R. Surpratman (Kubujati/Pen-arukan), Seririt.

Eating Out

Singaraja has many Chinese restaurants and a few serve Indonesian food. Most of them are found along Jl. Yen Achmad Yani, have menus in English and are inexpensive. For instance *Gandhi's*, Jl. Yen Achmad Yani 25, is famous for its Chinese food, as is *Kartika's* next door. Further west along the same street try *Arina* at No 53, *Cafeteria* at No 55 and *Cafe 59*.

The night markets have a huge range of *warung* and fruit stalls set up in back lanes between Jl. Durian and Jl. Gaja Mada. Lit by kerosene lamps, most of the stalls have little benches where you can sit and watch and eat. Enjoy the hustle and bustle, because this is Singaraja's night life.

Entertainment

There are no Balinese dance shows for visitors because all theatre performances are part of ceremonies, so finding this type of entertainment is purely chance. The tourist office does not supply information on entertainment.
There are however, three cinemas:
Singaraja Theatre, Jl. Surapati, ph 21 391.
Wijaya Theatre, Jl. Pramuka 42, ph 41 627.
Bioskop Muda Ria, Jl. Ngurah Rai.

Shopping

Singaraja is not a good place to shop, however, general items are much cheaper than those found in the south, so stock up.

There are two art/antique shops worth a browse: *Miranda's* Jl. Yen Achmad Yani; and *Srikandi,* Jl. Diponegoro 46.

Miscellaneous

Medical Services
Rumah Sakit Umum (public hospital), Jl. Ngurah Rai,
ph 41 046. Dr Kwari Dermawan, Jl. A. Yani 58.

Money Changers
A few hotels change money, but banks are the best bet. Generally banks do not give cash advances on credit cards.
Bank Negara Indonesia, Jl. Surapati, ph 41 340.
Bank Bumi Daya, Jl. Erlangga 14, ph 41 245.
Bank Dagang Negara, Jl. Yen Achmad Yani, ph 41 344.
Bank Pembangunan Daerah, Jl. Yen Achmad Yani 56, ph 21 245.
Bank Perniagaan Umum, Jl. Gajah Mada, ph 21 491.
Bank Rakyat Indonesia, Jl. Ngurah Rai 14, ph 41 245.
Bank Seri Partha, Jl. Ngurah Rai, ph 61 252.

Photo Developers
Fuji, Jl. Yen Achmad Yani.
Reflex, Jl. Diponegoro.

Post Office
Jl. Gaja Mada 158 (open Mon-Sat 8am-5pm), Sun 9am-1pm).
Jl. Jenderal Sudirman 68.

Telephones
The telephone/telegraph offices are located at Jl. Letkol Wisnu 2, and Jl. Gaja Mada 154 (next to the post office).

Sightseeing

Gedong Kirtya Library
On Jl. Veteran (next door to the Tourism Office), is a library that houses a collection of Balinese literature and religious texts all inscribed on palm leaves, known as *lontar*. Other manuscripts are among the earliest written documents found on the island. Opening times are Sunday to Monday 7am-1pm; Friday 7-11am; and Saturday 7am-noon.

Puri Agung Sinar Nadi
Behind the library is a textile factory housed in the "Western Court" of the former palace of the King of Singaraja. Here beautiful sashes and *kain* (the female equivalent to the sarong) can be purchased at reasonable prices — remember one piece of cloth can take a month to weave! There is another weaving factory, Berdikari, on Jl. Dewi Sartika.

East of Singaraja

Banyuning
Known for its pottery, this little village is situated a kilometre east of Singaraja. The pieces are unglazed as they have no kilns.

Sangsit
Located 8km (5 miles) east of Singaraja, the village has one of the finest temples in the regency, the *Pura Beji*. Built in the 15th century, it is dedicated to the rice goddess, Dewi Sri, and is owned by the members of the local irrigation board, or *subak*. Standing in the middle of a rice field, this temple illustrates the distinctive filigree style of architecture found in Buleleng.

Rice terraces near Ubud in Central Bali

Fishing on Lake Bratan.

Jagaraga
About 7km (4 miles) beyond the *Pura Beji* is the turn for Jagaraga. In 1849, trapped by Dutch forces, Djilantik's consort and her retinue walked into the enemy gunfire rather than submit to the foe. Today, the only visible sign of the Dutch presence is found in the *Pura Dalem* (temple).

Sawan
Several kilometres inland from Jagaraga, Sawan is noted for its manufacture of Balinese *gamelan* instruments. The village also has its own bamboo orchestra, known as an *angklung*. Visitors are more than welcome to watch the gong-makers at work.

Air Sanih
Adjacent to the beach is the pretty landscaped swimming pool known as Air Sanih. The icy cold water is said to flow from a natural spring that originates at Lake Batur, and the clear pool is ideal for a swim, as is the pint-sized kiddies' pool. Nearby, the manicured Botanic Gardens create a beautiful and serene place to spend the day. A *warung* and bungalows are available.

South of Singaraja

Beratan Village
Located south of Singaraja (travel down Jl. Veteran and turn right, heading for Denpasar) is this village of silversmiths. Noted for their original style, sometimes referred to as the "Buleleng style", the silversmiths craft ornate jewellery and ceremonial pieces, which border on the rococo. The style is probably not to everyone's liking.

Gitgit Waterfall
The dramatic waterfalls of Gitgit, 10km (6 miles) south of Singaraja, are just the thing for weary travellers. The road climbs steeply, affording views of lush hillocks, and the waterfall is located on a trail less than a kilometre from the main road.

Bali Handara Kosaido Country Club
About 13km (9 miles) south of Gitgit is the renowned Bali Handara Kosaido Golf Club, ph 288 944. Rated in the top 20 courses in the world. Green fees are US$60 for 18 holes, and a half-set of clubs can be hired for US$10. The Country Club is a

fine hotel with full amenities including a sauna and fitness centre. Rooms from US$80-$300.

Lovina Beach

Located 10km (6 miles) west of Singaraja is the tourist resort of Lovina, which actually includes the beaches (east to west) of Pemaron, Tukad Mungga, Anturan, Kalibukbuk, Kaliasem and Temukas. "Lovina" was supposedly coined in the 1960s by the last Raja of Buleleng, who felt that the love the people bore the land was reflected in the scenery. Since the late 1970s, restaurants and losmen have sprouted, and although tourism has increased, Lovina is very different from the south. An exquisite beach, the atmosphere is relaxed, the pace slow, and the night life (except for a few places in Kalibukbuk) is almost non-existent. As yet, there are few hawkers.

How to Get There

By Public Bemo
In Singaraja, bemo travel during the daylight hours to Lovina, picking up along Jl. Yen Achmad Yani, and the fare is Rp400.

To reach Lovina from Denpasar, Karangasem or Gilimanuk you must change at Singaraja.

By Car
Coming from the south or east, you have to drive through Singaraja to arrive at Lovina.

Accommodation

Accommodation has been listed by village (from east to west) to reflect each location. Many losmen-style hotels are situated on the beach, while newer hotels tend to be set away from the beach. In all cases, they're much cheaper than in the south. Peak season is from mid-June to late August and again in December. Accommodation should be booked well in advance. All rates, which should be used as a guide only, are based on one night and are in US$ and do not include the 10% government tax and service charges. First class hotels really don't exist, but again, prices are much cheaper than in the south, and are usually negotiable in the low season. **The telephone code is 0362.**

Pemaron and Tukad Mungga
Far away from the tourist concentration of Kalibukbuk and marking the eastern end of Lovina Beach, these villages have few amenities, and it's very quiet.
Baruna Beach Cottages, ph 23 745. Beachfront hotel. Rooms from $20.

Anturan
The tiny fishing village of Anturan is perfect for those wishing for quieter environs. The main turn-off is opposite the petrol station and *Harmony Restaurant*.
Bali Taman Beach Hotel, Anturan, ph 22 126. Set on the beach. Room $35. *Simon's Seaside Cottages (aka Yuda's)*, Anturan, ph 22 261. On the beach. Rooms from $25.

Banyualit
The Banyualit road is the site of new developments. There are some shops and restaurants. It is only a short walk to the beach.
Aneka Lovina Beach Bungalows, Banyualit, ph 23 827. A new hotel, it's set on the beach. Rooms from $55. *Banyualit Cottages*, Banyualit, ph 25 889. Rooms from $30. *Kalibukbuk Beach Inn*, Banyualit, ph 21 701. Clean and simple hotel fronts onto the beach, but is separated from it by a wall. Rooms from $15. *Palma Beach Cottages*, Banyualit, 23 775. Rooms from $45.

Kalibukbuk
Bordered by Ketapang and Bina Ria Streets, Kalibukbuk has some restaurants and bars, and most of Lovina's tourist facilities.
Rambutan, Jl. Ketapang, ph 23 388. Well-furnished rooms set apart amidst gorgeous gardens, with swimming pool and restaurant. Highly recommended. Rooms from $30.

Kaliasem
West of Kalibukbuk, the road steers towards the beach, where there's a concentration of restaurants and accommodation.
Lovina Beach Hotel, ph 23 473. Lovina's oldest hotel, right by the beach. Rooms from $20.

Local Transport
Bemo are the easiest and cheapest form of transport. They travel along the coastal road and will generally pick up anywhere.

Bemo travelling east to Singaraja cost Rp400, and west to Banjar cost Rp600. The other alternative is to hitch-hike, which costs about the same as a bemo.

Eating Out

Most of the restaurants are centred around Kalibukbuk, and that's where you'll find the "night life".

Arya's, Kakatua, Mailaku, Malibu - Extensive Western and Indonesian/Chinese menu with lots of different cakes. Has large video screen and live music. Also offers free transport to and from hotels in the Lovina area. *Wina's*. Usual offering of Western and Indonesian dishes but its bar attracts a few people.

Water Activities

Scuba diving gear can be hired from *Spice Dive* in Lovina, or *Lovina Marine Resort*, Bali Lovina Beach Cottages. *Prahu* can be rented from anywhere on the beach for about Rp8000 an hour, or from most hotels. Wear sneakers because the coral is sharp. It is advisable to swim early in the day as the water clouds.

Outlying Attractions

Singsing Falls

West of Lovina, about a kilometre along the main Seririt road, is the village of Labuanhaji and Singsing waterfall. Take a bemo from Lovina (Rp250) to the dirt road with the sign to Singsing Air Terjun. A short walk leads to the bottom pool -suitable for swimming, but only in the wet season.

Banjar

The village of Banjar, about 5km (3 miles) west of Lovina, is an easy couple of hours' walk. The village market has a wonderful array of oddities, and the people are extremely friendly.

Seririt

Located 22km (14 miles) from Singaraja, the once bustling trade capital of Buleleng is now a sleepy town. Devastated by the earthquake of 1976, it was subsequently rebuilt.

Pulaki

Further west, is the village of Pulaki, about 53km (33 miles) from

Singaraja, and the temple, *Pura Agung Pulaki*, is 2km (1 mile) from the main road. The large and striking temple, built between a sheer cliff and the lapping shore, is home to a band of rapacious monkeys. Take care with all belongings.

From Pulaki, there are more hot springs 4km (2.5 miles) down the road at Pemuteran, outside of the temple.

West Bali National Park

An hour's drive from Lovina is the Taman Nasional Bali Barat, the West Bali National Park. If not with an organised tour, it's a 15-minute drive to the guard-post (PPA) at Teluk Terima. Visitors must purchase a permit (Rp500) and a guide (Rp5000) is mandatory by law. The best source of information is found at the headquarters which are located at Cekik, 2km (1 mile) south of Gilimanuk (about as west as you can get). A government office, it's open during the week until 2pm, and closes at 11am on Fridays and noon on Saturdays. The staff are very helpful and enthusiastic, and there's even a small library and exhibition.

The national park has 76,312 hectares of untouched flora and fauna. This is the natural habitat of the rare *Jalak Bali* or "Bali Starling" (*leucopsar Rothschildi*). The wild Javan buffalo (*bos Javanicus*) is another rare species. Other wildlife include wild pigs, barking deer, leaf monkeys, and unique green fowl. The park is simply teeming with wildlife.

Banyuwedang

On the outskirts of the national park are the oft-visited springs of Banyuwedang. These glorious springs, according to local lore, have curative powers, and people come from miles around to splash in the salutary waters.

Pulau Menjangan

From the park's Buleleng entrance, it's a 15-minute drive to Teluk Terima where small motorised boats can be hired for the 30-minute crossing to Pulau Menjangan. This haven, also known as Deer Island, is the home of the Java Deer. There are no *warung*, no bemo, and few people — an idyllic sanctuary, really. Remember to take a packed lunch. More enchanting than the deer, are the beautiful, psychedelic reefs.

Jembrana

Jembrana would probably be ignored by travellers if it were not for the ferry terminal at Gilimanuk. Little of its mountainous jungle has been explored and myths of the regency's strange inhabitants abound. Negara is the capital of Jembrana, and as in the village of Gilimanuk, Hinduism has yielded to Islam.

From the South to Negara

Driving from the south through Tabanan, the road eventually ends at the intersection at Antosari. The road north leads past rice terraces to Pupuan, then Seririt, then hugs the north coast to Singaraja. South it stretches past Soka and Payan, then hugs the south coast to Mendoya, meandering inland to Negara, and finally arriving at Gilimanuk. But not before some wonderful views across to Java. The town of Pekutantan (20km [12 miles] east of Negara) is the last place to turn north for Singaraja.

Negara

The capital of the regency, Negara possesses a few government offices, a couple of losmen and a few small warung. To a visitor it seems like a town in slumber. That is, until September, after the rice is harvested, when Negara is enlivened with spectacular bull races. Negara is 95km (59 miles) from Denpasar. Bemo depart from Tabanan (Rp900) or from Denpasar's Ubung terminal (Rp1500).

Palasari and Belimgingsari

Many of the people living in these villages are Christian migrants from the overpopulated areas of eastern and southern Bali. The government granted them uncultivated land in the hope of developing the area. The biggest Catholic church in eastern Indonesia is located in Palasari, and there are other denominations as well. But this is Bali and many of the churches are adorned with typical Balinese motifs, featuring biblical characters rather than those from the Hindu epics.

Gilimanuk

Gilimanuk, on the westernmost tip of Bali, is the village where east meets west. Most of the domestic tourists enter and leave Bali via this port. In Singaraja, bemo leave the Banyusari terminal (Rp1000) for Gilimanuk; and from Denpasar, bemo depart from the Ubung terminal (Rp2200) for the two-hour journey. Gilimanuk is 128km (80 miles) from Denpasar via Tabanan; and 85km (53 miles) from Singaraja, via Seririt and the National Park.

The Ferry

Despite the fact that the strait separating Bali from Java is less than 3km and is only 60m deep, the waters can be treacherous. The crossing takes 25 minutes, and both private and government ferries ply the route, departing at 15 to 20 minute intervals.

For passengers, the ferry prices range from Rp400 for the deck, to Rp1200 for first class; and stowage for motorbikes cost Rp1000; cars Rp7000. The ferry docks in Java at Ketapang and buses leave from there for Surabaya.

Tabanan

The regency of Tabanan stretches from the south-west coast all the way to the slopes of Gunung Batukau. The second-highest mountain in Bali, it is seldom mentioned, but Batukau dominates inland views, and has a beautiful ancestral shrine, *Pura Luhur*. Most visitors only venture to Tabanan to witness the sunset at Tanah Lot; or to spend a night in the mystical mountains of Bedugul on the way to Lovina.

Tabanan is mainly an agrarian district and has **one of the highest yields of rice in Indonesia.** On the southern plains, rice is cultivated alternately with nitrogen-rich soybeans to revitalise the soil, and in the mountains, vegetables and flowers are grown. Some of the most stunning landscape is seen when driving from Denpasar through Bedugul to the north.

Mengwi

North-west of Denpasar, Mengwi was the capital of the former powerful 17th century kingdom. All that remains of that time is the *Pura Taman Ayun*, and although the temple is said to be magnificent, it warrants no special journey.

Sangeh Monkey Forest

Fifteen kilometres from Mengwi is the village of Sangeh, location of the famed monkey forest (Bukit Sari) and its temple, *Pura Bukit Sari*. Monkeys have a special status in the Hindu religion and a number of temples have monkey "guardians", including *Ulu Watu* and the *Pura Dalem* in Ubud.

Tabanan Town

On the much-travelled road from Denpasar, not far from the Badung border, is the town of Tabanan. The capital of the regency, Tabanan is a commercial and administrative centre with little testament to its illustrious past. It's only attraction is the Subak Museum, which provides a historical perspective of rice-farming co-operatives. A kilometre east of Tabanan, in Sanggulan village, is the Subak Museum. *Subak* are the rice-growing co-operatives found all over Bali, and the museum houses a historical perspective on the formation and evolution of communal rice farming. There are a few losmen and *warung* in the town, but this really is not a good place to stay overnight.

How to Get There

By Bemo

Bemo depart from Denpasar's Ubung terminal and cost Rp700.

By Car

Tabanan is located 21km (13 miles) from Denpasar. By car, take the main road north-west from Denpasar passing through the villages of Lukluk and Kapal.

Outlying Attractions

Marga Village

About 15km (9 miles) north-east of Tabanan is the village of

Marga. Here lies a national shrine to I Gusti Ngurah Rai, who in 1946, lead the Tabanan forces against the Dutch in a *puputan*.

Krambitan Village
West of Tabanan, 12km (7 miles) away, is the village known for its *Tektekan* performance. Not so much a dance as an exorcism, the performance is incorporated into the island's annual day of exorcism, *Nyepi*. Two palaces built by the Tabanan royal family are located here, and both offer rooms for rent. The old palace, *Puri Krambitan* (owned by the twin grandsons of the late king), has an ornate concert hall decorated with Chinese porcelain tiles. The second palace, *Puri Anyar*, holds performances of the *Calon Arang* trance dance which features Rangda the witch.

Yeh Panas
The springs, regarded as sacred by the locals, are located 12km (7 miles) north of Tabanan on the way to *Pura Luhur* on the slopes of Gunung Batukau. The hot sulphurous springs were used by the Japanese stationed in Tabanan during the war.

Tanah Lot

The regency's main attraction is the temple at Tanah Lot which is associated with the priest Nirartha. One of the six *Sad Kahyangan* temples, it is visited by more tourists than any other sight in Bali. On a good day, the setting sun can create a wondrous backdrop to the outcrop of rocks and temple. Gorgeous pinks and oranges are contrasted with the blackened formation. On a bad day, it's just disappointing. The diminutive rocky island is a short walk from the shore and accessible only during low tide. Not that that matters. The temple is locked and tourists are not permitted in. Most people only visit to take photographs, and by the way, the best shots are taken from the headland on the left when facing the temple.

By car from Denpasar, take the road which eventually leads to Tabanan and turn left at the stoplight at Kediri which leads right down to the car park at Tanah Lot.

Gunung Batukau

Called the "coconut-shell mountain", this extinct volcano is the biggest mountain in the western part of the chain that severs north Bali from the south. The volcano is 2275m (7464ft) high and is carpeted with dense rainforest. On its slopes lies *Pura Luhur*, one of Bali's six national temples belonging to the *Sad Kahyangan* group. Guides can be hired if you want help to climb the mountain, as the ascent can be very dangerous.

Bedugul

Once upon a time, tourists seeking the quietude of the mountains fled to Ubud. Thankfully, most of them hadn't heard of Bedugul and environs. In fact, it's still a well-kept secret. Bedugul is a serene little village huddled on the shores of Lake Bratan in the crater of the long-extinct volcano, Gunung Catur (2096m - 6877ft). As far from the tropical coastal landscape as is possible, **Bedugul** and its sister village, **Candikuning,** are true mountain retreats. By early afternoon, the still lake and surrounding mountains are often shrouded in thick, white clouds, creating a mystical ambience. Make sure you pack a jumper because it gets quite cold at night. The cool clime, high rainfall, and rich volcanic soils make Bedugul and vicinity a fertile area producing most of the flowers found on Bali.

How to Get There

By Bemo
Bemo depart from Denpasar's Ubung terminal for Bedugul and Candikuning, cost Rp1000. The trip takes about 1.5 hours.

By Car
Bedugul is 48km (30 miles) from Denpasar and 30km (19 miles) from Singaraja. The road from Denpasar to Bedugul eventually ends at Singaraja. The views are spectacular, especially before Bedugul, where high in the mountains, the landscape is filled with beautiful hillocks, majestic mountains and glassy lakes. Drive only during the daylight hours.

Accommodation
Prices based on one night's accommodation are in US$, do not include tax and service charges, and should be used as a guide only. **The telephone code is 0362**

Pacung Resort, Baturiti, ph (0368) 21 038. Rooms from $80.
Bedugul Hotel, Bedugul, ph 226 593. Rooms from $40.
Ashram Hotel, Candikuning, ph 22 439. Rooms from $25.
Bukit Mungsu Indah, Baturiti, ph Baturiti 22. Rooms from US$20.
There are many small losmen in Bedugul village, near the Botanic Gardens. Don't be reluctant to bargain.

Local Transport
Bemo operate between Bedugul and Candikuning, cost Rp300, but it's only a refreshing 20-minute walk between villages.

Eating Out
There are only a few *warung* in Bedugul and Candikuning, but all the hotels listed above have restaurants.

Sightseeing

Botanic Gardens
Half a kilometre from the lake (towards Denpasar) is the *Kebun Raya Eka Karya Bali*, or Botanic Gardens.

Pura Ulun Danu Bratan
On the shores of Lake Bratan, Candikuning, is *Pura Ulun Danu*, dedicated to the goddess of the lake, Dewi Danu. Much revered for her powers over fertility, she also favours the people with the vital waters of the lake. Built right on the shores of Lake Bratan, two courtyards, one with an 11-tiered pagoda, are surrounded by water. When the clouds descend, obscuring much of the mountains, the temple has an ethereal atmosphere — much more dramatic than other oft-visited temples. The main complex on the shore, *Pura Teratai Bang*, is a temple of "origin" and is dedicated to Brahma. Admission is Rp500 and remember to wear a sash. Water-proof shoes are a must - muddy all year.

Japanese Caves
Across the lake from Candikuning (adjacent to the Bedugul Hotel) are the Japanese Caves. These caves excavated by Indonesian POWs during WWII, who were shot when they completed their task. The caves are accessible by canoe.

Glossary

aben cremation or the cremation ceremony.
adat traditional law or custom; unwritten code of conduct governing behaviour, inheritance, ownership of land, rituals of birth, marriage and death, rice cultivation, courtship etc. *Adat* is the law of the land and the oldest and most respected law.
Agama Bali Balinese Hindu religion otherwise known as Tirta Agama, Religion of the Holy Water.
agung great, big.
air panas literally, hot springs.
aling aling a wall behind the entrance gate to a family compound or temple which prevents demons from entering - it seems demons have problems negotiating corners.
alun alun the main town square, usually an expanse of lawn for sporting events and festivals etc.
angklung an ensemble of bamboo instruments.
anjing a dog, usually a pet; see *cecing*.
arak distilled palm or rice brandy.
Arjuna one of the five Pandawa brothers in the *Mahabharata*.

babi guling spit-roasted suckling pig.
bade funeral tower.
bale open-air pavilion, supported by posts.
bale agung a large pavilion where the village elders gather.
bale banjar village clubhouse where the banjar meets, and the site of community events; also where the *gamelan* orchestra rehearses.
Bali Aga indigenous, pre-Hindu inhabitants who resisted the cultural, social and political influences of the Majapahit Empire.
balian healer or traditional leader.
banjar village council consisting of married men who organise local affairs.
banten offerings to the gods.
banteng wild cattle of Indonesia.
banyan a sacred tree for the Balinese, usually a fig, with tangled roots which sprawl for metres around the tree. Also the tree under which Buddha found enlightenment. The *banyan* is supposedly eternal, feeding itself from the seeds, which drop on the ground. Temples and houses are often built near the site of a *banyan* tree.
bapak mister, father; the polite form of address to an older man.
baris warrior dance.
barong based on the 10th century Javanese king, Erlangga. Although a monstrous-looking creature, the Barong is a goodie who struggles against the evil witch Rangda (Erlangga's mother Mahendratta), in the *calon arang* myth. The *barong* is also a dance which features these characters.
Bedulu the last ruler of the Pejeng dynasty, defeated by the Majapahit minister, Gaja Mada in 1343AD.
Beh! an exclamation of surprise.
bemo a privately owned truck used for public transport.
betel slightly narcotic nut of *areca* palm, chewed with the leaf of the *sirih* vine and lime paste. *Pedanda* often chew the concoction, which leaves a red stain around the mouth.
betutu bebek roast duck.
Bima a warrior from the *Mahabharata* epic. One of the five Pandawa brothers, and a symbol of invincibility.
Boma deity of the earth.
Brahma four-headed Hindu god of creation, leader of the Hindu trinity.
Brahman the highest caste in Bali - the priestly caste.
brem black-rice wine.
Bupati head of one of the eight regencies on Bali.

Calon Arang mythical struggle between Mahendratta (the witch, Rangda), the Queen of Udayana, and her son Erlangga (the Barong), now depicted in the Barong dance.
candi bentar split gate entrance to temples.
cecing a mangy, homeless dog, despised by all.
cili palm-leaf effigy of the rice goddess, Dewi Sri.
colt a minibus for hire.

dalang shadow-puppet master.
danau lake.
dedari angels.
desa a village in the countryside.
dewa a god or honoured ancestor.
Dewa Agung title of utmost ruler of Bali.
dewi a goddess or divinity.
Dewi Danau goddess of the lake.
Dewi Sri goddess of rice and fertility.
dokar pony-drawn cart.
Durga consort of Siwa; goddess of death and destruction.

Eka Desa Rudra a ceremony held every hundred years at the "mother temple" to purify the entire island. Last performed in 1979.
endek woven cloth.
Gaja Mada a prime minister of the Javanese Majapahit Empire who conquered Bali in 1343AD.
Galungan the most important yearly festival on Bali, lasting ten days, to mark the new year

Glossary

of the "oton" calender and is a celebration of creation.
gambuh ancient form of dance from which most dances are derived; rarely performed.
gamelan a generic term for any Balinese orchestra using bronze or wooden percussion instruments.
Ganesha the fat-bellied son of Siwa; god of homes and learning.
gang alley.
Garuda a mythical bird, like a cross between an eagle and a roc. Siwa's mount. Also the emblem of the Indonesian Republic and name of the international airline.
geko chameleon-like lizard found in Balinese homes, restaurants, known for the "hiccupping" noises it makes.
gedong large building, pavilion or museum.
Gelgel a Balinese kingdom during the 15th, 16th and 17th centuries.
geringsing a rare cloth in which both the weft and the warp are tie-dyed before weaving. Found only in the *Bali Aga* village of Tenganan.
gunung mountain.
guru teacher.
halus refined, elegant and noble behaviours and cultural traits.
Hanuman the white monkey king who upholds good in the *Ramayana* epic.

ibu mother, also a term of deference for older women.
ikat a tie-dye technique applied to either the warp or weft where the threads are tightly bound so as not to absorb the dye. The process is repeated to add different colours and patterns.
Indra god of the rain and thunder.

jaba outside; used to describe the *Sudra* caste of people outside of the *Triwangsa*, the three high castes.
jaja Balinese rice cakes.
jalan street.
jam karet rubber time (a literal translation). Reason for "elasticity" in timetables, etc.
jeroan inner temple sanctuary.
joged the flirting dance, originated in Buleleng.
jukung small outrigger canoe.

Kabupaten one of the eight administrative districts based on the realms of the rajas.
kain length of fabric tied around the waist, falling to the ankles - similar to a sarong.
kain poleng black and white chequered cloth often tied around statues. The cloth admits both lightness and darkness, acknowledging both good and evil.
kaja north; towards Gunung Agung which is sacred, heavenly and positive - a pole of the axis upon which most buildings are constructed.
kala evil; also the son of Siwa and the god of malice.
kangin east; direction of the rising sun.
kantor office.
karma Hindu belief that destiny is determined by actions in this life and previous lives.
kasar a term for crude, impolite, coarse or inelegant behaviour.
kauh west; direction of the setting sun.
Kawi literary language known as Old Javanese, now only used in Balinese theatre.
kebaya ceremonial blouse. Traditionally, Balinese women were bare-breasted, but after the Dutch invasions women started to wear the Malay *kebaya*.
kecak the monkey dance, an excerpt from the *Ramayana* epic. A choral performance characterised by the "chukka, chukka" of monkeys.
kelod south; towards the sea, which is evil, negative and unlucky - opposite to the *kaja* pole.
kretek Indonesian clove cigarette, very sweet and numbing (due to the anaesthetic properties of the cloves).
kris a double-edged ceremonial dagger.
Krishna a manifestation of Wisnu, and a popular god in his own right.
kulkul a drum, often perched in a *banyan* tree which warns of danger, heralds or calls.

Kuningan the last day of the ten day *Galungan* ceremony, usually for ancestral deities.

lawar a ceremonial food concocted of shredded vegetables and meats.
legong graceful dance performed by young girls.
leyak a roaming, mischievous spirit.
lingga a phallic image and the symbol of Siwa.
lontar palm-leaf books.
losmen a small homestay or guesthouse available for rent and much cheaper than hotels.

Mahabharata an Indian Hindu epic poem describing the origins of the Hindu gods. The climax recounts the legendary battle between the Pandawa brothers, the "goodies" and their cousins, the Korawas, the "baddies". The poem was translated into *Kawi* in the Middle Ages, and is featured in literature, art and dance.
Majapahit great Hindu Empire established in Java, later moving to Bali in the 14th century. The kingdom had a profound effect on the culture, art and political organisation of Bali.
mandi a tub for bathing; to bathe.
meru tiered shrine.

negara a state, realm, capital, court, town or village.
Nirartha, Danghyang a Javanese priest who crossed to Bali after the fall of the Majapahit Empire. He acquired great fame through his teachings and gathered many disciples. He is associated with the temples at *Ulu Watu* and *Tanah Lot*, to name two.
nusa island.
Nyepi a day of silence to confuse evil spirits.
odalan temple anniversary festival.
oton a Balinese year of 210 days.

padi rice field.
padmasana high lotus throne used by the gods when they descend from heaven, often found in the inner sanctum of a temple.

Pancasila "The Five Principles"; a political philosophy introduced by Sukarno before Indonesian Independence as a basis for a constitution. Most Balinese have to recite the five creeds before they can be employed in any government office. And all of them will admit they believe in the creeds, especially the belief in one god. But in reality, the *pancasila* (for the Balinese anyway), is a foreign philosophy imposed by a Muslim government.
pantai beach.
paras soft volcanic stone used for statues.
pedanda Brahman priest.
pemangku non-Brahman temple curator or priest.
pendet welcoming procession.
penjor tall bamboo poles adorned with bamboo decorations that arch over streets during Galungan.
potong gigit tooth-filing ceremony.
prahu small wooden sailing boat or outrigger.
puputan literally, "the end"; a ritualised fight to the death or a mass suicide charge.
pura temple.
puri palace.

Ramayana an Indian epic which tells of the struggles between the hero Rama (Wisnu reincarnated) and the evil King Rawana, who abducts Rama's consort.
Rangda witch who struggles for supremacy against the Barong in the *Calon Arang* myth. She is based on Udayana's queen, Mahendratta, who is said to have practised black magic. As Rangda the witch, she is pitted against the Barong, Mahendratta's son Erlangga.
regency one of eight administrative districts on Bali based on the old kingdoms of the rajas. Also known as *Kabupaten*.
rijstaffel literally, "rice table" in Dutch. A smorgasbord of over forty Indonesian rice dishes, but the presentation is Dutch.

sad kahyangan state temples dedicated to the island, including *Pura Besakih, Pura Uluwatu, Pura Tanah Lot, Pura Goa Lawah, Pura Batukau, Pura Pusering Jagat.*
Sanghyang Widhi the Hindu Godhead; the omnipotent Hindu god. All deities, including Wisnu, Brahma and Siwa are manifestations of the cosmic force of Sanghyang Widhi. Well, that's according to intellectual Hindus intent on reconciling the *pancasila* with Hinduism.
Saraswati goddess of learning, literature and wisdom, and wife of Brahma.
Satrya the second-highest of the Hindu Bali caste, the warrior and ruling class.
sawah rice field.
sebel ritually unclean.
sirih a leaf of a species of pepper which is chewed by older Indonesians; the teeth and lips become rust-stained.
Siwa one of the Hindu trinity (Shiva for Indian Hindus). He is the Destroyer of the World, and is probably the most venerated because of his destructive powers. Siwa's emblem is the *lingga* or phallus.
subak village irrigation co-operative which oversees cultivation, irrigation and farming disputes.
suci holy, ritually clean.
Sudra those people outside of the Triwangsa caste system, which is about 90% of the population; Sudra is rarely used, most people refer to Sudra as *jaba*.
Surya the sun or the sun god.
suttee the rite of self-immolation by a widow at her husband's cremation; outlawed by the Dutch in the 19th century.
swastika the wheel of the sun, and the symbol for the Hindu religion in general.
tempeh soybean cake.
tingklik small bamboo xylophone.
topeng mask or mask dance.
Triwangsa Bali's three high castes, the *Brahmana, Satrya*, and *Wesya*, traditionally differentiated from the *Jaba* or *Sudra*.
tuak rice or palm wine.
warung food stall.

wayang kulit the two-dimensional leather puppets or the shadow-puppet play.
Wesya third-highest caste in the *Triwangsa*, originally merchants.
Wisnu one of the holy trinity, and the guardian of the world. known in India as Vishnu.
wuku a period of seven days; thirty *wuku* make up the 210-day Balinese year.

Yama god of the underworld.
yeh water, river, waterway.

List of Maps

Bali	frontpiece	Klungkung	172
Badung	76	Legian & Kuta	90-91
Bangli	180	Nusa Dua	118
Candi Dasa	192-193	Sanur	126-127
Indonesia	endpaper	Ubud	146-147
Karangasem	188		

Index

General

Accommodation 58
Art 36-37
Artists 148
Bahasa Indonesia 20-24
Bali-belly 48-49
Balinese calendar 29-30
Banking & business hours 44
Banks 43
Bargaining 68-69
Baris 32-33
Barong 32
Batik 38,70
Bedulu, King 10
Bicycles 62
Bungy jumping 71
Car rental 60-61
Carving 37-38
Caste system 17
Churches 52-53
Climate 9
Conduct 50
Consulates 42-43
Cremation 28-29
Cruises 65
Customs allowance 41
Dance and drama 32-34
Departure tax 42
Dewa Agung 11
Distances 62
Diving 72
Djilantik 12
Doctors 49
Dokar 60
Dress requirements 50
Drink 65-68
Drugs 51
Dutch East India Trading Company 12
Economy 39-40
Eka Dasa Rudra 15
Electricity 50
Entry regulations 41
Erlangga, Prince 10
Exit regulations 42
Family, The 18-19
Festivals & Holy Days 30-31
Food 65-68
Fruit 67-68
Galungan 30-31
Geography 7
Geringsing 39
Golf 71-72
Health 47-49
Health regulations 41
Hinduism 24-29
History 9-16
How to get there 55-57
Immigration 43
Independence 14-16
Inoculations 47-48
Joged Bung Bung 33
Kebyar Deduk 33
Kecak 33
Kuningan 30-31
Lange, Mads 12
Language 20-24
Legong 33
Literature 24
Local transport 59-63
Magazines 46
Mahendradatta, Princess 10
Majapahit Empire 10-11
Measurements 50
Medical care 49
Money 43
Motorbike rental 61-62
Music 34-35
Naming 18
Newspapers 46
Ngurah Rai 14
Nyepi 31
Odalan 30
Painting 36-37
Paintings 70
Pendent 34
Performing arts 31-36
Photography 51-52
Police 51
Post offices 46
Precautions 49
Public bemo 59
Puppetry 35-36
Puputan 13-14
Radio 47
Rice cultivation 40
Rites of Passage 26-28
Shipping 50
Shopping 68-71
Silver 71
Snorkelling 72
Songket 39
Surfing 73-74
Taxis 59
Telephones 44-46
Television 46-47
Temples 25-26
Textiles 38-39
Theft 52
Time 50
Tipping 51
Toilets 51
Tooth filing 27
Topeng 34
Tourism 39-40
Tourist information 57
Tours 63
Travel insurance 52
Udayana, Prince 10
Village, The 19-20
Water 48
Water parks 74-75
Water skiing 74
Water sports 72
Whitewater rafting 74
Wildlife parks 75
Woodcarving 71

Places & Attractions

Air Sanih 209
Amlapura 187,197
Antonio Blanco's Gallery 162
Anturan 215

Badung 77-138
- History 77-78
Bali Barat National Park 75,213
Bali Handara Kosaido Country Club 209-210
Bangli 181-186
Bangli Town 181-182
Banyualit 211
Banyuning 208
Batuan 142-143
Batubulan 140-141
Batur 184-185
Bedugul 218-219
- Accommodation 218-219
- How to get there 218
- Local transport 219
- Sightseeing 219
Bedugul Botanic Gardens 219
Bedulu 165
Belimbingsari 214
Bemo Corner 99
Beratan Village 209
Besakih 64,112
Bhatara Turun Kabeh 199-200
Bukit Peninsula 113-124
Buleleng 203-213
- Cultural character 203
- History 203-204

Candi Dasa 190-197
- Accommodation 191-195
- Eating out 195-196
- Entertainment 196
- How to get there 191
- Shopping 196
- Water activities 197
Candikuning 218

Catuh Mukha Statue 87
Celuk 141
Celukan Bawang 219
Coral Pyramid 135

Denpasar 78-88
- Accommodation 80-81
- Bemo transport system 81
- Eating out 82-83
- Entertainment 84
- How to get there 79-80
- Local transport 81-82
- Nightlife 83-84
- Night markets 83
- Shopping 84-85
- Sightseeing 85-88
- Tourist information 80

Eka Dasa Rudra 200

Galleries 159-162
Gedong Kirtya Library 208
Gelgel 175
Gianyar 139-170
- History 139-140
Gianyar Town 169-170
Gilimanuk 215
Gitgit Waterfall 209
Goa Gajah 164-165
Goa Karangsari 178
Goa Lawah 175-176
Gunung Agung 198,201
Gunung Batukau 217-218
Gunung Batur 183
Gunung Kawi 167-168

Indonesia Jaya Reptile & Crocodile Park 75

Jagaraga 209
Japanese Caves 219
Jembrana 214-215
Jimbaran 113-115
Jimbaran Bay 115-116

Kaliasem 211
Kalibukbuk 211
Kamasan 175
Karangasem 187-202
- History 187
Kerta Gosa 174
Kesiman 88
Kintamani 112,185-186
Klungkung 171-179
- History 171-173
Klungkung Town 173-176
Kuta
- Accommodation 95-97
- Bars 107
- Discos 107-108
- Night Clubs 107-108
- Pubs 107
- Restaurants 102-104
Kuta & Legian Resort Area 88-112
- Entertainment 108-109
- Getting your bearings 92
- How to get there 92
- Shopping 109-111
- Sightseeing 111-112
- Tourist information 93

Lake Batur 183-184
Legian
- Accommodation 95-97
- Restaurants 102-104
Le Mayeur Museum 135
Lempad Gallery 159
Lovina Beach 210-212
- Accommodation 210-211
- Eating out 212
- How to get there 210
- Local transport 211
- Water activities 212

Mas 143
Mengwi 216
Monkey Forest Temple 163
Moon of Pejeng 166
Mother Temple 64,198-201
Museum Bali 86
Museum Gedong Arca 167
Museums 159-162

Negara 214
Neka Museum 160-161
Nusa Dua 117-122
- Accommodation 119-120
- Eating out 121
- How to get there 119
- Local transport 120
- Nightlife 121
- Shopping 122
- Water sports 122
Nusa Lembongan 138, 179
Nusa Penida 138, 176-179
- Accommodation 178
- How to get there 177-178
- Local transport 178
- Sightseeing 178-179

Padangbai 189
Palasari 214
Pejeng 164, 165-167
Peliatan 143-144
Pemaron 211
Penelokan 182-183
Pengosekan 144
Prasati Belanjong 135
Pulaki 212-213
Pulau Menjangan 213
Puputan Square 85
Pura Besakih 198-201
Pura Gunung Lebah 163
Pura Jagatnatha 86-87
Pura Kehen 182
Pura Moaspahit 87
Pura Pedarman 168
Pura Peed 178
Pura Pemecutan 87
Pura Penataran Agung 199
Pura Petitenget 112
Pura Ulun Danu Bratan 163
Puri Agung Sinar Nadi 208
Puri Kangin 197-198
Puri Lukisan Museum 160
Puri Saraswati 162-163
Puri Saren 162

Sangeh Monkey Forest 216
Sangsit 208
Sanur 124-13

- Accommodation 125-130
- Dance performances 133-134
- Eating out 130-132
- How to get there 125
- Local transport 130
- Nightlife 132-133
- Shopping 134-135
- Water sports 136
Sawan 209
Seminyak
- Accommodation 94-95
- Bars 106
- Night Clubs 106
- Pubs 106
- Restaurants 101-102
Seniwati Gallery 161
Serangan Island 136-138
Seririt 218
Singaraja 204-210
- Accommodation 205-206
- Eating out 206
- Entertainment 207
- How to get there 205
- Local transport 206
- Shopping 207
- Sightseeing 208-210
- Tourist information 205
Singsing Falls 212
STSI (Academy of Dance) 88
Sukawati 141-142
Suluban Beach 117

Tabanan 215-219
Tabanan Town 216-217
Taman Burung Bali Bird Park 75
Tanah Lot 64,112,217
Tanjung Benoa 123-124
Teges 143
Tenganan 189-190
Tirta Empul 168-169
Tirta Gangga 198
Trunyan 184
Tuban
- Accommodation 98-99
- Bars 108
- Night Clubs 108
- Restaurants 104-105
Tukad Mungga 211
Tulamben 201-202
Turtle Island 136-138

Ubud 112,145-163
- Accommodation 149-152
- Eating out 153-156
- Entertainment 156-157
- History 145-148
- How to get there 149
- Local transport 152-153
- Nightlife 156
- Shopping 157-159
- Sightseeing 162-163
- Tourist information 149
Ubud Palace 162
Ujung Water Palace 198
Ulu Watu 112,116-117

Werdhi Budaya Cultural Centre 88
Yeh Pulu 165

Surfing at Nusa Lembongan

Local market at Kuta

INDONESIA